The Ecumenical Luther

CONCORDIA ACADEMIC PRESS

THE ECUMENICAL LUTHER

THE DEVELOPMENT AND USE
OF HIS DOCTRINAL HERMENEUTIC

RICHARD P. BUCHER

CONCORDIA PUBLISHING HOUSE · SAINT LOUIS

ACADEMIC PRESS

To my family, my joy in the Lord,
without whose encouragement
this book would not have come to be.—RPB

Manufactured in the United States of America

Library of Congress Cataloging-in-Publication Data

Bucher, Richard P.
    The ecumenical Luther : the development and use of his doctrinal hermeneutic / Richard P. Bucher.
        p.   cm.
Includes bibliographical references.
    ISBN 0–7586-0325-8
    1. Luther, Martin, 1483–1546. 2. Lutheran Church—Doctrines. I. Title.
BX8068.A1B83 2003
230'.41'092—dc21   2003012913

1 2 3 4 5 6 7 8 9 10   12 11 10 09 08 07 06 05 04 03

CONTENTS

FOREWORD

The title of this book, *The Ecumenical Luther*, initially appears to be an oxymoron or at least counter-intuitive. After all, Luther's thunderous "Nein" to various doctrinal positions of the papacy, as well as to Erasmus, Müntzer, Zwingli, and the Anabaptists—not to mention his attacks on Schwärmerei of every stripe—does not appear to be very ecumenical. Indeed, Luther's assertion—and Luther delighted in assertions![1]—that "we can be saved without love . . . but not without pure doctrine and faith" makes him a sticky wicket in ecumenical dialogues, especially when he continues with the claim that it is specious and the devil's argument that cautions against "offending against love and the harmony among the churches."[2] Such assertions by Luther, often complemented by assigning his opponents to the devil, as well as threats to break their necks with doctrine, make him an unlikely candidate for ecumenist of the year.

Our present religious culture still stands in the shadows of Pietism and its stepchildren, the church growth movement and the apparently unquenchable appetite for works on spirituality of dubious doctrinal content. The classical Pietists, such as Spener, certainly appreciated Luther's Reformation of doctrine, but they argued that doctrinal reform needed to be completed by reform of life, by regeneration. The ecumenism of Pietism, with its interiorization and individualization, was and continues to be the ecumenism of religious experience. The early ecumenical movement's motto that "creeds divide, but deeds unite" echoes the priority of life over doctrine. To such an ecumenical orientation Luther would reply, "The proper role of the gospel is not to make people pious, but rather only to make Christians. To be a Christian is quite simply to be pious."[3] The opposite pole of this orientation to unity on the basis of shared experience is the more recent effort to add this, that, or the other "theological" thing to approximate Luther and his tradition to Roman Catholic and/or Orthodox teaching. Thus some of Luther's heirs, too, have difficulty reconciling his emphasis on doctrine with their own concerns and agendas. But Luther's "issue was teaching the truth. By comparison, nothing else really mattered. . . . 'For I know—God be praised—what my position is and where I shall stay. . . . If they [his opponents] do not need my doctrine, I need their grace still less, and I will let them rage and rant in the name of all devils, while I laugh in the name of God.' "[4] Luther has never been accused of indifferentism!

This "stiff-necked" Luther is well known. What is not so well known is why and how Luther understood doctrine. Thus Richard Bucher renders a great service to both Luther studies and Luther's contribution to ecumenical dialogue with this study of Luther's definition and use of doctrine. Bucher goes beyond the usual Luther citations that highlight his emphasis on doctrine to explore Luther's doctrinal hermeneutic, how Luther defined doctrine and determined whether or not a particular church teaching must be believed by all Christians. The key "interpretive lenses," Bucher argues, through which Luther judged and defined a necessary doctrine are his scriptural and evangelical canons. The former is based "on the right Scripture rightly interpreted," and the latter posits "that only a teaching necessary for salvation could be an article of faith."

Furthermore, Bucher presents Luther's development of his doctrinal hermeneutic in the historical context of his early writings, his dialogue with the *Unitas Fratrum*, the controversy with Zwingli over the Lord's Supper that came to a head at the Marburg Colloquy, and his "testament" and preparation for a proposed ecumenical council in the Schmalkald Articles. Bucher thereby allows the reader to see Luther's development in context and to grasp what Luther perceived to be at stake. The question, then, of Luther's understanding and use of doctrine is significant for understanding church history and historical theology, as well as for suggesting models for contemporary ecumenical dialogue that steer between the Scylla of false irenicism and the Charybdis of false polemicism. Last, but by no means least, Bucher notes throughout his study that Luther's concern for doctrine was never a theological parlor game; rather, it was a drive to express a pastoral theology that liberates burdened consciences.

Carter Lindberg
Professor Emeritus of Church History
Boston University School of Theology

PREFACE

In his masterful *Eucharist and Church Fellowship in the First Four Centuries*, Werner Elert observed that "[t]he early church was never in doubt that unity in doctrine is a prerequisite of altar fellowship. No one who taught false doctrine might receive Holy Communion in an orthodox congregation."[1] But this correct observation begs the question: Unity in which doctrine(s)? Or, "On what doctrines must Christians agree to be in fellowship with one another?" It is all well and good to insist that agreement in doctrine presupposes altar fellowship. This is meaningless, however, unless all parties know what that "doctrine" is. Is the "doctrine" that requires agreement every teaching of the canonical Scriptures? Is it every teaching that the *magisterium* of the church has called "doctrine"? Or is it only the doctrines included in the ecumenical creeds, in the *regula fidei* (rule of faith), or in the Lutheran Confessions? If so, why these particular doctrines? What is it about the doctrines of the creeds and the rule of faith that caused the ancient church to deem agreement on them necessary for unity? Did the doctrines of the creeds and the *regula fidei* share a common definition, or were they included because the exigencies of history forced the church to give them an inflated importance? It is not particularly helpful to say that only essential or fundamental doctrines (that is, dogma) need be commonly confessed and believed. The designation of some doctrines as "essential" inevitably leads to the same kinds of questions, namely, who or what decides that a particular doctrine is essential? How is this determined?

These are the questions that I pondered beginning with my formation at Concordia Theological Seminary, Ft. Wayne, Indiana. These also are the questions that eventually led me to the doctoral program in theology at Boston University School of Theology under the tutelage and guidance of Dr. Carter Lindberg. Specifically, I wanted to know how Martin Luther might answer these questions. I wanted to know whether and, if so, how the great reformer defined essential or necessary doctrine—doctrine that is necessary for salvation and unity. This seemed an important point of departure because Luther's intensive interest in doctrine is well known. The result of this research was my doctrinal dissertation, out of which this book has grown.

Thanks and gratitude is owed to several people for their support, encouragement, and guidance during the writing of this book. First and foremost, I wish to thank my wife, Amy, and our children, Amanda and Samuel, for their patience and encouragement, which never wavered during the long process of research and writing. I also am deeply in the debt of my *Doktor-Vater*, Carter Lindberg, who throughout my acquaintance with him has personified a rich balance of academic brilliance with gracious wit and constant encouragement. I chose Boston University as the site of my graduate work because of him, and I wasn't disappointed. I also wish to thank my editors at Concordia Publishing House, Mark Sell and Dawn Weinstock. Their many suggestions to this novice author proved invaluable and improved the manuscript considerably. Finally, a word of gratitude is owed to my former congregation, Trinity Lutheran Church, Clinton, Massachusetts. If not for the willingness of this people of God to "share" me with my doctoral studies, this book would not exist. To God alone be the glory and praise.

1

INTRODUCTION

"The significance of doctrine for Luther can scarcely be overestimated."[1] So said the dean of Luther scholars Bernhard Lohse in his magisterial *Martin Luther's Theology*. Lohse highlighted what has often been observed about Martin Luther: Doctrine, rather than ethics or morality, was the focus of his life's work.[2] Indeed, this was Luther's self-evaluation. In the autumn of 1533, as he looked back on what he had accomplished, Luther remarked that he considered his emphasis on doctrine to be his life's work.

> Doctrine and life must be distinguished. Life is bad among us, as it is among the papists, but we don't fight about life and condemn the papists on that account. Wycliffe and Huss didn't know this and attacked [the papacy] for its life. I don't scold myself into becoming good, but I fight over the Word and whether our adversaries teach it in its purity. That doctrine should be attacked—this has never before happened. This is my calling. Others have censured only life, but to treat doctrine is to strike at the most sensitive point . . . .
>
> . . . When the Word remains pure, then the life (even if there is something lacking in it) can be molded properly. Everything depends on the Word, and the pope has abolished the Word and created another one. With this I have won, and I have won nothing else than that I teach aright. Although we are better morally, this isn't anything to fight about. It's the teaching that breaks the pope's neck.[3]

According to Luther, fighting over doctrine was his calling. But what did Luther mean by *doctrine*? How did he define it?

The ecumenical movement has resulted in a renewed focus on the definition and nature of Christian doctrine. For example, Gerhard Ebeling made the astute observation that questions of doctrinal differences inevitably lead to questions of the meaning of doctrine. Ebeling stated: "The doctrinal differences that divide the church can at least amount, and perhaps indeed ultimately always do amount, to differences concerning the real meaning of the concept 'doctrine' as such."[4] According to Ebeling, a criterion that would determine which doctrines were divisive and why was needed.[5] In the same spirit, Eeva Martikainen has written that churches should be asking questions about the nature of doctrine and its significance for unity. Doctrine is not just a formal legal entity: it is organically related to the gospel. For this reason we need to ask what the essence, structure, and content of doctrine is, and what its significance is for faith, the life of the church and for spirituality and church unity. Without basic research into the nature of doctrine, the suitability and acceptability of various ecumenical models for the perspectives of the different churches will not be properly assessed.[6]

Thus defining doctrine and striving for unity have gone hand in hand.

So it was with Luther. His interest was not merely doctrine but the definition of doctrine. Luther gradually developed a method to determine whether a church teaching was a necessary doctrine, that is, an article of faith, a doctrine that must be believed by all Christians. As Luther conversed with the tradition he had inherited, as he pondered and taught the Bible, and as he reacted to his literary opponents, his method of defining necessary doctrines came into focus. I call this method Luther's *doctrinal hermeneutic*. In this method, *hermeneutic* takes on its basic sense of "definition" or "interpretation," which is the meaning of *hermeneuo* and its cognates.[7]

Luther's doctrinal hermeneutic was composed of two interpretive canons that he applied to the teaching in question to determine whether it was an article of faith: a scriptural canon and an evangelical canon. In its most basic sense, the scriptural canon stated that a necessary doctrine must be based only on Scripture, not on human words. The evangelical canon in its basic form posited that only a teaching necessary for salvation could be an article of faith. As his doctrinal hermeneutic developed, Luther nuanced each canon in important ways. For example, when his opponents based their teachings on suspect Bible passages or on suspect interpretations, Luther emphasized that necessary doctrine must be based not only on Scripture but also on the right Scripture rightly interpreted. Sometimes Luther applied the canons separately; at other times he applied them concurrently. In short, the scriptural and evangelical canons became interpretive lenses through which the reformer judged and defined whether a doctrine was one that must be believed.

As it does today, Luther's efforts to define doctrine often occurred within the context of dialogues for unity. Luther used his doctrinal hermeneutic not only to indicate what was necessary for salvation but also what was necessary for unity. Through an examination of three ecumenical[8] dialogues in which the reformer participated, we will see how Luther applied his doctrinal hermeneutic. These dialogues are (1) the dialogue with the *Unitas Fratrum* in the 1520s, (2) the dialogue with the Swiss and South Germans at the 1529 Marburg Colloquy, and (3) the dialogue with the Roman church via the 1537 Schmalkald Articles.

The Significance
of Luther's Doctrinal Hermeneutic

Given the massive amount of literature available on every facet of Luther's theology and life, it is surprising how little has been written about his understanding of doctrine. When Luther scholarship has drawn attention to his heavy emphasis on doctrine, it frequently has done so superficially in a paragraph or a section of a chapter. Luther's understanding of doctrine has not been examined for its own sake, but it has been brought in as minor evidence for a larger topic. Many studies of Luther do not even address his understanding of doctrine. For example, biographies of Luther typically say nothing about it.[9] The two genres of Luther research that do speak about the reformer's view of doctrine—at least in passing—are studies of Luther's theology and studies of Lutheran theology.

Studies of Luther's Theology

Many studies of Luther's theology have understood doctrine as an important theme in the reformer's theology. In his venerable two-volume work on Luther's theology, Julius Köstlin included a section on Luther's understanding of fundamental articles and how these articles related to one another. Köstlin repeated, as have many other scholars, Luther's belief that all articles of faith comprise a singular whole.[10]

Gerhard Ebeling's introduction to Luther's theology contained only several passing references to Luther and doctrine. For example, Ebeling referred to Luther's distinction between doctrine and life.[11] Slightly more helpful was a section on the relationship between doctrine and the Word of God in Ebeling's *Word and Faith*. Here Ebeling rightly pointed out that at times Luther equated doctrine with God's Word while at other times the reformer stated that doctrine must be normed by the Word of God. This section was disappointing, however, because Ebeling used Luther's concept of doctrine only as a point of departure. Ebeling's real goal was to define doctrine for his own day.[12]

In *Let God Be God*, Philip Watson included a helpful, albeit brief, section entitled "Luther's Concern for Doctrine" in which he drew attention to Luther's distinction between doctrine and life and concluded that contending for right doctrine was Luther's personal view of the Reformation. More helpful was Watson's assertion that "[t]his for Luther is the supreme test of his own doctrine and all other doctrines—whether they set forth in one way or another the glory of God alone."[13] Unfortunately, Watson did not develop this perceptive thought.

Paul Althaus briefly addressed Luther's understanding of doctrine in *The Theology of Martin Luther*. In an introductory chapter, Althaus noted that Luther advocated that articles of faith must be based on Scripture alone. In a chapter entitled "Righteousness in Faith," Althaus highlighted Luther's insistence that the doctrine of justification is the most important doctrine, the chief article on which the church stands or falls, and the summary of Christian doctrine that illumines all other doctrines.[14]

In *Where God Meets Man*, Gerhard Forde provided a rationale for Luther's emphasis on pure doctrine in a short section entitled "Doctrine and Freedom." According to Forde, Luther stressed pure doctrine to preserve Christian freedom, but the reformer is not quoted to substantiate Forde's position.[15]

STUDIES OF LUTHERAN THEOLOGY

A number of scholars also have referenced Luther's understanding of doctrine in studies on Lutheran theology. Although these works don't address Luther or his theology directly, they deserve attention because they touch on the reformer's conception of doctrine. For example, in his seminal work *The Theology of Post-Reformation Lutheranism*, Robert Preus briefly drew attention to Luther's conviction that Christian doctrine is a unified whole. But he did so only to demonstrate that the theology of the Lutheran dogmaticians of the sixteenth and seventeenth centuries (his main topic of study) agreed with that of Luther.[16] Luther's view of doctrine was not further developed. Similarly, Kurt Marquart has also referred to Luther's understanding of doctrine in *The Church and Her Fellowship, Ministry, and Governance*. Chapter 7 in Marquart's book featured an excellent discussion of the meaning of *doctrine* and *articles of faith* in the theology of the Lutheran Confessions. Marquart referred to Luther's distinction of doctrine and life and his belief that doctrine is a singular unity but only in passing. Marquart's main concern was to demonstrate the teaching of the Lutheran Confessions, not the teaching of Luther.[17] As he discussed the unity of the church in *Church and Ministry*, Eugene Klug demonstrated Luther's penchant for stressing pure doctrine by quoting at length a passage from the reformer's 1531 Galatians commentary. Because Klug was demonstrating the Lutheran (not Luther's) theology of church and ministry, Luther's comments about doctrine in the Galatians commentary were not explicated further.[18]

Other scholars have highlighted Luther's understanding of doctrine in the context of explaining the Lutheran doctrine of justification. In *Justification and Rome*, Robert Preus devoted his first chapter to "The Centrality of the Doctrine of Justification and Its Hermeneutical Role." In making his case, Preus assembled several statements from Luther's writings that demonstrated that, for Luther, the article of justification was the central doctrine and one that had a crucial hermeneutical role to play: "[A]ll other articles flow into and out of this one article, and without it the others are nothing."[19] Francis Pieper also punctuated Luther's understanding of justification as the chief doctrine in *Christian Dogmatics*.[20]

Surprisingly, the only monograph devoted to Luther's understanding of doctrine is Eeva Martikainen's *Doctrina: Studien zu Luthers Begriff der Lehre*. It is a thorough examination that, among other things, compares Luther's view of doctrine to the scholastic use of *doctrina* in the Middle Ages and examines Luther's contrast between the Law and theological doctrine. Martikainen also explores several specific Christian teachings (for example, the Trinity, the creeds, faith, and love) to shed light on Luther and doctrine.[21]

STUDIES OF LUTHER'S THEOLOGY FROM AN ECUMENICAL PERSPECTIVE

Because the focus of this book is Luther's doctrinal hermeneutic as it related to his ecumenical work, we need to consider the literature that already has addressed this aspect of the reformer's work. *Luther for an Ecumenical Age*,[22] a collection of essays on various aspects of Luther's theology, was one of the first serious attempts to examine the reformer's theology in an ecumenical context. However, as the book's forward made clear, the essays were not intended to examine Luther's ecumenical stance *per se*. Rather, they were written to raise the question of the place and value of Luther's theology for the twentieth-century ecumenical movement. *Luther for an Ecumenical Age* set the tone for later studies, including *Luther, Reformer for the Churches*[23] and *Luther's Ecumenical Significance*.[24] These studies offered helpful analyses of different themes in Luther's theology (for example, ecclesiology, Scripture, anthropology, *simul iustus et peccator*), interpretations of that theology, and the corresponding ecumenical potentials and pitfalls. The studies also were helpful because they shed new light on aspects of Luther's theology vital to any ecumenical rapprochement. Each study approached Luther's theology by addressing it topically, then evaluating the usefulness of these *loci* for contemporary ecumenical discussions and challenges.

This book goes beyond these efforts in several ways. First, except for the Martikainen study, none of the literature surveyed treats Luther's understanding of doctrine as the main topic of research. Each of the works addresses some other subject of Luther's (or Lutheran) theology—therefore, references to "Luther and doctrine" are understandably brief. When Luther is quoted to demonstrate his view of doctrine, the same few passages—all from his later writings—are recycled repeatedly.[25] In contrast, Luther's view of doctrine is the main focus of this book, which allows a more thorough examination. Moreover, examples from Luther's early writings are offered to show that beginning in his formative years, Luther was developing his concept of doctrine. Second, this book examines

Luther's concept of essential articles of faith. As Martikainen has shown, Luther used the word *doctrine* in various ways; here the focus is on those teachings that Luther considered necessary doctrines—necessary for salvation and unity among Christians. Third, this book reveals that Luther's writings contain a deliberately nuanced method of determining what makes a church teaching a necessary doctrine, a fact not considered by other authors. Fourth, this book demonstrates Luther's ecumenical significance not in a particular theme of his theology but in his dogged methodological insistence on basing unity only on necessary doctrines. Fifth, this book reveals how Luther applied his doctrinal hermeneutic in specific ecumenical contexts.

Because this book sheds light on Luther's ecumenical methodology, it contributes to contemporary ecumenical thought through its focus on the definition of necessary doctrine as the basis for unity. In many contemporary ecumenical discussions, too little attention has been given to the nature of essential doctrine, that is, to what makes a particular church teaching necessary for unity. At the heart of many an impasse are competing views of what is essential and why. Luther's doctrinal hermeneutic may stimulate helpful thinking in this area.

PRIMARY SOURCES

The primary sources are, naturally, the writings of Martin Luther, especially those produced between 1518 and 1529 and Luther's key writings and correspondence pertaining to the three ecumenical dialogues identified previously. For example, this book focuses on Luther's treatise "The Adoration of the Sacrament" because it is a key document in the ecumenical exchange with the *Unitas Fratrum*. The Marburg Articles, the reconstructed dialogue of the colloquy, and key eucharistic treatises of Luther and Zwingli are the focus of study in the case of the Marburg Colloquy. Finally, Luther's 1537 Schmalkald Articles, which the reformer prepared as an ecumenical platform for an anticipated church council, are the primary entry point in the study of Luther's dialogue with Rome.[26]

The focus on Luther's writings in the years 1518 to 1525 is deliberate because Luther scholarship has usually regarded these years as formative for the reformer's theology. Moreover, it is well known that the older Luther emphasized doctrine, and when scholars have quoted the reformer to show this emphasis, his later writings are cited. Even in this early period, however, Luther's doctrinal hermeneutic can be identified, though in a developing form. Luther later applied this hermeneutic to ecumenical dialogues.

CONTENT SUMMARY

The primary method of examination is twofold. Keeping in mind the social milieu, literary genre, and occasion of each text, this book analyzes Luther's writings to identify those places in which he speaks of essential doctrine and defines it. Because Luther consistently used certain vocabulary to describe essential doctrine (for example, *Artikel, Hauptartikel, Lehre, notwendig, notwendigkeit, articulis, doctrina*), these key words and phrases are investigated. Then several key ecumenical dialogues in which Luther was involved are examined to reveal how Luther spoke of and used his doctrinal hermeneutic in an ecumenical context.

The first part of chapter 2 examines the terminology of "necessary doctrine." Medieval doctrinal terminology is briefly examined before considering the unique vocabulary that Luther employed to describe doctrine. The second part of chapter 2 considers evidence for Luther's doctrinal hermeneutic found in his 1518 to 1525 writings. Because Luther gradually developed his method of defining doctrine, especially as he reacted to his literary opponents, this section begins with an examination of the argumentation of the Catholic controversialists so the emergence of Luther's doctrinal method can be viewed in its proper context. The remainder of chapter 2 examines in detail evidence for the scriptural and the evangelical canons that comprised Luther's doctrinal hermeneutic.

Chapters 3 through 5 examine key ecumenical dialogues in which Luther participated to show how the reformer used his doctrinal hermeneutic in an ecumenical setting. These chapters demonstrate how Luther put into practice his belief that unity must be based on essential doctrine.

Chapter 3 analyzes Luther's dialogue with the *Unitas Fratrum* (Unity of Brethren), which occurred from 1522 to 1524. The Unity of Brethren, spiritual heirs of Jan Hus, is the best early example of a group actively seeking unity with Luther and vice versa. The dialogue with the *Unitas Fratrum* was a key experiment in unity for Luther. The first section of chapter 3 sketches the beginnings of, the theology of, and Luther's initial contacts with the *Unitas Fratrum* to enable a better understanding of this partner in ecumenical dialogue. The discussion focuses on the theology of Lukas of Prague because he was the chief spokesman for the Brethren. Because Luther wrote and submitted his treatise "The Adoration of the Sacrament" to the *Unitas Fratrum* as a platform for unity, the second section of chapter 3 analyzes this document to demonstrate the Wittenberg reformer's doctrinal hermeneutic in action.

Chapter 4 examines Luther's dialogue with the evangelicals from Strasbourg and Zurich at the 1529 Marburg Colloquy. The dialogue at Marburg concerned the differing views of the Lord's Supper held by

Luther and the Wittenbergers, on the one hand, and the Swiss reformers and the South Germans—including Huldrych Zwingli, Martin Bucer, and Johannes Oecolampadius—on the other. The chapter opens with an examination of the origins of the dispute over the Lord's Supper. The second section of chapter 4 considers the evidence for Luther's doctrinal hermeneutic in several of his eucharistic treatises preceding the meeting at Marburg and his comments at the Marburg Colloquy itself. Evidence for both his scriptural and evangelical canons is demonstrated to ascertain what impact Luther's doctrinal hermeneutic had on the dialogue.

Chapter 5 focuses on the 1537 Schmalkald Articles, a document authored by Luther in preparation for an ecumenical council with the Roman Church. The Schmalkald Articles is an excellent example of how the mature Luther employed his doctrinal hermeneutic in an ecumenical setting. The first section of chapter 5 explores the origins of the Schmalkald Articles: Why was this document written? What was it intended to be? Contrary to the traditional interpretation that the Schmalkald Articles was primarily a polemical confession of faith,[27] this chapter argues it originally was intended to be an ecumenical document. The events that led to the calling of the council and Luther's correspondence with his prince, John Frederick, support this position. The second section of chapter 5 examines the text of the Schmalkald Articles. Although a detailed theological analysis of each article is not possible, sufficient attention is given to determine whether Luther was insisting on necessary doctrine (as defined by his doctrinal hermeneutic) for unity.

Given the enormity of the potential sources for this book, two major limitations must be mentioned. First, though a thorough study of all of Luther's writings would be optimal, it is not realistic. Therefore, this book focuses on those documents authored by Luther between 1518 and 1529, with the exception of the 1537 Schmalkald Articles. Second, many theological and social issues related to the three dialogues discussed in this book must be ignored. Instead, the discussion focuses on that which has a bearing on the ecumenical nature of these events and, therefore, on Luther's doctrinal hermeneutic. A third limitation concerns the contemporary ecumenical application of this book. Obviously, only those church bodies that view doctrinal consensus as normative for ecumenical dialogue will find a doctrinal methodology useful. Understandably, those groups that emphasize nonfoundational theological norms and that employ a hermeneutic of suspicion toward whatever functions or is named as essential will not find this book relevant.

LUTHER'S
DOCTRINAL HERMENEUTIC
AS FOUND IN HIS
1518 TO 1525 WRITINGS

During the years 1518 to 1525, Martin Luther developed a method of determining whether a doctrine was necessary to be believed. At the heart of this method of judging doctrine were two canons—one scriptural, the other evangelical—that formed the basis of Luther's doctrinal criteriology. As Luther developed his method, each canon was further nuanced to become the interpretive lenses through which the reformer judged whether a particular doctrine must or may be believed. This is Luther's doctrinal hermeneutic.

Documents written by Luther between 1518 and 1525 reveal that such a doctrinal hermeneutic existed at various stages of development. This assertion must be made with a certain degree of caution, lest one falls prey to a kind of textual eisegesis. To a certain extent, one can agree with Norman Cantor that "[w]e tend to discover the past we set out to find."[1] It is temptingly easy to choose selectively from the vast literature of history so one may superimpose personal cultural or theological agendas on the sources and have history say what one wants it to say. Such a temptation is especially alluring in Luther research.[2] Thus before the evidence is brought forth, this chapter must deal briefly with a method of locating and evaluating the evidence.

To argue that Luther developed a definition of what makes a doctrine necessary to be believed depends on being conversant with the terminology that he used to describe such a doctrine. What words or phrases did Luther use when he wanted to indicate that he was speaking of essential doctrine? Because Luther was a child of the late Middle Ages, one needs to be familiar with the vocabulary used by Luther's predecessors. If it can be reasonably proven that the high and late Middle Ages used certain words and phrases to describe doctrine that must be believed, then it is justifiable to assume that the same words and phrases identify discussion of necessary doctrine in Luther's writings.

Of course, Luther did not develop his doctrinal hermeneutic in isolation. He did not arrive at this complex of ideas in the calm, detached environs of his study. Instead, what is true about Luther's theological development in general also holds true for his doctrinal hermeneutic: Two sources combined in its formation. Luther developed his doctrinal hermeneutic from his study of Scripture and, especially, the gospel of justification by grace through faith. He also developed it in reaction to literary and political opponents who repeatedly accused him of heresy and unbelief and threatened Luther with excommunication because of the doctrines he put in writing. This led the reformer to think through the whole question of necessary doctrine because voices within the tradition he had inherited had declared that only those who persistently disobeyed the most important doctrines were guilty of heresy. The most prominent group of Luther's opponents in this period (1518 to 1525) were the Catholic controversialists. Their chief accusations and condemnations of Luther, therefore, are briefly explored to identify what precipitated Luther's reaction.

The first part of this chapter briefly examines the vocabulary of doctrine in vogue in the late Middle Ages before turning to an exploration of the language that Luther used. Part two demonstrates and describes Luther's doctrinal hermeneutic, locating the evidence within the social and theological context, especially the context of Catholic controversialist critique.

THE VOCABULARY OF NECESSARY DOCTRINE

THE VOCABULARY OF DOCTRINE IN THE LATE MIDDLE AGES

Since the Roman Catholic Council of Vatican I, *dogma* has been the word most often associated with doctrine that all Christians are to believe,[3] though in recent years Roman Catholic scholarship has tended to discard or reinterpret the word so it is less juridical.[4] Was a similar word used in the late Middle Ages? If not, what words or phrases did theologians of that period employ to designate a necessary doctrine?

As Albert Lange has shown, though *dogma* was occasionally used in the Middle Ages, the most common term was *articulus fidei*.[5] To what kind of doctrines did "articles of faith" refer? Jaroslav Pelikan has provided a succinct answer.

> The basic truth of theology consisted in the articles of faith. . . . The term "article of faith" could refer to a particular catholic truth stated explicitly in the creed or added to the creed by the authority of the church over the course of centuries; or it could be "the sum total of all catholic truth," which was complete and integral already and brooked

no addition by anyone. The articles of faith included those truths that were expressly taught in Scripture and such truths as could be necessarily inferred from Scripture: on this everyone agreed, but not on the question whether there were also some articles of faith not contained in Scripture but transmitted apart from Scripture through authentic tradition. In addition to the articles of faith of whatever sort, however, there were teachings that the church permitted as belonging to "the piety of faith" but did not require, as, for example, various pious beliefs about the Virgin Mary. Even among the articles of faith, not all were of equal importance with the fundamental doctrines of the Trinity and the person of Christ.[6]

Thus the expression *articulus fidei* was the terminology used when the church required belief, as contrasted with "pious beliefs" or "opinions" that had not yet reached the status of articles of faith. However, because some imprecision existed about the definition of *articulus fidei*, confusion was inevitable.[7]

The opposite of an article of faith was a heresy. Thus William of Ockham could write that a "catholic truth" was one "held to be catholic by all Christian and catholic peoples." A heresy was "something contrary to divine Scripture or to the doctrine of the universal church." Such a heresy had to be held pertinaciously.[8] In addition to defining heresy, William also mentioned in passing that "catholic truth" and "the doctrine of the universal church" were still other ways that theologians of this period signaled a teaching that must be believed.

THE VOCABULARY THAT LUTHER USED TO IDENTIFY NECESSARY DOCTRINE

What words or phrases did Luther employ to define doctrine that was required? Not surprisingly, Luther wrote like a medieval man when he spoke of doctrine—but he didn't always use the terms in conventional ways.

Articles of Faith

Like his medieval forebears, when Luther wanted to speak of doctrines that all Christians must believe, he most often used the phrase "article(s) of faith."[9] At times, Luther clearly used this terminology to refer to one of the statements of the Apostles' Creed, such as in "Discussion on How Confession Should Be Made," in which the reformer gave the following advice: "The man about to make confession (who is celebrated far and wide) should do away completely with the confusion of distinctions such as these: . . . [sins] against the seven sacraments, against the seven gifts of the Holy Spirit, against the eight Beatitudes, against the nine alien sins, against the twelve articles of faith."[10] Similar to this was Luther's reference in "Bondage of the Will" to the statement "I believe . . . in the life everlasting" as one of the "chief articles" of the faith: "This life or eternal salvation, however, is something that passes human comprehension, as Paul quotes from Isaiah [64:4], in 1 Corinthians 2[:9] . . . . It is also included among the chief articles of our faith, where we say [in the creed]: 'And the life everlasting.' "[11]

Luther also used the phrase "article of faith" when he protested against some teaching widely assumed to be an article of faith, arguing that it was only opinion. An example of this contrast between articles of faith and opinion is the reformer's observation in "To the Christian Nobility of the German Nation" concerning the teaching of transubstantiation: "For it is not an article of faith that bread and wine are not present in the sacrament in their own essence and nature, but this is an opinion of St. Thomas and the pope."[12] Luther voiced a similar complaint in "Babylonian Captivity of the Church": "We do not object to their being free to invent, say, and assert whatever they please; but we also insist on our liberty, that they shall not arrogate to themselves the right to turn their opinions into articles of faith, as they have hitherto presumed to do."[13] In an introductory manner, these examples demonstrate that "article(s) (of faith)" was an important phrase by which Luther indicated that a teaching was foundational to the Christian faith.

Luther did not use *article* only to refer to doctrine that must be believed. Like his contemporaries, he could use the word "article(s)" to refer to any statement, religious or secular. For example, the individual points in a list of political grievances were referred to as "articles." Luther also occasionally referred to teachings of lesser importance as articles, as can be seen in his criticism of Andreas Bodenstein von Karlstadt: "[H]e compels us to turn from the great important articles to minor ones, so that we with him lose time and are in danger of forgetting the main articles."[14] These exceptions aside, Luther most often used "articles of faith" to refer to doctrine that all Christians must believe.

Doctrine vs. Life

Another way in which Luther referred to important doctrine was his distinction between doctrine (*doctrina, Lehre*) and life. In this paradigm, *doctrine* referred to that which was God's, specifically his salvific Word, the Scriptures. *Life* denoted what belonged to human beings, their behavior, morals, and love for one another.

In his conciliatory letter of dedication to Pope Leo X, which was published with "Freedom of a Christian" in 1520, Luther had this distinction in mind when he wrote: "I have no quarrel with any man concerning his morals but only concerning the word of truth. In all other matters I will yield to any man whatsoever; but I have neither the power nor the will to deny the Word of God."[15] Less than two months later, the same distinction between doctrine and life, more sharply worded, was directed against Leipzig cleric Hieronymus Emser:

> But I wanted to have nothing to do with your own or with anyone else's life, and I do not want to have anything to do with it now. I do not deal with [someone's] life, I deal with his teaching. An evil life is most harmful to itself. But evil teaching is the greatest evil on earth, and it leads souls to hell in large numbers. I do not care whether you are godly or evil. I shall attack your poisonous and deceitful teaching, which opposes God's word, and, with God's help, I shall counter it well.[16]

Here the importance of doctrine for Luther comes sharply into view. One can tell he had necessary doctrines in mind, rather than trivial ones, because of his anxious comment that evil doctrine leads souls to hell. Only doctrines on which salvation depends could do such a thing.

Luther found justification for this distinction in the Scriptures, especially in the writings of Paul. When radical theologian and revolutionary Thomas Müntzer[17] had lifted up Luther's alleged impiety as the reason for rejecting Luther's doctrine, the reformer responded in a letter to his Saxon princes:

> It is not a fruit of the Spirit to criticize a doctrine by the imperfect life of the teacher. For the Holy Spirit criticizes false doctrine while bearing with those who are weak in faith and life, as Paul teaches in Rom. 14[:1ff.] and 15[:1] and everywhere else. I am not so much offended by the unfruitfulness of the spirit of Allstedt as I am by his lying and his attempt to establish other doctrines. I would have paid little attention to the papists, if only they would teach correctly. Their evil life would not cause much harm. When this spirit goes so far as to be offended at our sickly life and makes this a ground for boldly judging our doctrine, he has shown sufficiently his true character.[18]

Whether the perceived opponent was on the right or the left, Luther wanted all concerned to know that doctrine, not life, was his highest priority.

Luther's use of *doctrine* was multifaceted. Although he typically contrasted doctrine with life, he also could use doctrine to denote any kind of religious teaching or practice, just as his medieval predecessors had done. Thus in "A Sermon on the Three Kinds of Good Life for the Instruction of Consciences," he spoke of "churchyard" doctrines that were only concerned with external works, such as ceremonies, clothing, and food and drink.[19]

Necessary vs. Unnecessary

Perhaps the most obvious way that Luther distinguished between doctrines was by using the adjective *necessary* (*nottige, notwendig, notwendigkeit, necesse, necccessaria*), which he often contrasted with what is *unnecessary*. In

"Defense and Explanation of All the Articles," Luther attempted to respond to his teachings that had been condemned by the papal bull *Exsurge Domine*.[20] In this context, the reformer asked the pointed question, "Has papal authority the power to make unnecessary matters necessary articles of faith, and can it make heretics of people in matters which are not necessary for salvation?"[21] In a less polemical atmosphere, Luther spoke to the question of necessary doctrine when he gave a piece of practical advice: "Now concerning private confession before communion, I still think as I have held heretofore, namely, that it neither is necessary nor should be demanded. Nevertheless, it is useful and should not be despised."[22]

To a great extent, Luther used the terminology of the late Middle Ages when he wanted to refer to doctrine that a Christian must believe. If the words he used to denote necessary doctrine were not novel, the manner in which the reformer used those words, and the concepts behind them, was unique. Luther's specific contribution was the manner in which he defined necessary doctrine. It was at this point that he broke away from his medieval moorings and eventually sailed into a new sea.

MARTIN LUTHER'S DOCTRINAL HERMENEUTIC

Bernhard Lohse has stated what has often been observed by Luther scholars: "To a great extent, then, Luther set forth his theology within specific disputes . . . he always developed his theology in relation to and in debate with the various questions of his day. Clearly we must always note what is unexpressed but in fact assumed, and as a result is of considerable weight as a basis for theological argument."[23] That is to say, Luther developed and sharpened many accents of his theology as he reacted to the arguments, accusations, condemnations, and methodologies of his opponents. Understanding the various contexts of the controversy can help make Luther's theological emphases intelligible.

Especially is this true of Luther's doctrinal hermeneutic. In the years 1518 to 1525, Luther displayed a keen interest in defining the nature of doctrine. Luther was motivated to think through the nature of doctrine because of the attacks of his literary opponents. His doctrinal hermeneutic took shape as he reacted to the accusations and methodologies of the Catholic controversialists[24] and other opponents. In fact, the arguments that Luther came to use in defining doctrine only make sense within this context.

THE CATHOLIC CONTROVERSIALISTS
AS THE CONTEXT FOR LUTHER'S DOCTRINAL HERMENEUTIC

Before the publication of Luther's "Ninety-five Theses," there is little evidence that Luther attempted to define the nature of doctrine. Afterwards, there is a noticeable increase in the frequency of such discussion. Why? The answer is the Catholic controversialists. These theologians were the literary defenders of the old faith, who, beginning with the Indulgence Controversy, sought to refute what they believed to be the heretical emphases in Luther's teachings. Their accusations and argumentation forced Luther to think through the nature of doctrine. Specifically, they contributed to Luther's doctrinal hermeneutic in two ways. First, they accused Luther of heresy concerning teachings that had not yet been elevated to the status of binding dogma. Second, the methodology the controversialists used to defend teachings of the old faith that were questioned by Luther indirectly drove the reformer to clarify his emerging methodology in defining necessary doctrine.

The first works of the Catholic controversialists that were directed against Luther were a result of the publication of the "Ninety-five Theses," which was Luther's critique of certain aspects of indulgence theory and practice. In the theses, Luther had restricted the power of the pope in three ways: (1) He denied that the pope could remit any punishments except those specifically stated in canon law (Theses 5, 61). (2) He denied that the pope could remit any guilt—only God could do so (Theses 6, 76). (3) He denied that the pope could remit punishments in purgatory (Theses 25–26). Although these questions had been addressed in two papal bulls—*Unigenitus* of 1343 and *Salvator noster* of 1476—no binding or definitive doctrinal decision had been given.[25] This didn't stop the first Roman polemicists—Johann Tetzel[26] (ca. 1465–1519), Sylvester Prierias[27] (1456–1523), Johann Eck[28] (1486–1543), and Konrad Wimpina (1460–1531)[29]—from accusing Luther of heresy for offending the power of the pope.

In January 1518, a set of 106 theses appeared. They had been authored by Konrad Wimpina and were debated by Johann Tetzel in Frankfurt. The theses charged Luther not only with error but also with blasphemy (of which heretics are guilty) for limiting the power of the pope and denying purgatory.[30] In April or May 1518, Tetzel published a refutation of Luther's "Sermon on Indulgences and Grace"[31] and for the first time likened Luther to John Wycliffe and Jan Hus as a heretic. Tetzel demanded that all twenty points of the sermon be condemned, and he fully expected that the pope, church, and universities would recognize Luther as a heretic.[32] Attached to this refutation was a set of 50 theses, also prepared by Tetzel, in which he stated that anyone who doubted the infallibility and supreme authority of the pope or who diverged from the Roman doctrine of the church, including the doctrine of indulgences, was a heretic.[33]

In March 1518, Luther received "Obelisks,"[34] which also contained accusations of heresy. Written by Johann Eck, "Obelisks" called Luther a

Bohemian; a heretic; rebellious, presumptuous, and impudent; and a despiser of the pope. Even the title of the work was accusatory. Obelisks or daggers were notations used during the Middle Ages to mark false or heretical statements in texts.[35]

These accusations of heresy provided the background and early motivation that drove Luther to develop his doctrinal hermeneutic. The accusations forced Luther to think through carefully what made someone a heretic, which in turn made him carefully think through essential doctrine. After all, only one who errs against formally established articles of faith is a heretic.

But it was not only the Catholic controversialists' accusations of heresy that stimulated Luther to develop his doctrinal hermeneutic. David Bagchi has argued persuasively that a key difference between Luther and the Catholic controversialists was the authorities they used and the way in which they used these authorities.[36]

When Tetzel, Wimpina, Eck, or Prierias accused Luther of heresy, they supported their accusations with authorities they considered sufficient for necessary doctrine but which Luther did not: the scholastic theologians and the papacy. Bagchi's analysis of the first wave of Catholic controversialist literature revealed that it was filled with proofs from the scholastic fathers. Luther would not accept the authority of the scholastic fathers because he had rejected many of the premises of scholastic theology in his September 1517 "Disputation against Scholastic Theology."[37] As Luther had written to Eck in "Asterisks": "I have asserted nothing, but have disputed and have tried to do so in a Catholic way. I desire, not that my proposition be accepted as certain, but only that the opinion of scholastics need not be accepted as certain."[38] For Luther, the writings of the scholastic theologians were at best *opiniones* and were not to be included among the traditional sources of doctrine (Scripture, church fathers, and canon law)—and the controversialists sharpened him in this understanding.

To an even greater degree, the controversialists' accusation of heresy against Luther was supported by the power of the pope. This is perhaps most clearly illustrated from Prierias's *Dialogue against the Presumptuous Conclusions of Martin Luther*,[39] which Luther received on August 7, 1518, along with a summons to appear in Rome on suspicion of heresy. The most germane section of the *Dialogue* is the introduction, which was entitled "On the Power of the Papacy." The introduction listed four *fundamenta*, or methodological preconditions, on which Prierias based his work. The second *fundamentum* asserted the inerrancy of the pope in his *ex officio* pronouncements and also the inerrancy of a church council duly convoked by the pope. The third *fundamentum* declared: "Whoever does not hold to the doctrine of the Roman church and to the pope as the infallible rule of faith, from which also Holy Scripture derives power and authority, is a heretic."[40] In this bold statement, Prierias sought to establish the pope as the highest of authorities—an authority greater than Scripture itself. The pope was guarantor of the church's rule of faith, and anyone that deviated from him was a heretic. Again, Luther could not accept this position. At a time when Luther remained in flux over doctrinal authorities, Prierias's assertions could only push him in the opposite direction as he continued to think through the sources of and authorities of doctrine.

Luther differed with his opponents not only on authorities but also on the method used to relate these authorities to one another. David Bagchi stated:

> What distinguished Luther's approach to theology from his opponents was his reductionism, his adoption of a methodological razor that prevented the multiplication of authoritative theological sources beyond necessity.
>
> . . . This reductionist or "analytic" approach stands in marked contrast with the "synthetic" approach of the Catholic controversialists—scholastic, humanist, and scholastic humanist alike. They held to a principle that Fraenkel has aptly characterized as "the more, the better." They were utterly baffled by the grounds on which Luther made qualitative distinctions between theological authorities.[41]

The controversialists' synthetic or consensus approach led them to view all sources of ecclesiastical truth—Scripture, church fathers, canon law, and scholastic doctors—as one harmonious whole. All were trustworthy witnesses to the same catholic truth. As the Roman polemicists argued with Luther over the necessity of a particular doctrine, the assumption behind their argumentation "was that the truth of a doctrine was directly related to the numbers, the antiquity, the sanctity, and the erudition of those who upheld it."[42] However, as Luther increasingly emphasized the scriptural principle, and as his following grew, the Roman polemicists came to see the weakness of this argument.

The most reliable justification for the synthetic approach was custom (*mos* and *consuetudo*, sometimes translated as "use"). The opening lines of Gratian's *Decretum* had declared custom second only to divine and human law. The controversialists also loved to cite Augustine's dictum that "the custom of the people of God has the force of law." Custom turned out to be an amazingly flexible argument, as Bagchi noted:

> The surprising thing about custom, at least as understood by the controversialists, is that it did not have to be old: it simply had to be "received." It is true that *consuetudo* was sometimes preceded by the adjective *longa* in the literature, but long usage was seen as a bonus. It was entirely consistent with this understanding of custom for Tetzel and Prierias to argue that whatever is said to be Catholic (by someone

with authority to speak on behalf of the church, for example a preacher) thereby becomes Catholic.[43]

. . . This precedential function of custom was, I think, paradigmatic for the Catholic controversialists' understanding of doctrine. In the same way as they believed what was was therefore right, they also believed that what was taught was therefore true.[44]

The synthetic methodology of the Catholic controversialists, buttressed by their use of custom, must be kept in view as one considers evidence for Luther's doctrinal hermeneutic because his attempt to define the nature of necessary doctrine was, to a large extent, a reaction against this very different method of determining doctrine.

THE CASE FOR LUTHER'S DOCTRINAL HERMENEUTIC

During the years 1518 to1525, Luther developed a doctrinal hermeneutic, a unique method by which he defined the nature of necessary doctrine. His method had both a scriptural and an evangelical canon, and these two canons must be discussed separately to enable a more focused analysis of the development and nuances of each. However, this strategy could incorrectly imply that Luther never used the canons simultaneously, which is a false impression. Instead, Luther often employed the scriptural and the evangelical canons side by side.

THE SCRIPTURAL CANON

The first canon of Luther's doctrinal hermeneutic was that a necessary doctrine of the Christian faith must be based on Scripture alone, the right Scripture, and the right Scripture rightly interpreted. This threefold formula, exactly as stated, does not come from Luther's writings, yet it describes a pattern apparent in Luther's writings during the period 1518 to 1525. As Luther wrestled with the nature of necessary doctrine, he gradually nuanced his scriptural canon in this threefold manner. At first, however, Luther's approach to defining doctrine was not measurably different from that of his contemporaries.

In the early period of his writings (1518 to early 1519), the reformer was rather unremarkable when he spoke of the definition of doctrine. At first, Luther was almost in lockstep with the mind of the late Middle Ages. Like many scholastic theologians, he held that for a teaching to be a necessary doctrine, it must be based on Scripture, the church fathers, councils, canon law, and reason. Yet even at this early stage, Luther made it clear that neither the writings of the scholastics nor the decrees of the pope by themselves could be a part of the definition of necessary doctrine.

This becomes apparent in the August 1518 "Explanations of the Ninety-Five Theses." Because the "Ninety-five Theses" had been misunderstood and criticized by many, Luther went to work in early 1518 to explain further his positions. He had finished the first draft of "Explanations" in February, but the bishop of Brandenberg, Jerome Schulze, demanded that Luther delay publication, a demand with which the reformer complied. The final edition of the document, probably somewhat revised, came off the presses in August at a time when the literary war with the Catholic controversialists was in full swing. "Explanations" is widely viewed as one of Luther's most important treatises in his formative years. It is also a suitable stage on which to view the initial development of his doctrinal hermeneutic.

In "Explanations," Luther often appeared conventional in his descriptions of the authorities by which one defined doctrine. In the opening declaration, he testified:

> I desire to say or maintain absolutely nothing except, first of all, what is in the Holy Scriptures and can be maintained from them; and then what is in and from the writings of the church fathers and is accepted by the Roman church and preserved both in the canons and the papal decrees. But if any proposition cannot be proved or disproved from them I shall simply maintain it, for the sake of debate.[45]

Luther sounded as if he was of one mind with the definition of doctrine that he had inherited. Later in "Explanations," as he sought to explain his teaching that the pope could not remit any punishments except those spelled out in canon law, Luther wrote: "[I]t is utterly absurd to teach anything in the church for which a basis cannot be found in the Scriptures, in teachers, in the canons, or at least human reason."[46]

As late as January 1519, in a letter to Elector Frederick the Wise, Luther was still working on the basis of the same fourfold authority.

> The new decretal just issued [*Cum postquam*, 9 November 1518] at Rome concerning the matter of indulgences seems to me very peculiar. . . . Fourthly, and this is the most important point, it does not, as all other laws usually do, cite some passages of Scripture, the Fathers, or Canon Law, or give any logical argument, but offers only empty words which do not deal with my problem . . . . Since the church ought to give a basis for its doctrine, as St. Peter commands [1 Pet. 3:15], and is forbidden in many ways to accept anything unless it is tested, as St. Paul states [1 Thess. 5:21], I cannot acknowledge such a decretal as a firm and sufficient doctrine of the holy church.[47]

In this scheme, Scripture was perhaps the most important basis for necessary doctrine, but it still was only one basis among several.

Where Luther already parted company with his tradition (at least with the Catholic controversialists) was over the authority of the scholastic doctors. Luther said they could in no way be a basis for defining official doctrine because they wrote only *opiniones*. In the opening declaration of "Explanations," Luther had written:

> I add one consideration and insist upon it according to the right of Christian liberty, that is, that I wish to refute or accept, according to my own judgment, the mere opinions of St. Thomas, Bonaventura, or other scholastics or canonists which are maintained without text or proof. I shall do this according to the advice of Paul to "test everything, hold fast to that which is good," although I know the feeling of Thomists who want St. Thomas to be approved by the church in everything. The weight of St. Thomas' authority is known well enough. From this declaration I believe that it is made sufficiently clear that I can err, but also that I shall not be considered a heretic for that reason, no matter how much those who think and wish differently should rage or be consumed with anger.[48]

By these words, Luther dismissed scholastic doctors as a source or norm of necessary articles. What they wrote were "mere opinions," not certain truth. If the reformer disagreed with the opinions of the scholastic doctors, therefore, he might be in error, but he could not be called a heretic because only the person who contradicted an article of faith could be a heretic. What the scholastic doctors wrote had to be tested or proven, and here, as he would often do, Luther quoted 1 Thess. 5:21. Whereas Luther later used this verse to refer to Scripture only, the immediate context strongly suggests that he was thinking of testing the scholastics by the traditional authorities mentioned above. The comment about the "Thomists who want St. Thomas to be approved by the church in everything" was a clear attack on several of Luther's Dominican controversialist opponents—such as Tetzel, Wimpina, Prierias, and Cajetan—who set Thomas Aquinas against Luther's teachings.[49]

Luther's "Explanations" also demonstrates that, at this point in his formation, the reformer regarded a general council as the authority that defined new articles of faith. For example, when Luther's controversialist opponents used recent scholastic theologians to prove that Luther had departed from the teaching of the church, he caustically responded:

> I come to the usual argument, which is the strongest of all, when I ask by what authorities they prove that punishments other than the canonical are waived through the power of the keys. In answer they point out to me Antoninus, Peter de Palude, Augustinus de Ancona, Capreolus.[50] . . . Indeed it is as if those men were of such importance and authority that whatever they think must be immediately counted among the articles of faith. Rather they ought to be reproached for having brought forth these claims to our shame and harm, claims which they have invented in accordance with their pious desire, paying absolutely no attention to that faithful admonition of the Apostle, "Test everything; hold fast what is good."

... For since this matter would be an article of faith if it had been set-tled, therefore it is not up to the teachers to define it, for it must be supported also by the decision of a general council.[51]

Later in "Explanations," Luther made it clear that just as new articles of faith could not be based on the scholastic teachers, neither could they be based solely on papal decree.

At this point the following objection is raised:

First, Sixtus IV is said to have decided that the method of intercession in no way lessens the over-all value of indulgences.

My answer is this: First if anyone wishes to be obstinate about this, he should say, "Prove what you say, Holy Father," especially since it is not for the pope alone to decide new articles of faith, but, according to the laws, to make judgments and decisions about questions of faith. This, however, would be a new article of faith. Therefore that decision would be a matter for a general council much more than the doctrine of the conception of the Holy Virgin[52] would be, especially since the latter constitutes no danger, while determining new articles of faith on the part of the pope could be a grave and great danger for people. Otherwise, since the pope is only human and can err in matters of faith and morals, the faith of the whole church would be constantly in danger if it were necessary to believe as true whatever might occur to the pope to be true.[53]

Luther did not disqualify the pope from any role in the defining of doctrine; rather, he stated that articles of faith could not be based on the decisions of the pope *sola*. Luther again stated that only a general council could decide new articles of faith. The pope was eliminated as the sole definer of doctrine because he "is only human and can err in matters of faith and morals." Because he could err, it would put the church "in dan-ger if it were necessary to believe as true whatever might occur to the pope to be true."

From "Explanations" alone, Luther's use of Scripture to define doc-trine was hardly radical. In this early phase, however, we begin to see an advance in Luther's thinking. Sometimes Luther speaks of only Scripture and reason in defining doctrine. Responding to the criticism that his teaching was proven wrong by the teaching of Bonaventura, Luther remarked:

The second objection to my argument is this: St. Bonaventura in Book 4, chapter 20, says that one must not resist strenuously if anyone should maintain that the pope has power over purgatory.

I answer, first, that the authority of St. Bonaventura is not sufficient in this matter. . . . Third, Bonaventura speaks rightly, because he

expresses his opinion by adding the words, "only if that claim is supported by the clear authority of the Scriptures or reasonable proof."[54]

It can be seen that Scripture is beginning to occupy a central place in
deciding doctrine, though Luther approvingly quoted Bonaventura that
"reasonable proof" could also suffice.

A similar advance in Luther's thinking can be observed as he raises
Scripture above canon law. Although in "Explanations" Luther had previously placed Scripture and canon law side by side as authorities, later in
the same treatise he offered a more nuanced statement: "Canon laws, like
all other man-made laws, are, according to chapter 29, bound by the circumstances of time, place, and persons, as everybody knows. It is only
about the word of Christ that it has been said, 'Thy word, O Lord,
endures forever, thy truth to all generations.' "[55] In this presentation, it
was the time-boundedness of canon law that made it inferior to the "word of
Christ," which was eternal and applicable for all generations. Therefore,
the word of Christ was to be preferred when deciding articles of faith.

Luther's continued development of his scriptural canon becomes more
evident in the November 1518 "Proceedings at Augsburg." This document was Luther's account of his hearing before Cardinal Cajetan,[56] which
took place in the city of Augsburg, October 12–14, 1518. As papal legate,
Cajetan was in Augsburg for the August imperial diet, but he also had
been commissioned by Pope Leo X to summon Luther to Augsburg as a
notorious heretic. Cajetan's commission stated that if Luther did not
recant, he was to be taken prisoner.[57] Luther's prince, Elector Frederick
the Wise, intervened on Luther's behalf, eliciting a promise from Cajetan
that Luther would be shown benevolence and mildness and, regardless of
the outcome of the hearing, would be allowed to return to Wittenberg.
The hearing[58] focused on two disputed points: (1) Luther had denied that
the merits of Christ constituted the treasury of indulgences (Thesis 58 of
the "Ninety-five Theses"), a position that contradicted *Unigenitus*, the
1343 *Extravagante*[59] of Clement VI. (2) Luther had taught justification by
faith alone or, more specifically, that a person taking the Lord's Supper
had to have certain faith that he received forgiveness there.[60] As Luther
reported the events surrounding this hearing, his scriptural canon was in
clear evidence.

In the opening section of "Proceedings at Augsburg," Luther claimed
that he told Cajetan that "[t]he Scriptures, which I follow in my Thesis 7
[of "Explanations"], are to be preferred to the bull in every case."[61] In a
written statement that Luther delivered to Cajetan during the hearing, he
again put forth his scriptural canon, elevating Scripture above human
words.

Indeed, I did not possess the extraordinary indiscretion so as to discard so many important clear proofs of Scripture on account of a single ambiguous and obscure decretal of a pope who is a mere human being. Much rather I considered it proper that the words of Scripture, in which the saints are described as being deficient in merits, are to be preferred to human words, in which the saints are said to have more merits than they need. For the pope is not above, but under the word of God, according to Gal. 1[:8]: "Even if we, or an angel from heaven, should preach to you a gospel contrary to that which you received, let him be accursed." Furthermore, it was not unimportant to me that the bull stated that this treasure was committed to Peter, concerning which there is nothing either in the gospel or any part of the Bible.[62]

In the exchange on the question of the treasury of merits, Luther contrasted the authority of Scripture with Cajetan's authority of canon law and papal decree. As in "Explanations," Luther clearly placed Scripture (which he directly identified as the Word of God) above and before both canon law and papal decree and, at least potentially, above all human words. The words of Scripture must take precedence in defining and debating doctrine.

Later in "Proceedings," Luther stated his scriptural canon more boldly. After quoting Rom. 5:19 to prove that one is justified by the obedience of Christ's works apart from indulgences, Luther set forth a definite priority: "To maintain this concerning the merits of Christ is contrary to the clear meaning of the Scriptures. Therefore I do not care whether this statement is contrary to an *Extravagante* or an *Intravagante*. *The truth of Scripture comes first*. After that is accepted, one may determine whether the words of men can be accepted as true."[63] This position represents the first part of Luther's scriptural canon. When the words of men and the words of Scripture disagree about a given doctrine, the truth of a doctrine is determined by Scripture. God's Word has the highest priority; everything else is subordinate.

Scriptural Canon I: The Necessary Teaching Must Be Based on Scripture, Not on the Words of Men

When Luther discussed articles of faith, he consistently stated that necessary teaching should be based only on Scripture, not the words of men. This insight is the first part of Luther's scriptural canon. In the course of his ongoing literary battles with the Catholic controversialists (and to a lesser extent with certain radical reformers), Luther further nuanced his definition of necessary doctrine.

What irked Luther about his opponents was not that they put forth the words of men but that whatever the words of men said were considered to be articles of faith. As he sarcastically complained to the Louvainian Jacobus Latomus:[64] "[There are] as many principal articles of faith as there are sayings of the fathers, decrees of the councils, ordinances of the pope, and opinions of the professors. You see from this that the world is almost drowning in a flood of such principal articles of faith."[65] For Luther, however, "nothing should be asserted in [questions of] faith without scriptural precedent."[66] Doctrine should be based only on Scripture. "Scripture alone is the true lord and master of all writings and doctrine on earth. If that is not granted, what is Scripture good for? The more we reject it, the more we become satisfied with men's books and human teachers."[67] These were among the opening words of Luther's famous "Defense and Explanation of all the Articles," in which the reformer attempted to defend forty-one of his teachings that had been condemned as heretical by the June 15, 1520, bull *Exsurge Domine*.[68] Later in "Defense and Explanation," Luther made it clear that Scripture was the ultimate judge in deciding and defining doctrine: "Scripture is our court of appeal and bulwark; with it we can resist even an angel from heaven—as St. Paul commands in Gal. 1[:8]—let alone a pope and a council! . . . Listen, you papists! Paul curses an angel from heaven if he teaches contrarily to Scripture, and am I not to have the power to scorn a man if he so teaches?"[69] That doctrine should be based only on Scripture was not merely the entrenched position of Luther the hardened polemicist, it was also the stance of Luther the preacher: "We should have a pure faith that believes nothing without a foundation in Scripture. Everything which we are to believe is abundantly contained in Scripture."[70]

In "Defense and Explanation," Luther applied the first part of his scriptural canon to the questions of purgatory and whether Peter had been bishop in Rome. These two examples are instructive because Luther personally believed that both were true—yet he refused to consider them to be articles of faith. He summarized his position on purgatory in this way:

> I have discussed all this in order to show that no one is bound to believe more than what is based on Scripture, and those who do not believe in purgatory are not to be called heretics, if otherwise they accept Scripture in its entirety, as the Greek church does. . . . The pope and his partisans play this game only in order to fabricate many wild articles of faith and thus make it possible to silence and suppress the true articles of the Scripture.[71]

Because purgatory could not be proven from Scripture, it was not a binding belief. No one could be called a heretic for disobeying such a teaching. According to Luther, purgatory was a "fabricated" and "wild" article of faith.[72]

On the question of whether Peter had been bishop in Rome, Luther drew the following conclusion:

Although I maintained that St. Peter was in Rome, and still do, I would not want to die for it as an article of faith. Moreover, I do not know how it could be either maintained or proven; indeed, no one (as far as I know) can prove it. It is not an article of faith, and no one is a heretic if he does not believe St. Peter was in Rome.

. . . For if it cannot be proven with certainty by Scripture that St. Peter was in Rome (which is not possible), the papacy already lies in mud and amounts to nothing. For just as unnecessary as it is to believe that St. Peter was in Rome, since Scripture does not say so, so is it equally unnecessary to believe that the pope is the heir to his see and [therefore] the pope. . . . That is why I come to the conclusion here that it is unnecessary to consider the pope either the pope or the heir to St. Peter's see until they verify with Scripture that St. Peter was in Rome.[73]

Luther was clear: Because the teaching that Peter was bishop in Rome for twenty-five years could not be proven with certainty from Scripture, such a teaching was not an article of faith. Therefore, it was not necessary to believe it. Moreover, neither was it necessary to believe that the pope was the heir to Peter's see.

Why did Luther give such preferential treatment to Scripture to the great detriment of the controversialists' consensus of authorities? The reformer provided several answers. First, only Scripture was fully trustworthy because only Scripture had never erred.

This is my answer to those also who accuse me of rejecting all the holy teachers of the church. I do not reject them. But everyone, indeed, knows that at times they have erred, as men will; therefore, I am ready to trust them only when they give me evidence for their opinions from Scripture, which has never erred. This St. Paul bids me do in 1 Thess. 5:21, where he says, "Test everything; hold fast what is good." St. Augustine writes to St. Jerome to the same effect, "I have learned to do only those books that are called the holy Scriptures the honor of believing firmly that none of their writers has ever erred. All others I so read as not to hold what they say to be the truth unless they prove it to me by holy Scripture or clear reason."[74]

Included in this first answer was a second one. Scripture itself commanded Christians to use Scripture to test all doctrine. Although Luther had previously applied 1 Thess. 5:21 ambiguously, now there was no question that it spoke only of Scripture. "St. Paul taught us this when he wrote, 'Test every doctrine; hold fast to what is good.' He did not say that one should hold fast to everyone's teaching, but that one should test them all and hold fast to what is good. . . . If, however, we should test them, as St. Paul says here, what kind of touchstone should we use other than Scripture?"[75]

A third answer was that only Scripture could define necessary doctrine because only Scripture brought certainty that what one believed was pleasing to God. Thus Luther could remark in "Avoiding the Doctrines of Men":

> This is the very worst feature about the doctrines of men and the life built upon them, that they are without foundation and warrant in the Scriptures. Men cannot know whether what they are doing is good or wicked, for their whole life is an uncertain venture. If you ask them whether they are certain that what they are and do is pleasing to God, they admit that they do not know, they must take the chance.[76]

The reason for this certainty, of course, is that Luther believed Scripture to be the word of God, so those who based doctrines on it could be certain that such doctrines were pleasing to God.

Luther could speak of the traditional authorities generally as the words or doctrines of men. When his opponents emphasized a particular authority as key, however, Luther responded with equal specificity. When cleric Hieronymus Emser[77] stated that what the fathers taught could form the basis of the doctrine that only certain Christians were priests, Luther responded with an emphatic no: "But I could not be satisfied with the passages from the fathers because they do not constitute articles of faith and are not binding, except insofar as they are founded on Scripture."[78]

When the Franciscan monk Augustine Alveld[79] claimed that whatever the pope declared was sufficient for doctrine, Luther denied this claim.

> I shall accept whatever the pope establishes and does, on condition that I judge it first on the basis of Holy Scripture. For my part he must remain under Christ and let himself be judged by Holy Scripture. But the Roman knaves come along and put him above Christ, make him a judge over Scripture, and say that he cannot err. They want to make everything he dreams about in Rome, and indeed everything they might ever think of, into articles of faith for us.[80]

Scripture as judge determined what were articles of faith, not the pope.

When *Exsurge Domine* accused Luther of teaching that Christians might oppose anything a council proposed, the reformer clarified his teaching on the authority of a council: "My papists attack this article with such hate and venom, as though I intended to teach that anybody might arbitrarily and without reason oppose the councils—a thought which was never either in my mind or on my pen. I have said that when anything contrary to Scripture is decreed in a council, we ought to believe Scripture rather than the council."[81] Luther already had addressed this in "Babylonian Captivity of the Church" when he took up the issue of transubstantiation, which had been declared an article of faith by the Fourth Lateran Council of 1215.[82] It is not within the pope's power, nor that of any general council, Luther argued "to make new articles of faith."[83] This marked a significant advance from his previous position.

Luther also specifically came out against basing articles of faith on usage (custom). Emser claimed that only those who were ordained were priests, and he attempted to substantiate this on the basis of ancient usage. Luther's scriptural canon would not allow such an argument: "Therefore learn, dear goat, that no usage can change or reinterpret anything in Scripture in articles of faith. Instead, usage applies only to external, changeable works and manners, in which neither the Christian nor the priestly estate, but only offices, services, and similar works are indicated and realized."[84] Although valuable in other areas, usage could not be a basis for articles of faith. Only Scripture could provide the basis for doctrine.

Luther was forced to grapple with another claim to authority for doctrine, though not one that the controversialists had suggested. The "new prophets" who had become active in Saxony between 1522 and 1524 claimed their doctrine came directly from the Holy Spirit. When they appealed to Joel 2:28 ("I will pour out my Spirit on all people"), Luther's scriptural canon came into play.

> We now have no revelation of the Holy Spirit other than the Holy Scripture. They must not establish some new kind of doctrine which they pretend to establish by the authority of the Holy Spirit. After all, if Christ is going to establish a new kind of preaching, He will not do this in darkness nor in the heart of one or another person. Rather, He will declare it with an open sign, lest anyone be able to have doubts about it.[85]

New revelations of the Spirit could not establish doctrines, unless there were clear and public miracles to substantiate them.

FIVE ARGUMENTS AGAINST BASING ARTICLES OF FAITH ON SCRIPTURE ALONE

As Luther's opponents grasped the scriptural canon of his doctrinal hermeneutic, they responded with at least five arguments that rejected it as insufficient.[86] Consideration of Luther's refutation of these five arguments is important because it shows how he continued to develop the first part of his scriptural canon.

1. Scripture Is Obscure. A stock argument of the controversialists was that one could not base necessary doctrine on Scripture alone because Scripture was obscure. Therefore, other authorities were needed to illumine and interpret Scripture. Luther responded to this argument by repeatedly stressing the essential *claritas scripturae*.[87] Luther averred that the idea that Scripture needed to be illumined was absurd.

> Who told them that the fathers are clearer than Scripture and not
> more obscure? . . . If the Spirit spoke in the fathers, he spoke even
> more in his own Scripture. And whoever does not understand the
> Spirit in his own Scripture—who will believe that he understands him
> in the writings of someone else?
>
> . . . Therefore, one must know that Scripture without any glosses is the
> sun and the whole light from which all teachers receive their light, and
> not vice versa.[88]

Luther did not state that every passage was clear but that the subject
matter—Christ, the Gospel, what was necessary for salvation—was abundantly clear. Thus "[t]he Scriptures are common to all, and are clear
enough in respect to what is necessary for salvation, and are also obscure
enough for inquiring minds."[89]

Luther echoed this same thought in 1525 in "Bondage of the Will."[90]
He admitted to Erasmus[91] that there were many passages in the Scriptures
that were obscure "not because of the majesty of their subject matter, but
because of our ignorance of their vocabulary and grammar."[92] These texts,
however, "in no way hinder a knowledge of all the subject matter of Scripture."[93] For Luther, the obscurity was in the reader and interpreter, not in
the Scriptures. Once the subject of Scripture was known, the Scriptures
would become clear. That subject was the gospel of Jesus Christ.

> For what still sublimer thing can remain hidden in the Scriptures,
> now that the seals have been broken, the stone rolled from the door of
> the sepulcher, and the supreme mystery brought to light, namely, that
> Christ the Son of God has been made man, that God is three and
> one, that Christ suffered for us and is to reign eternally? Are not these
> things known and sung even in the highways and byways? Take Christ
> out of the Scriptures, and what will you find left in them?[94]

Luther qualified what he had written about the *claritas* of Scripture by
stating that "there are two kinds of clarity in Scripture, just as there are
also two kinds of obscurity: one external and pertaining to the ministry of
the Word, the other located in the understanding of the heart."[95] His
comments on the external clarity of Scripture particularly have bearing on
the reformer's scriptural canon. Erasmus had asked how Christians were
to test the spirits concerning the doctrine of free will and on what authority Christians should depend.[96] Luther responded:

> There is therefore another, an external judgment, whereby with the
> greatest certainty we judge the spirits and dogmas of all men, not only
> for ourselves, but also for others and for their salvation. This judgment
> belongs to the public ministry of the Word and to the outward office,
> and is chiefly the concern of leaders and preachers of the Word. We
> make use of it when we seek to strengthen those who are weak in faith
> and confute opponents. This is what we earlier called "the external

clarity of Holy Scripture." Thus we say that all spirits are to be tested in the presence of the Church at the bar of Scripture. For it ought above all to be settled and established among Christians that the Holy Scriptures are a spiritual light far brighter than the sun itself, especially in things that are necessary for salvation.[97]

Luther demonstrated that his scriptural canon had nothing to do with a kind of crass, individualistic interpretation of Scripture that was then being manifested by the heavenly prophets.[98] True or false doctrine was to be decided before the bar of Scripture but in the presence of the church. A corporate interpretation was not rejected, as long as that interpretation submitted to Scripture and interpreted it rightly.

2. The Spirit-Led Church Gave Birth to the Scriptures; Therefore, the Church Is Superior to the Scriptures. Another argument against basing articles of faith only on Scripture stated that because the church had established the canon, the church was above Scripture. Luther responded to this position and, in so doing, further articulated his scriptural canon. Amid discussion of whether ordination was a sacrament, Luther declared:

> The church has no power to make divine promises of grace, as some prate, who hold that what is decreed by the church is of no less authority than what is decreed by God, since the church is under the guidance of the Holy Spirit. For the church was born by the word of promise through faith, and by this same word is nourished and preserved. That is to say, it is the promises of God that make the church, and not the church that makes the promise of God. For the Word of God is incomparably superior to the church, and in this Word the church, being a creature, has nothing to decree, ordain, or make, but only to be decreed, ordained, and made. For who begets his own parent? Who first brings forth his own maker?[99]

For Luther, what made the Word superior was that it brought the church into existence, not vice versa. By this statement, Luther reminded his Roman opponents that the Word of God in the Scriptures was the same Word of God that was first spoken by Christ and the apostles and that continued to be spoken through the office of preaching. The church, both then and now, was the child, born again through the Word of promise, the Gospel. The church was creature, but the Word was parent and creator. As such, it alone could create doctrine.

3. Scripture Is Insufficient for Establishing Doctrine, as Christ Himself Declared. Another favorite argument of the controversialists against Luther's scriptural canon was the alleged insufficiency of Scripture. Scripture was insufficient, the controversialists argued, because it did not contain everything needed for the doctrine and practice of the church. Nor was it intended to because Christ had said so in John 14 and John 21.[100] Christ, therefore, had further revelation to give. Luther replied that to take this position would land the Romanists in the error of the Manichaeans, who like the "new prophets" also had claimed to be bringing forth additional promised revelation of the Spirit. Moreover, this position had been refuted by a correct interpretation of John 14:26: "St. Augustine overcomes this masterfully and proves in *Against Felix* that everything the promised Holy Spirit should teach was fulfilled and written down by the apostles."[101]

4. Augustine's Statement. One of the most recurrent arguments used against Luther's scriptural canon was a saying of St. Augustine: "I would not believe the true Gospel, unless the authority of the catholic church did not move me."[102] To the catholic controversialists, this proved that the church had more authority than the Scriptures. Luther's refutation was twofold. First, "Even if Augustine had said so, who gave him the authority that we must believe what he says? What Scriptures does he quote to prove his statement? What if he erred here, as we know that he frequently did, just as did all the fathers? Should one single sentence be so mighty as to refute all the texts [of Scripture]?"[103] Second, if the controversialists were interpreting Augustine correctly, then Augustine would be contradicting himself: "For in very many places he [Augustine] exalts the Holy Scriptures above the statements of all teachers, above the decrees of all councils and churches, and will have men judge him and the teachings of everyone else according to the Scriptures."[104]

5. The Scriptures Are the Doctrines of Men Also—For They Were Written by Men. The last argument of the Catholic controversialists affirmed that because the authors of Scripture were men, their writings were also doctrines of men. If one listens to their writings, therefore, one should listen to other doctrines of men. Luther regarded such reasoning as blasphemy and argued that if this were taken to its logical conclusion, "we had best go our way, following our own fancy and really believing nothing at all, but simply regarding everything as the doctrine of men."[105] Luther would not allow this argument because it failed to reckon with the substantial difference between the Scriptures and other human writings: "They cannot even distinguish between a man who speaks for himself and one through whom God speaks. The words of the apostles were committed to them by God and confirmed and proved by great miracles, such as were never done for the doctrines of men. . . . And the Scripture, although they too are written by men, are neither of men nor from men but from God."[106]

Scriptural Canon II: The Necessary Teaching Must Be Based on the Right Scripture

Luther's ongoing controversies convinced him that a more nuanced argument was needed: Necessary doctrine must not be based only on Scripture, but on the right Scripture.

THE SCRIPTURE MUST BE CLEAR

First, one had to base an article of faith on passages of Scripture that were "clear."[107] Obscure or figurative passages, which Luther knew Scripture contained,[108] would not sustain faith at such a time: "Figurative language proves nothing."[109] Already in "Babylonian Captivity," Luther had written: "We ought to see that every article of faith of which we boast is certain, pure, and based on clear passages of Scripture. But we are utterly unable to do that in the case of the sacrament under consideration."[110] Luther was discussing the Roman sacrament of ordination, which, according to his definition, did not pass the test. Nor did the teaching of free will. In "Bondage of the Will," Luther rejected the dogmatic status of free will because it could not be proven by clear passages of Scripture.

> Consequently, if the dogma of free choice is obscure or ambiguous, it does not belong to Christians or the Scriptures, and it should be abandoned and reckoned among those fables which Paul condemns Christians for wrangling about. If, however, it does belong to Christians and the Scriptures, it ought to be clear, open, and evident, exactly like all the other clear and evident articles of faith. For all the articles of faith held by Christians ought to be such that they are not only most certain to Christians themselves, but also fortified against the attacks of others by such manifest and clear Scriptures that they shut all men's mouths and prevent their saying anything against them.[111]

Luther's pastoral care shines through in his insistence that articles of faith be based on clear passages of Scripture. This was necessary so every Christian could be certain that such articles were true. It also was necessary because the articles of faith based solidly on Scripture could be fortified against various attacks.[112]

The second part of Luther's scriptural canon was also behind his sarcastic dismissal of the divine right of the papacy.

> First, since everything that is done in the church is proclaimed in clear and plain passages of Scripture, it is surely amazing that nothing is openly said in the whole Bible about the papacy. This is especially strange since my opponents consider the papacy the most important, most necessary, and most unique feature in the church. It is a suspicious situation and makes a bad impression that so many matters of lesser importance are based upon a multitude of reliable and clear passages of Scripture, while for this one doctrine no one has been able to produce a single clear reason.[113]

Not only was the divine origin of the papacy disqualified as necessary doctrine because it lacked scriptural support, it was highly suspicious and ultimately disqualified because it could not be supported by clear passages of Scripture.

THE SCRIPTURE MUST BE CANONICAL

According to Luther, a necessary doctrine must be based on canonical Scripture, the sixty-six books of the Hebrew Old Testament and the Greek New Testament, not the apocryphal books. He first articulated this position at the Leipzig Debate during the discussion of the doctrine of purgatory.[114] Because his position on purgatory had been condemned by *Exsurge Domine*, Luther elaborated on his teaching in "Defense and Explanation":

> But their use of the passage in 2 Macc.12[:43], which tells how Judas Maccabeus sent money to Jerusalem for prayers to be offered for those who fell in battle, proves nothing, for that book is not among the books of Holy Scripture, and, as St. Jerome says, it is not found in a Hebrew version, the language in which all the books of the Old Testament are written. . . . But even were the book authoritative, it would still be necessary in the case of so important an article that at least one passage out of the chief books [of the Bible] should support it, in order that every word might be established through the mouth of two or three witnesses.[115]

Because Rome insisted that the teaching of purgatory was an article of faith, Luther insisted that it be based on the canonical books. One passage in an apocryphal book was not sufficient according to the second part of the reformer's scriptural canon.

THE SCRIPTURE MUST BE TEACHING, NOT EXAMPLE

Luther further nuanced his doctrinal hermeneutic by teaching that a necessary doctrine must be based on Scripture that is teaching, not example. Already in the 1521 "Judgment of Martin Luther on Monastic Vows," Luther emphasized that the apostle Paul's example could not determine doctrine: "I am not arguing whether Paul lived a life of celibacy, but whether his example should be made into a law or a matter of doctrine."[116] But the distinction between scriptural teaching and scriptural example was sharpened especially by Luther's polemic against Andreas Bodenstein von Karlstadt[117] (ca. 1480–1541) in "Against the Heavenly Prophets in the Matter of Images and Sacraments."[118]

Karlstadt embraced the Wittenberg Reformation in 1517, and for a while was Luther's valued assistant. With Luther, he debated Johann Eck of Ingolstadt (1486–1543) at Leipzig in 1519, helped reform the University of Wittenberg's curriculum, and published numerous treatises supporting Wittenberg's new theology. The mantle of leadership fell on Karlstadt in May 1521 when, following his stand at the Diet of Worms, Luther was declared an outlaw by the emperor and was secreted away at the Castle Wartburg. During the ten months of Luther's absence, Karlstadt attempted to implement the teachings of the Reformation, as he understood them, in the liturgical life of the Wittenberg congregation.

Unrest followed, and Luther was forced to return to the city in March 1522. After preaching a series of eight powerful sermons (the "Invocavit Sermons"[119]), Luther calmed the church and community. Order was restored, and Karlstadt's reforms were halted.

Already at this time, Karlstadt's theology was heading in a different direction than Luther's. Karlstadt had been deeply influenced by Augustine and by German mysticism, and these writings had taken him down the path of spiritualism and biblical (Mosaic) legalism.[120] Also evident in Karlstadt's theology was a biblical literalism or biblicism that putrefied into legalism. The biblicism showed up when Karlstadt said that it is sin to do whatever Christ did not do. The legalism stemmed from Karlstadt's understanding of the place of Mosaic Law in the life of the Christian. Because it was Karlstadt's conviction that Christ did not abolish anything pleasing to God in the Law of Moses, the Christian was still obligated to keep that Law.

In one instance, Karlstadt argued that because Christ had not elevated the host in the Sacrament, Christians were forbidden to do so. Luther responded:

> [W]e are of the opinion that it is not necessary to do or refrain from doing all that Christ has done or refrained from doing. Otherwise we would also have to walk on the sea, and do all the miracles that he has done.
>
> . . . Therefore we will admit no example, not even from Christ himself, much less from other saints, for it must also be accompanied by God's Word, which explains to us in what sense we are to follow or not to follow it.[121]

Christians were to beware and to pay no attention to any example in Scripture, even that of Christ, if they did not hear God's Word commanding or forbidding it.[122] Articles of faith must not be built on examples unless a clear Word of teaching accompanied them.

THE SCRIPTURE MUST NOT BE THE MOSAIC LAW

Also arising from Luther's battle with Karlstadt was the conviction that necessary articles of faith should not be based on Mosaic Law, though Luther had adhered to this idea in some form since at least the 1519 Galatians commentary.[123] According to Karlstadt, images in the church were wrong and must be taken down because they transgressed the First Commandment and led people into idolatry. Therefore, not to remove, break, and destroy images was to sin against the Law of Moses. Basing his argument on 1 Tim. 1:9 and Acts 15:10–11, Luther responded that "the whole of Moses with all his laws" had been abrogated.

> Now then, let us get to the bottom of it all and say that these teachers of sin and Mosaic prophets are not to confuse us with Moses. We

don't want to see or hear Moses. . . . We say further, that all such Mosaic teachers deny the gospel, banish Christ, and annul the whole New Testament. I now speak as a Christian for Christians. For Moses is given to the Jewish people alone, and does not concern us Gentiles and Christians. We have our gospel and New Testament. If they can prove from them that images must be put away, we will gladly follow them.[124]

Luther was concerned that Karlstadt was attempting to argue that a doctrine was necessary solely because the Law of Moses said so. Luther's scriptural canon would not allow this. Interestingly, Luther applied this abrogation of the Law of Moses to the Decalogue, as well as to the so-called judicial and ceremonial laws of the Old Testament. Luther did not mean that God's Law did not apply to Christians, a position that would have contradicted his consistent Law-Gospel paradigm. Rather, the Ten Commandments did not apply directly to Christians as they did to the Jews, though the Decalogue was the best available summary of natural law. Natural law was not optional; instead, natural law was necessary because it revealed the sinfulness of each human being, which is a prerequisite for being justified through faith in Christ. Luther stated: "Thus we read Moses not because he applies to us, that we must obey him, but because he agrees with the natural law and is conceived better than the Gentiles would ever have been able to do. Thus the Ten Commandments are a mirror of our life, in which we can see wherein we are lacking, etc."[125]

THE SCRIPTURE MUST BE FOR ALL

Luther further applied the second part of his scriptural canon by stating that a necessary doctrine must be based on a Scripture that applied to everyone: "One must distinguish well whether the word pertains to only one or to everybody."[126] There are many words in Scripture that were spoken to historic individuals that in no way applied to all Christians. For example, Luther pointed out that "God commanded Abraham to put his son to death; but that does not make me Abraham and obligate me to put my son to death. God spoke also to David. It is all God's word. But let God's word be what it may, I must pay attention and know to whom God's word is addressed."[127] Luther suggested that this principle arose from his tussles with certain unnamed "prophets" (probably Thomas Müntzer), who were claiming that something was necessary for the Christians of the sixteenth century merely because it was in God's Word.

The word in Scripture is of two kinds: the first does not pertain or apply to me, the other kind does. And upon that word which does pertain to me I can boldly trust and rely, as upon a strong rock. But if it does not pertain to me, then I should stand still. The false prophets pitch in and say, "Dear people, this is the word of God." That is true;

we cannot deny it. But we are not the people. God has not given us the directive.[128]

What was necessary for all Christians had to be based on the right Scripture, one that is addressed to everyone.

Scriptural Canon III: The Necessary Teaching Must Be Based on the Right Scripture Rightly Interpreted

Luther had little patience for those who erected articles of faith on the shifting sands of suspect interpretation. In his writings, a consistent pattern emerged in which he refused to base necessary articles of faith on the wrong kind of interpretation.

SCRIPTURE INTERPRETS SCRIPTURE

In his hearing before Cajetan, Luther had complained about the cardinal's distorted interpretations.

> As a matter of fact, when I quoted the Scriptures to prove my points, that man began in a paternal way to conjure up glosses out of his own imagination. And while he so readily used the *Extravagante* against me, he clearly pretended not to know that canon on the basis of which the church prohibits anyone from interpreting the Scriptures solely on his own authority. According to Hilary, one should not read a meaning into the Holy Scriptures, but extract it from them.[129]

Luther was objecting to a particular kind of error in interpretation, namely, that Cajetan was interpreting Scripture on his own authority by forcing the meaning of the scholastic glosses on the text.

What was wrong for the cardinal was wrong for the pope as well. One reason Luther so often objected to the Romanists' claim that only the pope was authorized to interpret Scripture[130] was because he saw the pope interpreting Scripture according to his own authority. But didn't all expositors of Scripture interpret according to their own authority? No, and Luther turned to the fathers to prove his point: "That is the real art, to gather Scripture correctly. The father who can do this best is the best father. One should read the books of all the fathers with caution, not believing them but rather watching out whether they also cite clear passages and illumine Scripture with clear Scripture. How could they overcome the heretics if they had fought with their own glosses?"[131]

When the fathers interpreted Scripture with clear Scripture, they were interpreting according to the Holy Spirit's authority, not their own. Luther expounded on this as he commented on 2 Pet. 1:20–21.

> With these words all the fathers who interpret Scripture in their own way are refuted, and their interpretation is invalidated. It is forbidden to rely on such interpretation. If Jerome or Augustine or anyone of the fathers has given his own interpretation, we want none of it. Peter has stated this prohibition: You shall not give your own interpretation.

The Holy Spirit Himself must expound Scripture. Otherwise it must remain unexpounded. Now if anyone of the saintly fathers can show that his interpretation is based on Scripture, and if Scripture proves that this is the way it should be interpreted, then the interpretation is right.[132]

That Luther has doctrine in mind is made clear when he adds: "It is especially necessary for us to understand this well, lest we permit the right and the power shared by all Christians to pass judgment on all doctrine to be wrested from us, and lest we let it come to the point that we must wait until the councils decide what we are to believe and must follow them."[133] Thus necessary doctrine must be based on the right Scripture rightly interpreted. For Luther, this meant, above all, that Scripture (the Holy Spirit) interprets Scripture.

The Natural, Literal, and Grammatical Meaning

According to Luther, Scripture rightly interpreted also meant that one must interpret according to the literal sense. Luther had inherited the traditional fourfold medieval method of exegesis. Scripture was understood to have four meanings: the literal, the tropological, the allegorical, and the anagogical. Although Luther had uncritically used this fourfold method in his early lectures on the Book of Psalms,[134] he eventually dismissed it as useless for defining doctrine. In his 1519 Galatians commentary, Luther was beginning to appraise critically the tradition he had received.

> There are usually held to be four senses of Scripture. They are called the literal sense, the tropological, the allegorical, and the anagogical, so that Jerusalem, according to the literal sense, is the capital city of Judea; tropologically, a pure conscience or faith; allegorically, the church of Christ; and anagogically, the heavenly fatherland.
>
> . . . This kind of game may, of course, be permitted to those who want it, provided they do not accustom themselves to the rashness of some, who tear the Scriptures to pieces as they please and make them uncertain.[135]

In 1519, Luther was willing to allow the use of the fourfold method but not as a basis for establishing doctrine. "But these interpretations should not be brought forward with a view to establishing a doctrine of faith. For that four-horse team (even though I do not disapprove of it) is not sufficiently supported by the authority of Scripture, by the custom of the fathers, or by grammatical principles."[136]

Eventually Luther discarded the fourfold method and insisted that only the literal, natural, plain, and grammatical meaning of the text should be used, especially in articles of faith, because "the natural meaning of the words is queen, transcending all subtle, acute sophistical fancy."[137] In an age when the prevailing exegetical method was to lay stress on the hidden or spiritual meaning of Scripture, Luther's approach was radical. More than once the reformer reminded his opponents not to be like Origen, who "was rightly repudiated long ago because, ignoring the grammatical sense, he turned the trees and everything else written concerning Paradise into allegories."[138] Luther's oft-repeated interpretive rule of thumb was that "[i]n no writings, least of all the divine, is it right in mere whimsy to grasp at figurative meanings. These ought to be shunned, and the pure, simple, original sense should be sought, unless the context or an evident absurdity forces one to recognize a figurative expression."[139] For Luther, understanding a passage figuratively was to be the last resort, not the first, an approach used only after being forced from the grammatical meaning. Only the literal, plain, grammatical meaning was a suitable basis on which to build an article of faith.

In the 1525 commentary on Deuteronomy, Luther summarized what he had learned.

> This admonition I have often given elsewhere I repeat here and shall give again: that the Christian reader should make it his first task to seek out the literal sense, as they call it. For it alone is the whole substance of faith and Christian theology; it alone holds its ground in trouble and trial, conquers the gates of hell (Matt. 16:18) together with sin and death, and triumphs for the praise and glory of God. Allegory, however, is too often uncertain, and is unreliable and by no means safe for supporting faith.
>
> . . . Hence the rule of Paul should be observed here, that allegories should be kept in second place and be applied for the strengthening, adorning, and enriching of the doctrine of faith, or, as he says in 1 Cor. 3:11ff., they should not be the foundation but be built on the foundation, not as hay, wood, and stubble but as silver, gold, and gems. This is done when, according to the injunction of Rom. 12:6, prophecy is according to the analogy of faith, namely, that you first take up a definite statement set down somewhere in the Scriptures, explain it according to the literal sense, and then at the end connect to this an allegorical meaning which says the same thing. Not as though the allegorical meaning proved or supported the statement of doctrine; but it is proved or supported by the statement, just as a house does not hold up the foundation but is held up by the foundation.[140]

For Luther, an allegorical or figurative interpretation could not support a statement of doctrine; only a literal interpretation could do so.

An "unnatural" or nonliteral way of understanding a text, Luther believed, was often prompted by reason refusing to believe what the text asserted. One should simply accept that all articles of faith were beyond reason's ability to grasp, proceed on the basis of the simple understanding, and believe.

> But if we are so to treat our faith that we bring our pet ideas into Scripture and deal with Scripture according to our understanding, attending only to what is common to the crowd and generally accepted notions, then no article of the faith will remain. For there is none in Scripture that God has not placed beyond the reach of reason. . . . [I]n reality reason balks at the Word of God and the articles of faith.[141]

According to Luther, human reason was the mortal enemy of faith. Left to its own devices, reason could do nothing but create heresy.[142]

THE EVANGELICAL CANON

For Luther, a teaching that was a necessary article of faith must be based only on Scripture, the right Scripture, and the right Scripture rightly interpreted. This is his scriptural canon. Luther had another canon, however, that he used to test whether a doctrine was necessary: the evangelical canon. This canon states that only teachings necessary for salvation, in harmony with the Gospel, or which keep the conscience free can rightly be considered articles of faith. An article of faith must be necessary for salvation. If believing or not believing it saved or damned one, then it was a necessary doctrine. Luther had, however, numerous ways of expressing this canon.

What Is Necessary for a Christian Must Make One Christian

As early as his 1518 lectures on Hebrews, Luther had drawn the distinction between man-made doctrines and the Gospel. All man-made laws and doctrines were powerless to change human beings, according to Luther. By contrast, "the Gospel preserves nothing of the old man but destroys him completely and makes him new."[143] According to this definition, the Gospel made a Christian; therefore, it was true doctrine. In "On the Papacy in Rome," Luther responded to Alveld's claim that all those outside the Roman fellowship were heretics and not Christians:

> For whatever is necessary to being a true Christian must make one. If it does not make a true Christian then it must not be necessary, just as I am not made a true Christian by being in Wittenberg or in Leipzig. Now if it is clear that the external unity of the Roman assembly does not make Christians, then being outside of it certainly does not make heretics or schismatics either.[144]

When Emser declared that those who did not follow Roman custom and law were heretics, Luther retorted: "And even if they [Roman usage and law] were to belong to universal Christendom, it would still not be an error of faith not to keep them. To obey human laws does not make a

Christian; not to obey them does not make a non-Christian."[145] Just as Luther had already rejected the argument of custom with his scriptural canon, he did the same with his evangelical canon.

When members of the Strasbourg clergy wrote Luther in 1524, asking his opinion of Karlstadt's theological views, the reformer emphasized his evangelical canon in his response:

> My sincere counsel and warning is that you be circumspect and hold to the single question, what makes a person a Christian? Do not on any account allow any other question or other art to enjoy equal importance. When anyone proposes anything ask him at once, "Friend, will this make one a Christian or not?" If not, it cannot be a matter of major importance which requires earnest consideration.[146]

Necessary for Salvation

In a related manner, Luther asserted his evangelical canon by explicitly stating that a doctrine could not be considered necessary (that is, an article of faith) unless it was necessary for salvation. In the same context, Luther often would insist that it was not heretical to disagree with something not necessary for salvation.

In the autumn of 1520, the reformer was ready to live peaceably with Rome and to submit to her assertions, provided that such assertions did not violate his evangelical canon.

> We do not object to their being free to invent, say, and assert whatever they please; but we also insist on our liberty, that they shall not arrogate to themselves the right to turn their opinions into articles of faith, as they have hitherto presumed to do. It is enough that we accommodate ourselves to their rites and ceremonies for the sake of peace; but we refuse to be bound by such things as if they were necessary to salvation, which they are not. Let them lay aside their despotic demand, and we shall yield free obedience to their wishes, in order that we may live in peace with one another.[147]

The particular doctrine under discussion when Luther penned these words was the Roman sacrament of ordination. According to Luther, such a teaching could never be an article of faith because it was not necessary for salvation.

One of Luther's "errors" condemned by the bull *Exsurge Domine* was his statement that it would not be heresy to disagree with an opinion of the pope and a large majority of the church, provided the opinion didn't deal with something necessary for salvation. In his 1521 "Defense and Explanation of All the Articles," the reformer took up this question again.

> Why will they not allow me to hold this article, since it speaks only of things not necessary to salvation? In regard to the conception of our Lady they have admitted that, since this article is not necessary to sal-

vation, it is neither heresy nor error when some hold that she was conceived in sin, although in this case council, pope, and the majority hold a different view. Why should we poor Christians be forced to believe whatever the pope and his papists think, even when it is not necessary to salvation? Has papal authority the power to make unnecessary matters necessary articles of faith, and can it make heretics of people in matters which are not necessary for salvation?[148]

It had become axiomatic for Luther that heresy was only that which contradicted an article of faith, and an article of faith was only that which was necessary for salvation. Moreover, a Christian should be obligated to believe only what was necessary for salvation. Luther's Roman opponents condemned his statement because they worked with a different doctrinal hermeneutic. For example, Pope Sixtus IV had forbidden debate on the immaculate conception of Mary. His prohibition, however, had nothing to do with the necessity of that doctrine for salvation; rather, it was because the matter had not yet been "decided by the Roman Church or the apostolic see."[149] Luther interpreted the pope's decree in light of his evangelical canon. The conception of Mary did not have dogmatic status because it was not necessary for salvation. Given the different definitions of doctrine, a parting of the ways was inevitable between Luther and those who opposed him.

Justification as Criterion

An important component in Luther's evangelical canon that is observable in his writings from 1518 to 1525 is the idea of a kind of hierarchy of doctrines. For Luther, this was not a sophisticated ordering of doctrines into categories such as fundamental and nonfundamental, as the later Lutheran dogmaticians would do.[150] Nor was his hierarchy merely a matter of giving priority to the doctrines of the Trinity and the person of Christ, as his medieval forebears had done.[151] For Luther, one doctrine in particular was clearly the most important: the Gospel of Jesus Christ. This treasure and gift of God was the highest of doctrines.[152] What was Luther's definition of Gospel?

> That, I say, is our gospel, that Christ made us righteous and holy through that sacrifice and has redeemed us from sin, death, and the devil and has brought us into his heavenly kingdom. We have to grasp this and hold it fast through faith alone. We have preached this and reiterated it so often that everyone can know it well and can conclude from it that all our own works undertaken to expiate sin and escape death are necessarily blasphemous. They deny God and insult the sacrifice that Christ has made and disgrace his blood, because they try thereby to do what only Christ's blood can do.[153]

Christ by his death made us righteous; we grasp this through faith alone; all this is apart from our works—this is Luther's doctrine of justification by grace for Christ's sake through faith. The teaching that the just shall live by faith was, for the reformer, "by far the most important article."[154] The "chief article and the best part of the Gospel" is the teaching "that we are redeemed by the blood of Christ, that our sins have been taken away, and how He has been given to us as a gift. This cannot be grasped in any other way than through faith. The apostle spoke about this when he said, 'Christ also died for sins once for all' ([1 Peter] 3:18)."[155]

Luther similarly located the theological concepts of "faith," "Christian," and "Christ" within the matrix of justification. As he stated in "Preface to Romans": "Faith is a living, daring confidence in God's grace, so sure and certain that the believer would stake his life on it a thousand times."[156] This faith, however, was unabashedly intolerant: "Faith in Christ cannot tolerate grace and justification coming from our own works or the works of others, for faith knows and confesses continually that grace and justification come from Christ alone."[157] In fact, "faith and works stand at opposite extremes in the matter of justification."[158] What, then, does it mean to be a Christian, and what is Christ? "This is the definition of being a Christian: simply believing you are justified by the works of Christ alone without any works of your own, believing you have been freed from your sins and saved. Similarly, by definition this is what Christ is: 'He who saves his people from their sins,' he who gives them his own merits and complete justification."[159]

Yet in giving highest priority to the gospel of justification by grace through faith, Luther was actually investing it with an important interpretive function. According to his evangelical canon, the doctrine of justification was the chief article, and, as such, it was the criterion[160] by which the reformer defined whether other teachings were necessary doctrines. For Luther, "[t]he doctrine of God teaches faith,"[161] by which he meant justifying faith. All doctrines, if they were divine and necessary doctrines, were connected to justifying faith in the Gospel of Jesus Christ. Therefore, any and all doctrines that contradicted this chief article could not be necessary doctrines and were to be summarily rejected. Luther understood this to be the import of Gal. 1:8–9: "Therefore let us say confidently with Paul: 'Damned and accursed be every doctrine from heaven, from earth, or from whatever source it is brought—every doctrine that teaches us to trust in works, righteousness, and merits other than those that belong to Jesus Christ.' "[162]

The criterion of justification was much in evidence in a letter of encouragement written by Luther to the Christians of Livonia in August 1523.

> From this you have gone on and learned that all the doctrines that have been proposed to us hitherto in order to make us righteous and save us by works, by the laying aside of sin and the doing of penance

(such, for example, as the appointed fasts, prayers, pilgrimages, masses, vigils, charitable endowments, monkery, nunnery, priestcraft), all such things are devils' doctrine and blasphemy, because they pretend to do for us what only the blood of Christ, through faith, can do. Thus they ascribe to man's doctrines and works that which belongs only to the Word and works of God.[163]

One by one, doctrines that the Romanists had proposed to the Livonians as necessary were critiqued and rejected. Luther rejected them as "devils' doctrine" because they contradicted the Gospel. They claimed to do what only faith in Christ's blood could do, that is, justify and save human beings.

In this context, Luther considered the teaching of the Law as a necessary doctrine. According to Luther's scriptural canon, one did not accept doctrines as necessary if they were based only on Mosaic Law. This did not mean, however, that natural law was not necessary. Luther made this clear in "Against the Heavenly Prophets." Near the beginning of this treatise, he listed what he considered to be the two "most important and necessary articles."[164] The second article was the gospel of justification by faith alone. The first article was "the law of God, which is to be preached so that one thereby reveals and teaches how to recognize sin (Rom. 3[:20] and 7[:7]), as we have often shown in our writings."[165] Natural law, as revealed in the Decalogue, was an important article of faith because it was a prerequisite for justification by faith. Until the Law had done its work of showing sinners their sin, the message of the Gospel could not be preached. Thus the doctrine of the Law of God and, by derivation, the doctrine of original sin were necessary because they were connected to justification as prerequisites.

One of the best examples of how Luther used justification as an evangelical canon is in "Bondage of the Will," which was written against Desiderius Erasmus. E. Gordon Rupp was at least partially correct when he observed that in the debate over the freedom of the will, "Erasmus prodded Luther into some splendid epigrams and into uttering hermeneutic principles of worth."[166] The way Luther used justification as criterion is such a hermeneutic principle of worth.

It is well known that Luther and Erasmus differed on the importance attached to the question of free will.[167] At the beginning of *Diatribe*, Erasmus had clearly revealed that he considered the whole topic unnecessary.

This, I say, was in my judgment sufficient for Christian godliness, nor should we through irreverent inquisitiveness rush into those things which are hidden, not to say superfluous: whether God foreknows anything contingently; whether our will accomplishes anything in things pertaining to eternal salvation; whether it simply suffers the action of grace; whether what we do, be it of good or ill, we do by necessity or rather suffer to be done to us.[168]

On the other hand, Luther considered the question of whether the will does something or nothing in matters pertaining to eternal salvation as something absolutely necessary. It was

> the cardinal issue between us, the point on which everything in this controversy turns. For what we are doing is to inquire what free choice can do, what it has done to it, and what is its relation to the grace of God. If we do not know these things, we shall know nothing at all of things Christian, and shall be worse than any heathen. . . . For if I am ignorant of what, how far, and how much I can and may do in relation to God, it will be equally uncertain and unknown to me, what, how far, and how much God can and may do in me.[169]

Luther considered the subject of free will necessary to discuss because it had everything to do with how one is saved. As he saw it, the doctrine of free choice committed two errors that contradicted the gospel of justification by grace. First, as espoused by Erasmus, free choice led to a kind of semi-Pelagianism,[170] a belief that human beings, by their own power and worthiness, contributed something, however small, to merit righteousness and salvation. In the last section of "Bondage of the Will," Luther showed why free will must be rejected. He vigorously applied justification as a criterion.

> For what is sought by means of free choice is to make room for merits. *Diatribe* has shown this all along by her insistent demand: "If there is no freedom of choice, what room is there for merits? If there is no room for merits, what room is there for rewards? To what are we to ascribe it if a man is justified without merits?" Paul here replies that there is no such thing as merit, but all who are justified are justified freely (*gratis*), and this is to be ascribed to nothing but the grace of God. With the gift of righteousness, moreover, there are given also the Kingdom and eternal life. What about "endeavoring" now? What about your "earnest striving" and "works"? What about the merits of free choice? What use are they? You cannot complain of obscurity and ambiguity; the facts and the words are very clear and very simple.
>
> For suppose they do attribute as little as possible to free choice, nevertheless they teach that by means of this minimum we can attain to righteousness and grace. Nor have they any other way of solving the problem of why God justifies one man and abandons another than by positing free choice, and inferring that one has endeavored while the other has not, and that God respects the one for his endeavor but despises the other, and he would be unjust if he did anything else.
>
> . . . But Paul kills both these birds with one stone when he says that all are justified freely, or again, are justified apart from law and works of

law. For when he asserts that justification is freely bestowed on all who are justified, he leaves no one to work, or earn, or prepare himself, and he leaves no work that can be called congruous or condign; and thus by a single stroke of his thunderbolt he shatters both the Pelagians with their total merit, and the Sophists with their little scrap of merit. Free justification allows of no workers, because there is an obvious contradiction between "freely given" and "earned by some work."[171]

For Luther, the teaching of free will as espoused by Erasmus and the late scholastic tradition attributed salvation to the will, work, and efforts of man. Salvation was dependent, at least in part, on "doing what was within one."[172] This doctrine was ruled out by Luther's understanding of justification by grace, which declared that one's salvation was totally by God's grace, a gift given that was in no way dependent on anything about a human being or within a human being. In the words of Carter Lindberg: "The good news, Luther discovered, is that justification is not what the sinner achieves but what the sinner receives. That is, it is not the sinner who has changed, but rather the sinner's situation before God has changed."[173]

The second way Luther ruled out the doctrine of free will by the criterion of justification was that free will denied, or at least doubted, whether God necessarily foreknew all things. Luther believed such doubts or denials destroyed the reliability of God's promises.

> For if you doubt or disdain to know that God foreknows all things, not contingently, but necessarily and immutably, how can you believe his promises and place a sure trust and reliance on them? For when he promises anything, you ought to be certain that he knows and is able and willing to perform what he promises . . . . But how will you be certain and sure unless you know that he knows and wills and will do what he promises, certainly, infallibly, immutably, and necessarily?
>
> . . . Therefore, Christian faith is entirely extinguished, the promises of God and the whole gospel are completely destroyed, if we teach and believe that it is not for us to know the necessary foreknowledge of God and the necessity of the things that are to come to pass.[174]

As with the doctrine of the capability of human will, Luther did not critique the doctrine of God's necessity according to categories of reason, testimonies of church fathers, councils, or popes. He judged the doctrine according to its relation to the criterion of the gospel of justification by grace through faith in Christ.

The Conscience Must Remain Free

One final way that Luther used his evangelical canon to determine articles of faith was by considering what effect the proposed doctrine had on Christian freedom and the conscience of a Christian. According to Luther, evangelical freedom was a fruit of justifying faith and something extremely serious. To violate Christian freedom was, for Luther, "no less ungodly than to have denied the faith and to have apostacized, as we learn from Paul's letter to the Galatians."[175] Indeed, one's salvation depended on it: "This matter of Christian liberty is nothing to joke about. We want to keep it as pure and inviolate as our faith, even if an angel from heaven were to say otherwise. It has cost our dear, faithful Savior and Lord Jesus Christ too much. It is also altogether too necessary for us. We may not dispense with it without the loss of our salvation."[176]

What was Luther's definition of Christian freedom?

> Christian or evangelical freedom, then, is a freedom of conscience which liberates the conscience from works. Not that no works are done, but no faith is put in them. For conscience is not the power to do works, but to judge them. The proper work of conscience (as Paul says in Romans 2[:15]), is to accuse or excuse, to make guilty or guiltless, uncertain or certain. . . . Christ has freed this conscience from works through the gospel and teaches this conscience not to trust in works, but to rely only on his mercy.
>
> . . . And so, the conscience of a man of faith depends solely and entirely on the works of Christ.[177]

For Luther, Christian freedom meant having a free conscience, which in turn meant trusting only in the saving works of Christ, not in one's own works and performances. The moment one depended on anything other than Christ to be justified became the moment one's conscience was ensnared.

The question of doctrine was extremely important in this context because wicked and human doctrines attacked the freedom of conscience[178] and ultimately destroyed it.[179] Because of this, only articles of faith could "rule the conscience."[180] For Luther, the problem with the doctrines of men was that they made matters of conscience out of things that were not articles of faith, such as food, drink, clothing, and days.[181] This also was the reason that Luther and his party condemned the doctrines of men.

> We do not condemn the doctrines of men just because they are the doctrines of men, for we would gladly put up with them. But we condemn them because they are contrary to the gospel and the Scriptures. While the Scriptures liberate consciences and forbid that they be taken captive by the doctrines of men, these doctrines of men captivate the conscience anyhow. This conflict between the Scriptures and the doctrines of men we cannot reconcile.[182]

Christian freedom and the freedom of the conscience, therefore, became a gauge by which Luther determined whether doctrines in question were necessary doctrines. If such doctrines kept the conscience free, they qualified as articles of faith; if they ensnared the conscience by forcing it to depend on something other than Christ's Gospel for salvation, they were disqualified as necessary doctrines. Using this gauge of Christian freedom, Luther rejected the entire canon law: "Here you see the entire canon law as well as the dominion of the pope condemned as being against Christ, because they do nothing else but ensnare consciences in their own works and take them away from Christ, after having first destroyed their freedom as well as any teaching or knowledge of freedom."[183]

When Karlstadt vigorously renounced images, teaching that whoever did not remove and destroy them was sinning, Luther saw that the freedom of the conscience was at stake and reacted with indignation.

> Rather murderous spirits are not to be permitted to create sins and problems of conscience where none exist, and murder souls without necessity. For although the matter of images is a minor, external thing, when one seeks to burden the conscience with sin through it, as through the law of God, it becomes the most important of all. For it destroys faith, profanes the blood of Christ, blasphemes the gospel, and sets all that Christ has won for us at naught.[184]

To emphasize so passionately the removal of images, as if one's salvation depended on it, captivated and murdered the conscience because it tempted the Christian to depend on a work rather than on Christ alone.

Luther also perceived Karlstadt to be enslaving the conscience through his teaching that it was idolatrous to elevate the host in the Mass. According to Luther, such a position gave the impression that not elevating the host was necessary for salvation, something that the freedom of the conscience would not allow.

> For with teaching he manhandles consciences, which Christ has won with his own blood, and kills souls, which God has dearly purchased, with commandments and sins. For thereby the kingdom of Christ will be destroyed and everything the gospel has brought us exterminated. For Christ cannot remain in the conscience that goes whoring after alien teaching and the commandments of men. There faith must perish.

> . . . He is unable to deal properly with the main articles of Christian doctrine, and yet he presses such foolishness so severely on the conscience, with such bombastic words, as though these were the main articles on which everything depended.[185]

Luther also used Christian freedom as part of his evangelical canon when he cautioned against imposing any particular liturgical order as binding on all Christians. To do this, in his opinion, would be to risk captivating the conscience.

> Thus we think about the mass. But in all these matters we will want to beware lest we make binding what should be free, or make sinners of those who may do some things differently or omit others. All that matters is that the Words of Institution should be kept intact and that everything should be done by faith. For these rites are supposed to be for Christians, i.e., children of the "free woman," who observe them voluntarily and from the heart, but are free to change them how and when ever they may wish. Therefore, it is not in these matters that anyone should either seek or establish as law some indispensable form by which he might ensnare or harass consciences. Nor do we find any evidence for such an established rite, either in the early fathers or in the primitive church, but only in the Roman church. But even if they decreed anything in this matter as a law, we would not have to observe it, because these things neither can nor should be bound by laws. Further, even if different people make use of different rites, let no one judge or despise the other, but every man be fully persuaded in his own mind [Rom. 14:5]. Let us feel and think the same, even though we may act differently. And let us approve each other's rites lest schisms and sects should result from this diversity in rites—as happened in the Roman church.[186]

Because Luther approached liturgical reform conservatively, only changing what conflicted with the Gospel and with Scripture, the above quote does not mean that Luther was advocating an "anything goes" attitude toward worship. Great care was required in reforming the liturgy. But the above quote does make clear that at least at this stage, Luther did not consider a particular form of the Divine Service to be an article of faith, thus it should not bind the conscience. Freedom should remain supreme.[187] The last thing the reformer wanted was to return the liturgy to the position of a good work necessary for salvation, which he believed had happened with the Roman Canon of the Mass.

> For this is the damnable thing about the popish services: that men made laws, works, and merits out of them—to the detriment of faith— and did not use them to train the youth and common people in the Scriptures and in the Word of God, but became so engrossed in them as to regard them as inherently useful and necessary for salvation. That is the [work of the] very devil. The ancients did not institute or order them to that intent.[188]

CONCLUSION

Luther gradually developed a criteriology during the years 1518 to 1525 that defined what was necessary Christian doctrine and what was not. Yet

Luther's doctrinal hermeneutic did not emerge whole-cloth. Rather, his hermeneutic gradually took shape as he reacted to the arguments of his literary and political opponents, including the Catholic controversialists, radical reformers, and false brethren. Specifically, the tendency of Luther's opponents to indiscriminately elevate every controversial doctrine to the status of an article of faith drove Luther to nuance further his scriptural and evangelical canons. By 1525, Luther held that a doctrine was an article of faith only if it was based on the right Scripture rightly interpreted and only if it was necessary for salvation as measured by the criterion of justification.

What is not yet clear is the relationship between the scriptural and evangelical canons. Could they be used independently of each other, or were both needed to define necessary doctrine? More important, did Luther consider them to be equal, or did one have priority over the other?

At times, Luther applied only one canon to the doctrine in question and accepted or rejected that doctrine accordingly. For example, when addressing such teachings as the Roman priesthood, indulgences, or purgatory, Luther dismissed them solely on the basis of his scriptural canon. These teachings were not founded on Scripture; therefore, they could not be necessary articles of faith.[189] Luther could equally dismiss teachings such as appointed fasts, prayers, and pilgrimages as necessary doctrines solely on the basis of his evangelical canon. Such teachings were "devils' doctrine" because they claimed to do what only Christ's blood could do, that is, they claimed to save human beings.[190] Luther occasionally used both canons in tandem to accept or reject a doctrine, as he did in his opposition to the office of the papacy.[191]

Did Luther place one canon above the other? The answer is anything but clear. At best one can make a logical deduction that, admittedly, Luther himself never explicitly made. If one takes Luther's evangelical canon seriously, then it follows that it had the higher priority. If only those church teachings that make a Christian, that are necessary for salvation, and that are connected to the gospel of justification are necessary articles of faith, then it follows that all other teachings, even other teachings in the Scriptures, are not necessary articles of faith. Biblical teachings on fasting or financial giving satisfied Luther's scriptural canon, but because they were not necessary for salvation, they did not satisfy his evangelical canon. Therefore, such teachings could not be necessary doctrines.

In the years 1518 to 1525, Luther did not make such an explicit distinction between canons. He did write: "When anyone proposes anything ask him at once, 'Friend, will this make one a Christian or not?' If not, it cannot be a matter of major importance which requires earnest consideration."[192] Whether Luther was applying this kind of statement to scriptural teachings, however, is not obvious. At this stage in his development,

Luther had not yet sufficiently thought through the relationship between the scriptural and the evangelical canons to make definitive statements about which had priority over the other.

It is also noteworthy that though Luther often gave the oral Word of God priority over the written Word,[193] he consistently based necessary doctrine only on the written Word. Only the Scriptures, the written Word of God, could be the clear and objective basis to authenticate an article of faith.

Luther held that only those teachings that satisfied his doctrinal hermeneutic were necessary for salvation. But did he also use his doctrinal hermeneutic to determine which doctrines were necessary for unity among Christian groups? The next chapters examine representative six-teenth-century dialogues to demonstrate Luther's doctrinal hermeneutic in ecumenical settings.

3

LUTHER'S DIALOGUE
WITH THE *UNITAS FRATRUM*

In fall 1994, a Consultation in Geneva (Prague IV) was held to discuss the topic "Towards a Renewed Dialogue between the First and Second Reformations."[1] Heirs of the "first reformation"[2] (Waldensian, Czechoslovak Hussite Church, Czech Brethren, etc.) met with heirs of the "second Reformation" (Lutheran and Reformed) to discuss, in part, whether a better understanding of each reformation could be a worthwhile contribution to today's ecumenical movement. In reviewing the period 1522 to 1524, some participants touched on the dialogue held between Martin Luther and such sixteenth-century Hussite bodies as the Utraquists and the Unity of Brethren (*Unitas Fratrum*). The sense that somewhere in the relations between Luther and the Hussites lies an ecumenical plumb line to guide us is not new.[3]

Chapter 2 demonstrated that an intentionally nuanced doctrinal hermeneutic can be traced in Luther's writings from 1518 to 1525. He used this hermeneutic to determine which Christian teachings were necessary for all Christians to believe. But were such articles of faith necessary for unity as well as for salvation? Did Luther apply his doctrinal hermeneutic to unity discussions in which he participated, which would mean he based unity among Christian groups only on necessary doctrines?

This chapter demonstrates that Luther did seek to achieve unity with the Brethren during the period 1522 to 1524 on the basis of his doctrinal hermeneutic. Why choose the Brethren as a test case? Because they are an excellent example of another fellowship actively seeking unity with Luther and vice versa. The focus of discussion in this chapter is Luther's 1523 treatise "The Adoration of the Sacrament," which was the reformer's primary written contribution to the dialogue with the Brethren.[4] As defined by his doctrinal hermeneutic, the teachings Luther insisted on for unity in this treatise are necessary ones. The first part of this chapter will sketch the Brethren's beginnings, theology, and first contacts with Luther. The second part will focus on Luther's treatise "Adoration of the Sacrament."

UNITY OF BRETHREN: BEGINNINGS, THEOLOGY, AND CONTACTS WITH LUTHER[5]

By the early 1520s, the Unity of Brethren had existed as a separate body for approximately 50 years.[6] They had grown out of the various renewal movements that were prevalent in Bohemia and Moravia after the martyrdom of Jan Hus.[7] The Brethren were one of several small groups that had become dissatisfied with the Hussite Utraquist[8] church, led by archbishop Jan Rokycana (ca. 1390–1471). The Hussites, loosely united under the 1420 "Four Articles of Prague," had successfully steered the passage of the *Compacta* through the Council of Basle in 1436. The *Compacta*, a restricted version of the "Four Articles of Prague," gave the Utraquists the right to (1) freely preach God's Word; (2) administer the Lord's Supper in both kinds; (3) prohibit secular authority to priests and monks; and (4) call for repentance at all levels of Christian society and for the punishment of mortal sins. However, contrary to the Hussites' hope that the *Compacta* would be valid for all Christendom, the council ruled that the "Four Articles" were valid only for Christians in Bohemia who were willing to be governed by the agreement. This effectively created a special Czech Utraquist Church alongside the Czech Roman Catholic Church. Led by Rokycana, the Utraquist Church struck the Hussite middle course. The Utraquists attempted to be broad-minded enough to allow room for the many Hussite factions in Bohemia, but there was widespread dissatisfaction with this course. Thus many small lay groups began to form, groups that were seeking "a surer salvation" than the one offered by the Utraquists.

One of these groups, led by Rehor (Gregory), formed a congregation in the village of Kunvald in late 1457, and into it flowed various Hussite groups. Their actual break with the Utraquists and the Church of Rome came ten years later when they created a new priestly order, largely through the direction of Rehor. On March 26, 1467, they chose three priests from among themselves by lot. With this act, the Unity of Brethren became an officially separate entity. Later, for the sake of the weak in faith among the Brethren, the three priests were ordained by both a Roman and a Waldensian ordination.

The formation of unity and theology among the Brethren was influenced by Petr Chelcicky[9] (ca. 1380–?), an outstanding lay preacher whose writings they had enthusiastically read. In general, the theology of the Brethren stressed Communion in both kinds, encouraged a strict biblicism, opposed all authorities and writings that contradicted God's Law, observed the seven sacraments, rejected transubstantiation and a figurative conception of the Sacrament,[10] and showed a readiness to follow completely the teachings of Christ, especially as they were found in the Sermon on the Mount. The Brethren set high standards for priests and refused to let an evil priest consecrate the elements.[11] With Chelcicky, they opposed taking part in functions of the state. While avoiding chiliastic errors, their eschatology led the *Unitas Fratrum* to believe that they were living in the crisis of the last age. It has become commonplace to break the history of the *Unitas Fratrum* into six periods.[12] The year 1495 signals the end of the first period because in that year the Brethren

> consciously brought to an end this first stage of their journey as a period of moralistic excess and immoderation which would have dampened the prodigality of the grace of God. The Brethren then proclaimed in the light of Holy Scripture they recognized several shortcomings in the opinions of Brother Rehor and Petr Chelcicky as well, and that they did not intend to hold them any longer.[13]

This turning away from a moralistic and isolationist stance to enter an open stage in their history and theology was largely the work of Lukas of Prague (d. 1528). Lukas is widely considered the outstanding theologian of the Brethren and is hailed as its "second founder," the one who placed the "final stamp" on its theology.[14] His theological influence was so great that the second stage of Unity history, 1495–1531, has been dubbed "The Age of Lukas." It was his theology that Luther was engaging in the years 1522 to 1524, thus a brief description of that theology is in order.[15]

Although the distinction between "things essential" for salvation, "things ministrative," and "things incidental" was the "formal principle" for the Brethren's theology,[16] Lukas emphasized this in a significantly new way. More than the Old Brethren (1467–1495), he emphasized the objective nature of "things essential" by connecting them to the Apostles' Creed.

> To sum up, the essential things objectively comprehended are the love of God the Father, the righteousness merited by the Lord Jesus, and the gifts of the Holy Spirit. They are basic and essential because they are not in man's power. It is only through the gifts of the Holy Spirit, among which faith, love, and hope are foremost, that the believer is granted participation in the benefits of salvation.[17]

Lukas taught that Christ existed in four different modes of being: "bodily/naturally" (by which he sits at the right hand of God), "sovereignly" (as the God-man), "spiritually" (in the believer), and "sacramentally" (in which Christ is powerfully, truly, and spiritually in the Lord's Supper). Lukas spoke of faith in terms of "believing about God," "believing God," and "believing in God." Only this third faith was living faith and, therefore, made sinners righteous and gave eternal life. Faith was God's gift and was unconditioned by human merit. The second aspect of faith was the response of good works that one made to the hearing of

God's Word. Salvation was believed to have been won objectively by Jesus Christ and was appropriated by faith, which was a gift of the Holy Spirit. Lukas described faith as primarily the Spirit's work. When Lukas spoke of justification, he meant the actual righteousness in a human being, though he rejected the Thomistic concept that righteousness was a *habitus* of grace. This righteousness was by faith alone, though not imputed.

Under "things ministrative," Lukas wrote that the one church was both essential and ministrative. The essential church was the total number of the elect. The ministrative church was a mixed body of believers and unbelievers that formed congregations throughout the world. The ministrative church's mission was to bring people into the essential church. There was only one church but many "unities." Order and discipline were important, but such order was only *jus humanum*.

Among the church's ministries, the preaching of the Word was first in importance.[18] The sacraments, of which Lukas observed seven, were next. Lukas defined a sacrament in the traditional way: a visible sign of an invisible grace, founded by Christ, and given as a gift. Lukas was convinced that apart from the Word, the sacraments were meaningless. Faith was necessary to benefit from them.

Baptism had two intentions. The first was to bear witness to the righteousness that came from faith. The second was to incorporate an individual into the spiritual body of Christ. For this reason, though infants and young children should be baptized, they were baptized only for the sake of the second intention because they could not believe until they had "entered into reason." Thus Lukas and the Unity placed a stronger emphasis on confirmation as a supplement to Baptism.

Concerning the Lord's Supper, Lukas turned away from the early *Unitas* and held more closely to the Taborite conception: The Sacrament must be received by faith to be efficacious. Because Christ was truly present in the Supper according to his sacramental mode of being, Lukas rejected a memorial or symbolic view (as would later be held by Zwingli, the Anabaptists, or some Schwenkfelders). According to Lukas's view, however, the natural body of Christ—which had been crucified and was risen, ascended, and seated at God's right hand—was not present in the elements. So in what sense did one receive Christ in the Eucharist? Leaning on the work of E. Peschke,[19] Jaroslav Pelikan attempts to answer this question.

> If Peschke has caught his meaning, Lucas taught that the spiritual body received in the sacrament was not the same body betrayed by Judas and crucified on Good Friday, but that by the reception of that spiritual body one participated in the natural body as well. And so the presence of Christ in the Lord's Supper was neither spiritual nor symbolic nor sacramental nor real, but all of these.[20]

All the remaining articles of the Apostles' Creed (forgiveness of sins, resurrection of the body, and the life everlasting) were placed under the topic of "things incidental." This put them in the category of church ordinances that were not to be rejected if they did not contradict the things essential.

Luther originally considered the *Unitas* (his name for the *Unitas Fratrum* was the *Pighardi*) to be heretics.[21] The exact time of the Wittenberg reformer's first direct contact with the teaching of the Brethren is difficult to ascertain. Following Bartos and Müller, Thomson convincingly shows that Lukas of Prague's 1511 public *Apologia* to King Vladislav was widely disseminated, which would make it unlikely that Luther was not familiar with its contents.[22] Luther's lectures on the Epistle to the Romans (1516), his *scholia* on the Psalms from the period 1515 to 1516, and his 1518 "Resolutiones disputationum de indulgentiarum virtute" have also been said to present details that show a knowledge of and argument against Lukas and the *Unitas*.[23] All this builds a strong case that Luther was at least familiar with the theology of the Brethren quite early, long before the first face-to-face meeting in 1522.[24]

Luther's first face-to-face contact with the Brethren came in May 1522 when Jan Roh (German *Horn*), a deacon from Litomysl, and a companion visited Luther in Wittenberg. Roh had been introduced to Luther's writings by three Silesian monks who had been driven from Breslau because of their Lutheran doctrines. One of the monks was Michael Weisse.[25] Although unofficial, this was the first dialogue between the Brethren and Luther.

About this same time, Luther received correspondence from Paul Speratus, preacher at Iglau, who produced articles from among the Brethren that suggested they denied the bodily presence. When Roh assured Luther that despite the strange wording the Unity did believe in the bodily presence, Luther sent a letter to Speratus relating this information.[26] Speratus was not satisfied with Luther's answer because a discussion with Benes Optát, a Utraquist priest, had persuaded him that there was more to the Unity's doctrine of the Lord's Supper than Luther had concluded from his talk with Roh. Through Speratus, Optát himself asked Luther a question about the adoration of the Sacrament and the theory of concomitance that lay behind it. Luther sent another letter to Speratus, replying that the adoration of the host was an adiaphoron. From this letter, it is clear that Luther remained convinced that the Brethren believed as he did about the bodily presence.[27]

Although somewhat offended by his position on the adoration of the host, Lukas sent Luther, at his request, a Latin work that set forth the Brethren's teaching on the question.[28] Prior to this, Luther had received a Bohemian-German catechism from the Unity that stated their position on the Lord's Supper. As he stated in the introduction to "The Adoration of the Sacrament," the view of the Lord's Supper presented in this catechism "was a matter of real concern" to the Germans because it seemed to deny the bodily presence. Nor did the volume Lukas sent clear things up; instead, the Latin was unclear in places and its position on the Sacrament was also confusing.[29]

Luther decided that the best course of action would be a straightforward statement of his position on the question of the real presence. The result was "Adoration of the Sacrament," which was written in 1523. Luther intended this treatise not only to clarify his position on adoring the host but also to initiate real dialogue for unity. Luther stated this at the beginning of the treatise.

> I also asked of your messengers whether there were other matters in which you did not agree with us, in order that your people should not for that reason harbor animosity against us, nor we against you, but that each party should in brotherly fashion advise the other *to see whether we may reach a common mind*. It is true that I once called you heretics, while I was still a papist; but now I think differently. However, I shall now tell you what pleases me about you and wherein I think you are lacking.[30]

Indeed, as Luther made clear near the end, the point of his treatise had been to "reach the gist of the matter, and become one."[31] To prepare for his treatise, Luther had read Lukas's *Apologia* and appears to have used it as the basis for his comments.[32]

"THE ADORATION OF THE SACRAMENT": LUTHER'S DOCTRINAL HERMENEUTIC APPLIED IN AN ECUMENICAL SETTING

Lukas of Prague's *Apologia* was a long treatise, containing 480 Scripture verses in 59 folia.[33] Luther passed over many teachings and emphases on which he could have commented. This, coupled with his obvious desire for unity with the Brethren, strongly suggests that the teachings mentioned were carefully chosen, not randomly thrown on the table.

Luther organized his treatise as follows: After the introduction (275–77), the reformer discussed the Sacrament of the Altar (277–90); second, he discussed the adoration of the Sacrament (290–98); third, Luther mentioned teachings of the Brethren with which he agreed (298–300); and fourth, he told the Brethren which of their teachings were lacking, that is, were lacking for unity (300–303). In the conclusion, Luther urged the Brethren to learn and use the languages of scholarship, and he renewed the appeal for unity (303–5).[34]

THE SACRAMENT OF THE ALTAR

To set the question of the adoration of the Sacrament in the larger context, Luther began his treatise with a general discussion of the Sacrament. In the course of this discussion, he especially took aim at eucharistic errors that had arisen in the *Unitas Fratrum*. Already in the introduction, Luther had explicitly called the Sacrament an article of faith.[35] In the extended section that followed, however, Luther explained why the Sacrament was an article of faith by using the scriptural and evangelical canons of his doctrinal hermeneutic. Luther employed his scriptural canon when he considered the third error against the Sacrament, the teaching of transubstantiation.

> Of course, this error is not very important if only the body and blood of Christ, together with the Word, are not taken away—though the papists have earnestly contended and still contend for this their new doctrine. They label as heretic anyone who does not agree with them that it is a necessary truth, that no bread remains there—that monastic fantasy buttressed by Thomas Aquinas and confirmed by the popes. But while they insist so strongly upon this, and that out of pure arbitrariness and without any foundation in Scripture, we shall defy them and hold to the contrary that real bread and wine are truly present along with the body and blood of Christ. . . . For the gospel calls the sacrament bread.[36]

Luther rejected transubstantiation as an article of faith because it was based on human words not the Scriptures. Conversely, the teaching that true bread and wine along with the body and blood of Christ are present in the Sacrament was an article of faith for Luther because this teaching was based on the words of the Gospel.

For Luther, an article of faith had to be based on the right Scripture rightly interpreted. "Rightly interpreted" primarily meant that the natural, grammatical meaning of the text should be used unless one was compelled to adopt a figurative understanding. Luther took up this aspect of his scriptural canon when he addressed what he considered to be the first error against the Sacrament: "One must not do such violence to the words of God as to give to any word a meaning other than its natural one, unless there is a clear and definite Scripture to do that. That is what is done by those who without any basis in Scripture take the word 'is' and forcibly twist it to mean the same as the word 'signifies.' "[37] Such a teaching was dangerous for Luther because it denied the bodily presence and because to base the teaching of the Sacrament on a figurative interpretation was to nullify the Supper as an article of faith.

Luther's evangelical canon was his methodological emphasis that only a teaching that was connected to the Gospel, that was necessary for salvation, or that kept the conscience free could be an article of faith. Any teaching that failed the test must be declared to be an unnecessary doctrine. In "Adoration of the Sacrament," the Lord's Supper passed the test of Luther's evangelical canon because it was the Gospel. Luther spelled out the reason the papal teaching that made the Mass a sacrifice was so heretical: "Just as you cannot make out of the gospel a sacrifice or a work, so you cannot make a sacrifice or a work out of this sacrament; for this sacrament is the gospel."[38] Primarily the Words of Institution made the Sacrament Gospel for Luther at this point. These words were "the sum and substance of the whole gospel."[39] For Luther, the Lord's Supper was not only connected to the Gospel, it was the Gospel. As Gospel, the Sacrament not only told about forgiveness, grace, life, and salvation, it gave those things to the one who communed in faith: "It is a great degradation of the sacrament when a person ascribes nothing more to it than he ascribes to a good work. No good work can free us of our sins or give us grace or life or salvation. But this sacrament does give life, grace, and blessedness, for it is a fountain of life and of blessedness."[40] Thus it passed the test of Luther's evangelical canon; the teaching of the Mass as sacrifice did not.

THE ADORATION OF THE SACRAMENT

Because the Brethren had so firmly rejected the worshiping of Christ in the Sacrament, they had turned this rejection into a necessary doctrine. In the section on the adoration of the Sacrament, Luther not only told them that he disagreed, he told them why. According to Luther, the whole question of whether Christ should be adored in the Supper should remain a matter of freedom because Christ has neither commanded nor forbidden it in the Scriptures.

> For that reason we say now that one should not condemn people or accuse them of heresy if they do not adore the sacrament, for there is no command to that effect and it is not for that purpose that Christ is present. . . . On the other hand, one should not condemn and accuse of heresy people who do adore the sacrament. For although Christ has not commanded it, neither has he forbidden it.[41]

Luther's scriptural canon is in operation here. A necessary doctrine must be based on Scripture. Because the Brethren's rejection of the adoration of Christ in the Sacrament was not based on a clear command or prohibition in Scripture, it was wrong for them to make it necessary for salvation and to condemn as heretics those who did not comply.[42]

THE DOCTRINES WITH WHICH LUTHER AGREED

After completing the discourse on the Sacrament, Luther proceeded to indicate to the Brethren other teachings from Lukas's *Apologia* that he liked and didn't like. Significantly, but not surprisingly, the norm that

Luther used to determine the teachings he liked or found lacking was his doctrinal hermeneutic. Moreover, Luther wanted it known that he was offering his comments in the hope of unity. "I do this," said Luther, "in order to make your position and ours very clear and in order that we may daily draw nearer to each other."[43] This again shows that Luther envisioned unity with the *Unitas Fratrum* as the goal, and he framed his dialogue within this context.

The Articles of the Creed

Following the order of Lukas's *Apologia*, Luther gathered the teachings of the creed under the three articles. First, Luther commended the Brethren that they had the "right idea about God," namely, that they confessed that God the creator was triune. In Luther's discussion concerning the Second and Third Articles, he inserted material that demonstrated his evangelical canon at work. First, Luther added the phrase "and for our trespasses" before the phrase "suffered under Pontius Pilate." Second, he added the phrase "for our justification" after the phrase "on the third day rose again."[44] Third, Luther attached an interpretive statement at the end of the Second Article: "Thus it is not our work or merit or satisfaction that takes away our sins and earns us grace for eternal life, but solely his [Christ's] merit and the work that he has done for us."[45]

There were also evangelical additions to the Third Article. The first was the explicit definition of the holy Christian church as "the entire congregation of all those persons, whoever they may be, living or dead, who through the operation of the Holy Spirit partake of Christ's merit, suffering, and resurrection."[46] Membership in the church was related solely to the partaking of Christ's merit rather than to membership in any external organization. Second, Luther confessed that to "every member" of the church "belong the keys, the power to forgive sins, and to proclaim the gospel—privately, and publicly if one is required to do so by others having equal authority. Through this office of preaching and of forgiving sins, souls are resurrected here from sins and from death, and confidently await also the resurrection of the body and life everlasting through the same Holy Spirit."[47] In this dense formulation of the Third Article, Luther managed to succinctly articulate his understanding of the office of the keys, the priesthood of all believers, conversion by the power of the Gospel, and the certainty of life everlasting.

These interpretive additions to the Second and Third Articles of the creed were demonstrations of Luther's evangelical canon in action. They were his way of asserting that the articles of the creed were articles of faith because they taught and harmonized with the gospel of justification. Luther made this explicit at the end of the section on the creed: "These are the chief articles of the Christian faith. Where necessary they are sufficient for salvation, and without them no one can be saved. In these articles I find nothing blameworthy in you, and your *Apologia* is correct."[48] Salvation depended on the teachings of the creed, which in turn is what made them necessary articles of faith.

Other Teachings

The Brethren had several other teachings that Luther approved. Once more, the criterion on which he based his approval was his doctrinal hermeneutic. For example, Luther was pleased that the *Unitas* made nothing of purgatory and all the doctrines and practices that were based on it: "[T]he masses, vigils, foundations, altars, cloisters, and all its spreading corruption. For certainly no one is required to believe that there is a purgatory, because God has said nothing about it. . . . [I]n this matter we are not commanded either to know or to believe."[49] Here again was the scriptural canon: Purgatory was to be rejected as a necessary doctrine because God had said nothing about it, that is, it was not based on Scripture.

Next Luther voiced solidarity with the Brethren concerning their mariology and hagiology. Specifically, they neither honored nor prayed to Mary and the saints but trusted in Jesus Christ as the only mediator with the Father. Unlike the sophists, Luther refused to condemn the Brethren as heretics for these teachings. Why did he agree with them? Because praying to Mary and the saints was not supported by Scripture (scriptural canon) and the doctrine too easily contradicted the Gospel (evangelical canon). Therefore, the Brethren were right in not insisting on such teachings as essential.

> For there is nothing in the Scriptures about the intercession of dead saints, nor about honoring them and praying to them. And no one can deny that hitherto through services for these saints we have gone so far as to make pure idols out of the mother of God and the saints. We have placed more confidence in them, on account of the services and works which we have done for them, than we have placed in Christ himself, with the result that faith in Christ has perished.[50]

THE DOCTRINES THAT LUTHER FOUND TO BE LACKING

Next Luther addressed five doctrines of the Brethren that he found to be lacking. As in the previous section, so also here Luther judged the teachings of the Brethren by the criterion of his doctrinal hermeneutic.

The Sacrament of the Altar

Because Luther had already addressed the Sacrament in detail, he had nothing new to contribute: "[C]oncerning the sacrament of Christ's body I have indicated sufficiently above what I miss in you."[51] He asked for the Brethren to pray for the Wittenbergers, however, because they had not yet been able to implement "a proper Christian administration of the sacrament in both kinds."[52]

Infant Baptism

Luther correctly understood that the Brethren held that young children did not have faith; therefore, they baptized their young on the basis of future faith: "For you hold (as they tell me) that the young children do not have faith; nevertheless you baptize them."[53] But this was unthinkable to the reformer because "without faith the sacrament should not and cannot be received . . . . Before one baptizes, or at least at the same time, faith must be present."[54] The Brethren's position was wrong, according to Luther, because it contradicted clear Scripture, such as Mark 16:16 ("Whoever believes and is baptized will be saved"). Such a view on infant Baptism was also wrong because it contradicted the Gospel and denied salvation to children. If the Brethren were right and little children could not believe, then they also could not be saved because "without faith, no one has the kingdom of heaven."[55] Again Luther's doctrinal hermeneutic was employed to determine which teachings were necessary for salvation and unity.

Faith and Works

Although he could commend the *Unitas* for their distinction between believing about God, believing God, and believing in God, Luther told them that he was unable to determine whether they understood saving faith correctly. The problem was that the *Apologia* seemed to ascribe "a good deal to works."[56] The Wittenberg reformer regarded this as a serious question. Indeed, of the five doctrines that he considered lacking, Luther regarded this as the most important. The impression was being given that the Brethren were not basing justification and salvation on faith alone but were also depending on works.[57]

This impression led Luther to give a brief definition of justifying faith. Faith was a gift of the Holy Spirit, given outwardly through the Gospel. Such a faith was

> nothing else than a living trust and confidence in the merit that Christ has bestowed upon us. We rely upon it from the bottom of our hearts, without doing any works of our own. We are confident that it is not our own works but the work and merit of Christ that destroys our sins, overcomes death, and swallows up hell. This means that no work is required in order to believe in God or to have a true and living faith. Rather it is this living faith in God which subsequently does good works to one's neighbor, as Christ has done to him.[58]

Luther was defining faith in his characteristic way: as trust or confidence in Christ's merits, works, and death and as the source and cause of all good works. Because justifying faith was at the heart of his evangelical canon, it is not surprising that Luther saw this doctrine of faith as necessary for salvation and unity.

The Seven Sacraments

The fourth doctrine of the *Unitas Fratrum* that Luther viewed as problematic concerned the number of sacraments: "[Y]ou still have the seven sacraments from the church of the papists, although the Scriptures have no more than the two—baptism and the table of the Lord."[59] The other five were to be rejected as sacraments because "a sacrament must have two things for sure, God's Word and the external sign that has been duly instituted." Only Baptism and the Eucharist had these two things.[60] Luther objected to the Brethren making the other five sacraments[61] necessary for salvation because they were human teachings. In other words, the five sacraments failed Luther's scriptural canon: "Now it is certainly too much if we equate things instituted by men with things instituted by God. It would seem to follow that you cannot with good conscience reject some human ordinances, especially the pope's, if you accept certain of his institutions as necessary to saving faith. For you know that faith must and will rest on nothing else than on the sure Word of God."[62] Articles of faith must be based on Scripture alone.

Priestly Celibacy

Although Luther was pleased that the Brethren were choosing their own priests, he could not agree with them that priests should be forbidden to marry. Such prohibition denigrated marriage, making it seem to be "too despicable an estate to permit one to wait upon God in all kinds of divine service."[63] Priestly celibacy also contradicted the Gospel: "But it is still damaging to the gospel that you require them to go unmarried."[64] Such a practice damaged the Gospel because it forbade something that God had left free, thus ensnaring the conscience by making something sin that was not sin. In other words, Luther objected to forbidding priests to marry because it violated his evangelical canon.

Luther used his doctrinal hermeneutic as a criterion to judge certain doctrines of the Brethren to be lacking. The doctrines were lacking because they failed to satisfy Luther's scriptural or evangelical canons. Either they failed to insist on something as necessary doctrine that the Scriptures and the Gospel declared to be necessary (for example, they failed to teach "faith alone" or that infants are saved by faith) or they insisted on something as necessary that according to the Scriptures and the Gospel was not (for example, seven sacraments and priestly celibacy).

CONCLUSION

Luther's dialogue with the *Unitas Fratrum* was a key unity experiment because it demonstrated the reformer defining doctrines that are necessary for unity on the basis of his doctrinal hermeneutic. In "Adoration of the Sacrament," Luther not only addressed the individual doctrines that must be agreed on before unity could occur but also explained why the doctrines he addressed were necessary for unity. The mechanism that he used to determine the doctrines necessary for unity was his doctrinal hermeneutic. Those that he accepted as necessary were chosen because they were supported by Scripture alone and because they were necessary for salvation and part and parcel of the gospel of justification by faith. Those that Luther described as unnecessary received this categorization because they were not supported by Scripture, were not necessary for salvation, or contradicted the Gospel.

Luther's approach may have been well received by Lukas of Prague and the Brethren, given their longstanding emphasis on essential teachings. But because the Brethren defined essential teachings quite differently (as life as well as doctrine, Law as well as Gospel), it is not surprising that in his response Lukas gave no ground on the teachings Luther considered lacking, not the least of which was the adoration of the host.[65] It would remain for Jan Augusta and a new generation of Brethren leaders to engage Luther's vision for unity.

4

THE MARBURG COLLOQUY
AS A DEMONSTRATION
OF LUTHER'S
DOCTRINAL HERMENEUTIC

Any assessment of Martin Luther's ecumenical moves would be incomplete without an examination of his role in the Marburg Colloquy. This famous colloquy, held in the Marburg castle of Landgrave Philipp of Hesse[1] (1504–1567) October 1–4, 1529, deserves special attention for several reasons. It is a clear-cut case of Luther in face-to-face dialogue for the purpose of unity, something that rarely happened. Gathered in a large room of the Marburg castle for their one and only face-to-face meeting were the most famous and influential evangelical theological leaders of the German and Swiss reformations. On one side of the dialogue stood Luther, Philipp Melanchthon (1497–1560), and others in agreement with Luther's eucharistic theology.[2] On the other side stood the Swiss and South German leaders: Huldrych Zwingli[3] (1484–1531) of Zurich, Johannes Oecolampadius[4] (1482–1531) of Basel, and Martin Bucer[5] (1491–1551) and Wolfgang Capito[6] (1478–1541) of Strasbourg. They had gathered to overcome the vexing disagreement concerning the Lord's Supper that had sharply divided the groups since the mid-1520s.

Given Luther's posture before and during the Marburg proceedings, his behavior at the colloquy may appear anything but ecumenical. Luther adamantly opposed the Marburg Colloquy for two years. Only when urged by his own sovereign, Elector John, did he reluctantly accept the invitation of Philipp of Hesse.[7] Moreover, in his acceptance letter to the landgrave, Luther explicitly stated that he already had made up his mind and was not going to change it.

> For Your Sovereign Grace can easily see that all discussions are futile and the meeting vain, if both parties come with the intention of conceding nothing. Thus far I have found nothing other than that they want to insist on their position, though they have become very familiar with the basis of our position. On the other hand, having also become familiar with the basis of their position, I certainly know that I am unable to yield, just as I know that they are wrong. . . . For in

75

short, I cannot expect anything good from the devil, no matter how nicely he may appear to act.[8]

In another letter, Luther compared the approaching Marburg Colloquy to the meetings that took place in the days of Arius. Those meetings did more harm than good because they actually allowed the false teaching to spread.

Is there any indication that Luther had become more open-minded by the time the colloquy began? If there had been any suggestion of open-mindedness, it disappeared when, in the opening session, Luther declared that he had decided to attend the colloquy "not that I wished to change my conviction of which I am completely sure, but that I might demonstrate the reason for my faith and show where others are in error."[10] Because of this kind of evidence, "Luther is commonly regarded as having manifested throughout a position of dogged intransigence. He began by drawing the circle of chalk upon the table and writing within it the words 'This is my body,' and he ended by saying that the Swiss had a different spirit and he could not accord them a hand clasp fraught with theological implications."[11] What such an estimation fails to take into account, however, is that Luther did make an effort to compromise during the colloquy, going so far as to draft a compromise formula on the Lord's Supper that attempted to preserve what was important to the Swiss and South Germans.[12] The Marburg Colloquy, therefore, was a genuine dialogue for unity in which Luther participated. Through face-to-face discussions, a real attempt was made to overcome doctrinal disunity—the *res* of all genuine ecumenical discussions. That Luther was pessimistic about success at Marburg does not disqualify it as a moment of genuine ecumenism.

The Marburg Colloquy and Luther's eucharistic writings of the period clearly illustrate his doctrinal hermeneutic employed in an ecumenical setting. Moreover, his doctrinal hermeneutic illuminates why Luther took the hard stance at Marburg that he did. According to Luther, the Lord's Supper, including the bodily presence of Christ in the elements, was an article of faith, a doctrine necessary for unity and salvation. Luther came to this conclusion on the basis of his doctrinal hermeneutic rather than merely on the basis of pride or stubbornness in the heat of battle. He had been applying this same doctrinal hermeneutic to church teachings consistently throughout the Reformation.

METHODOLOGICAL CONSIDERATIONS

Key aspects surrounding the Marburg Colloquy necessitate a different approach to discerning Luther's doctrinal hermeneutic. First, though the dialogue with the *Unitas Fratrum* concentrated on numerous doctrines, the Marburg Colloquy focused primarily on one: the doctrine of the

Lord's Supper.[13] All parties understood that their differing views on the Lord's Supper were at the heart of the impasse. Because this is so, this chapter focuses solely on the Lord's Supper, showing Luther's explanation of why the Lord's Supper doctrine, especially Christ's bodily presence in the Supper, is an article of faith necessary for unity.

Despite the focus on a single doctrine, the Marburg Articles, which appears to be a primary Luther text, poses significant problems. First, the document was based on the Schwabach Articles, which the Wittenbergers had brought to Marburg. Johann M. Reu demonstrated long ago that it is incorrect to view Luther as the sole author of the Schwabach Articles and that portions must be ascribed to Melanchthon,[14] though as Wilhelm Maurer has established, the Schwabach Articles was definitely influenced by Luther's Confession of 1528.[15] Because Luther was not the sole author of the Schwabach Articles, this limits the Marburg Articles as a completely reliable gauge of Luther's theology. Second, the Marburg Articles was intended to be a bare-bones document that, at the request of Landgrave Philipp, was hurriedly drafted by Luther to highlight what consensus was possible between the dialogue partners. In such a brief document, Luther could not give detailed reasons why he included a particular article for consideration. Third, Ulrich Gäbler has correctly stated that no new aspects came out of the Marburg Colloquy (including the articles) beyond what already had been established in written form during the long debate on the Lord's Supper that preceded the colloquy.[16] By the time the two parties gathered in Marburg, Luther's position and argumentation on the Lord's Supper had been carefully worked out in several previous writings. The dialogue at Marburg and the Marburg Articles were simply epitomes of what Luther had presented thoroughly in treatises prior to the colloquy.

Instead of the Marburg Articles, several of Luther's key eucharistic treatises—in which he gives his rationale for including the Lord's Supper and especially Christ's bodily presence in the Supper as a necessary article of faith for unity—will serve as primary texts. Only then can we learn why Luther refused to budge at Marburg.[17]

This chapter does not pretend to be a comprehensive treatment of the Marburg Colloquy, the Eucharistic Controversy, or Luther's eucharistic theology. Many admirable treatments of these topics already exist.[18] Rather, this chapter demonstrates Luther's doctrinal hermeneutic at work in his eucharistic theology as he brought that theology to bear on the Eucharistic Controversy and the discussions at Marburg. After a brief look at the failure of the Marburg Colloquy to solve the dispute over the Lord's Supper, the first section of this chapter examines the medieval eucharistic tradition and the chronology of the Lord's Supper controversy to identify a source for the disunity. The second section examines

the evidence for Luther's doctrinal hermeneutic in his eucharistic treatises
and at Marburg. Evidence for both the scriptural and evangelical canons
of his doctrinal hermeneutic are assessed to determine how they influenced the dialogue with the Swiss and South Germans.

THE SEEDS OF DISUNITY

For three momentous days at Marburg, Luther and Melanchthon sat
across the table from Zwingli and Oecolampadius for the express purpose
of reaching agreement on the bodily presence of Christ in the Lord's
Supper.[19] Although the discussions were candid, thorough, and even
friendly, the colloquy ended on the afternoon of October 3 with no agreement. Even a last-minute compromise formula drafted by Luther on the
evening of October 3, in which he attempted to remove all that might
offend the Swiss and South Germans, failed to bring about agreement;
Zwingli rejected it.[20] The fifteenth article of the Marburg Articles
recorded the failed agreement:

> And although at this time, we have not reached an agreement as to
> whether the true body and blood of Christ are bodily present in the
> bread and wine, nevertheless, each side should show Christian love to
> the other side insofar as conscience will permit, and both sides should
> diligently pray to Almighty God that through his Spirit he might con-
> firm us in the right understanding. Amen.[21]

Highlighting this "failed agreement" does not deny that a consensus of
sorts occurred at Marburg. Consensus was reached on fourteen of the fifteen articles that comprised the Marburg Articles. Consensus was even
reached on five of six points in Article 15, the one that dealt with the
Lord's Supper.[22] But on the main point of contention in Article 15, the
point addressing Christ's bodily presence in the Supper, consensus was not
reached. Therefore, though in letters and sermons after the colloquy he
evaluated positively much of what had occurred at Marburg, Luther made
it clear that because the Swiss and South Germans had not accepted the
bodily presence of Christ in the Sacrament, he did not consider them fel-
low Christians. That this was Luther's estimation is made clear in his letter of October 4 to Nicholas Gerbel in Strasbourg:

> We defended ourselves strongly and they conceded much, but as they
> were firm in this one article of the sacrament of the altar we dismissed
> them in peace, fearing that further argument would draw blood. We
> ought to have charity and peace even with our foes, and so we plainly
> told them that unless they grow wiser on this point they may indeed
> have our charity, but cannot by us be considered as brothers and mem-
> bers of Christ.[23]

After so much effort, division remained over the question of Christ's bodily presence. But how had these reformers come to such a place of disunity? How could the single teaching of the bodily presence of Christ in the Sacrament have taken such a crucial place of importance so it alone would prevent unity among these evangelicals?

THE MEDIEVAL SETTING

The seeds of disunity that bloomed into discord and hostility during the 1520s were implicit in the medieval tradition of the Lord's Supper that all participants of the Eucharistic Controversy, including Luther, had inherited. Two very different theologies of Christ's presence in the Sacrament had more or less peacefully coexisted, but now they proved divisive in the sixteenth-century church as groups followed and expanded on one or the other tradition. One tradition stemmed from Ambrose of Milan (d. 397), the other from Augustine of Hippo (d. 430).[24]

Hermann Sasse has convincingly demonstrated that a real difference existed between the eucharistic theologies of Ambrose and Augustine and the liturgies that proceeded from them. These differences probably date to even earlier liturgical traditions. The "realist" or "metabolic" theory of Ambrose, which he shared with John Chrysostom, was that Christ's words in the Words of Institution effect a change (*transformatio, transfiguratio, mutatio*) of the bread into the body and the wine into the blood of Christ. Quite different was the "spiritualist" or "signification" theory of Augustine. Clearly influenced by Neoplatonism, Augustine made a sharp distinction between the *signum* and the *res* in the Sacrament, with all the emphasis placed on the invisible *res* (that is, body and blood) rather than the visible *signum* (bread and wine). Of equal importance was Augustine's emphasis on spiritual eating in the Supper and on the body of Christ being at one place at the right hand of the Father. As Sasse wrote: "The two types of understanding of the Sacraments existed side by side. The Real Presence of the body and blood of Christ could be understood in a more realistic or in a more spiritualistic way."[25]

The various debates over the real presence during the Middle Ages (between Ratramnus [d. 868] and Radbertus [d. 865] in the ninth century and between Berengar [d. 1088] and the Church of Rome in the eleventh century) and the sixteenth century can be explained by the combatants who followed either the Ambrosian or the Augustinian eucharistic tradition. A line runs from Augustine's "spiritualist" theory of the real presence to Ratramnus in the ninth century, Berengar in the eleventh, Wycliffe (d. 1384) in the fourteenth, and Cornelius Hoen (d. 1524) and Zwingli in the sixteenth. As Carter Lindberg has pointed out, Ratramnus used some of the same arguments that Zwingli later employed: that Christ had ascended into heaven and, therefore, could not be bodily present in the

Sacrament and that John 6:63 also ruled out the bodily presence. Berengar's claim that it was absurd to believe that Christ is present bodily in the elements, his interpretation of the *est* as *significat*, and his insistence that Christ can only be received spiritually in the Sacrament by faithfully remembering his passion and resurrection is strikingly similar to Zwingli's view.[26] Wycliffe also held to a figurative interpretation of the Words of Institution and to many of the same ideas that became characteristic of Zwingli.[27]

On the other hand, the Ambrosian "realistic" view was adopted by Radbertus in the ninth century and by the eleventh-century declaration *Ego Berengarius* (1079), which became the dogma of the Roman Church that settled the question of the real presence according to the Ambrosian "realistic" model. *Ego Berengarius*, which Berengar was forced to sign, unmistakably declared that the bread and wine, through the words of Christ in the Words of Institution and the "sacred prayer," are

> substantially converted (*substantialiter converti*) into the proper and life-giving flesh and blood of our Lord Jesus Christ, and that, after consecration, they are the true body of Christ which was born of the Virgin Mary and hung on the cross for the salvation of the world and which now sitteth on the right hand of the Father, and the true blood of Christ which was shed from his side, not only as a sign and by virtue of the sacrament, but in their proper nature and true substance.[28]

The disunity apparent before and during the Marburg Colloquy arose in part from the conflicting medieval traditions that Luther and his party and Zwingli and his had received and appropriated.

CHRONOLOGY OF A EUCHARISTIC CONTROVERSY

By the time the Marburg Colloquy convened, the disunity between Luther and those whom he called the Sacramentarians had been raging for about six years. Numerous treatises were published by both sides in an effort to convince the other side and the public of the correctness of their view. What began somewhat calmly erupted into a heated controversy by the end of the 1520s—a controversy that involved not only those few who participated in the Marburg Colloquy but also many others who jumped into the literary fray for the truth of the Sacrament.[29]

To understand the disunity that existed at the Marburg Colloquy, a chronological analysis of the key treatises in the Eucharistic Controversy is a necessity because neither Luther nor Zwingli developed his eucharistic theology all at once or in isolation. They developed it, at least in part, as they reacted to each other and to other combatants. As Bernhard Lohse wrote: "Naturally in essence both sides held to their point of departure.

The debate nevertheless forced the participants to develop their positions more precisely and thus to pay attention to opposing points of view."[30] A chronological analysis of these developments provides a clearer understanding of what Luther and Zwingli considered to be the major points in the discussion and why. A thorough examination of all the key treatises is, of course, impossible. What follows is an identification of and comment on those treatises that brought some new teaching or development to the controversy.

Exactly when did the Eucharistic Controversy between the evangelicals begin? Bernhard Lohse has noted that from 1517 to 1520, when the dispute with Rome was at its zenith, the evangelicals appeared to be united as they attacked the sacrifice of the Mass, Communion in one kind, and insisted on faith as a necessary prerequisite for receiving the Sacrament. In these years, "no attention was paid to differences among the evangelicals over sacramental doctrine."[31] If differences did exist, these did not become apparent until later.[32]

CORNELIUS HOEN

The beginning of the Eucharistic Controversy may date from the letter of the Dutch humanist Cornelius Hoen (Honius) that Luther received in 1522 and that Zwingli received in 1524.[33] In this letter, Hoen took up the tradition represented by Berengar and Wycliffe—that the Words of Institution must be understood symbolically—and introduced this tradition to the sixteenth-century church.[34] At the heart of Hoen's argument was the assertion that *is* in the Words of Institution must mean "signifies" because Christ's body is now at the right hand of the Father. The Lord's Supper is intended to be a visible pledge (like a wedding ring) that reminds us of Christ's promise to us and encourages us to trust that promise. It is faith that spiritually eats and drinks Christ's body and blood. For Hoen, Roman scholasticism had replaced this faith in Christ's promise with the belief that the bread and wine actually became Christ's body and blood after the consecration. When the host was adored, Hoen argued that such adoration led to idolatry. In his letter, Hoen cited numerous alleged examples of figurative language in the Bible, such as Matt. 11:14 (John is Elijah), John 19:26 (Behold your son), Matt. 16:18 (Peter the rock), 1 Cor. 10:4 (the rock was Christ), John 10:9 (I am the door), and John 15:1, 5 (I am the vine).

In April 1523, Luther reacted to Hoen's symbolic understanding of the Supper in "The Adoration of the Sacrament." This treatise carries special weight in Luther's literary corpus because it was the first time Luther dealt specifically with and rejected a figurative understanding of the Words of Institution: "In the first place there have been some who have held that in the sacrament there is merely bread and wine, such as people otherwise eat and drink. They have taught nothing more than that the bread signifies the body and the wine signifies the blood of Christ."[35] Earlier in the same treatise, Luther had defined the Wittenbergers' belief in the bodily presence, calling it a "substantial, natural" presence and stating "that Christ is truly present in the sacrament with his flesh and blood as it was born of Mary and hung on the holy cross, just as we Germans believe."[36]

In addition, several other arguments that would become characteristic of Luther's eucharistic theology are found in "Adoration of the Sacrament." First, Luther underscored the Words of Institution as the most important thing in the Sacrament.

> In the first place, we have often said that the chief and foremost thing in the sacrament is the word of Christ . . . . Everything depends on these words. Every Christian should and must know them and hold them fast. . . . This is why these words are far more important than the sacrament itself, and a Christian should make it a practice to give far more attention to these words than to the sacrament.[37]

The words of Christ are foremost in the Sacrament because these words are the Gospel[38] and because they have the power to do as they say: "[Y]ou should hold it to be a living, eternal, all-powerful Word that can make you alive, free from sin and death, and keep you so eternally; that brings with it everything of which it speaks, namely Christ with his flesh and blood and everything that he is and has. For it is the kind of Word that can and does do all these things, and therefore it should be so regarded."[39]

Second, Luther argued that the sinful intellect cannot grasp the bodily presence of Christ and fallen reason naturally rejects Christ's bodily presence in the Sacrament. Instead, Christians should cling in faith to the Words of Institution: "Now beware of such a view. Let go of reason and intellect; for they strive in vain to understand how flesh and blood can be present, and because they do not grasp it they refuse to believe it. Lay hold on the word which Christ speaks: 'Take, this is my body, this is my blood.' "[40] Luther considered reason to be a gift from God, but it was an abused gift when it refused to believe what the Scriptures declared.

Third, Luther maintained that Christians should hold to the "natural" or "plain" meaning of the words of Scripture, unless the immediate context, another biblical text, or an article of faith compelled a different interpretation.[41] Thus Luther wrote: "One must not do such violence to the words of God as to give to any word a meaning other than its natural one, unless there is clear and definite Scripture to do that. This is what is done by those who without any basis in Scripture take the word 'is' and forcibly twist it to mean the same as the word 'signifies.' "[42]

Fourth, according to Luther, the Lord's Supper was not a work we do for God; rather, it was God's work for us, through which he gives us grace, life, and forgiveness. In other words, the Lord's Supper is a means of grace. "It is a great degradation of the sacrament when a person ascribes nothing more to it than he ascribes to a good work. No good work can free us of our sins or give us grace or life or salvation. But this sacrament does give life, grace, and blessedness, for it is a fountain of life and of blessedness."[43] For Luther, the Eucharist does not merely remember a past gift, it is a present gift of forgiveness for all who believe.

Fifth, Luther emphasized that to receive the benefit of the Sacrament and to commune worthily, faith in the forgiveness offered in the Words of Institution was necessary. "For a sacrament is a matter of faith, because in it only the works of God proceed and are effected—through his Word!"[44] To underscore this, Luther ended the subsection on the adoration of the Sacrament with the words: "But the thing that we want to emphasize as of the utmost importance is faith in the words of the sacrament."[45]

Sixth, though in a simple form, Luther stressed what he would later call the *unio sacramentalis* (sacramental union—that the bread and body, wine and blood are one and exist together) by employing the analogies of red-hot iron and—for the first time—the person of Christ. "For we also find the same kind of twofold existence in the world of nature. We say properly concerning a red-hot iron: 'The iron is fire, and the fire is iron.' We do not say: 'The fire signifies iron, and the iron signifies fire.' In the same way we say concerning Christ: 'The man is God, and God is the man,' and not 'God signifies the man, or the man signifies God.' "[46] Thus what the communicant orally received was simultaneously bread-body and wine-blood, just as Jesus Christ was simultaneously God and man.

Already present in this significant treatise on the Lord's Supper were several key arguments that Luther would use repeatedly throughout the Eucharistic Controversy. The writings of Zwingli, Oecolampadius, and other opponents forced the Wittenberg reformer to sharpen and develop these arguments, but they already were present in "Adoration of the Sacrament" in nascent form. In his subsequent writings, Luther was able to build on and enlarge his doctrinal insights.

ANDREAS BODENSTEIN VON KARLSTADT

The next decisive phase in the Lord's Supper controversy was set in motion by the eucharistic writings of Andreas Bodenstein von Karlstadt. On September 18, 1524, Karlstadt was ordered by the counselors of Electoral Saxony to vacate the Orlamünde parish and leave the area. He then traveled to Strasbourg, Zurich, and Basel, where, in November, he published seven tracts, five of which concerned the Lord's Supper. These travels and his published works on the Lord's Supper brought Karlstadt into contact with and to the attention of other evangelical leaders, such as Bucer, Capito, Oecolampadius, and Zwingli. Luther's friends promptly notified him of Karlstadt's activities.[47]

Of special concern to Luther was the fact that Karlstadt's tracts rejected his understanding of the bodily presence of Christ in the Sacrament. One tract in particular, the *Dialogue*, forwarded the view that when Christ said, "This is my body," he was pointing at himself, not the bread. This view has since been traced to the thirteenth century and was apparently passed along by the Bohemian Waldensians. In addition, this argument had been used six months prior to the appearance of Karlstadt's tract by the circle of dissidents in Zwickau.[48] According to this position, the bread was merely bread; the Lord's Supper was a memorial meal.

The Strasbourg clergy, including Martin Bucer and Wolfgang Capito, wrote to Luther in late November, asking for his opinion on Karlstadt's views of the Lord's Supper, some of which they found acceptable. Luther responded in mid-December with "Letter to the Christians at Strassburg in Opposition to the Fanatic Spirit." His only comment about Karlstadt's position was that he, too, had been tempted to follow such a symbolic view five years earlier. Now, however, Luther wrote: "I am a captive and cannot free myself. The text is too powerfully present, and will not allow itself to be torn from its meaning by mere verbiage."[49]

Luther's real answer to Karlstadt's rejection of the bodily presence came in the second part of "Against the Heavenly Prophets in the Matter of Images and the Sacraments." Luther considered this lengthy treatise, completed and published in January 1525, to be a major statement on the bodily presence of Christ in the Sacrament.[50] The second part was directed primarily at Karlstadt's *Dialogue*.

"Against the Heavenly Prophets" is a marked advance in Luther's eucharistic thinking in several ways. It is the first time that he examined exegetically the principal Lord's Supper texts. His surveys of the Gospel texts (Matthew 26; Mark 14; Luke 22) are of limited value, unfortunately, because the bulk of his commentary was designed to disprove Karlstadt's imaginative exegesis.[51] Of more interest is Luther's extensive interpretation of 1 Cor. 10:16, a passage that Luther considered to be a powerful proof of the bodily presence of Christ in the Sacrament. He described it as "a verse which is a thunderbolt on the head of Dr. Karlstadt and his whole party. This verse has been also the life-giving medicine of my heart in my trials concerning this sacrament. Even if we had no other passage than this we could sufficiently strengthen all consciences and sufficiently overcome all adversaries."[52]

In the course of explaining this passage, Luther stressed that even the unworthy receive the objective body and blood of Christ (he cited 1 Cor. 11:29), a conviction that he continued to hold and sharpen as the

Eucharistic Controversy unfolded. Karlstadt denied this conviction. As an example, Luther referred to Judas: "This happened at the Supper to Judas the traitor who participated with the other disciples in the body and blood of Christ and partook with them. For he received it, ate, and drank just as the other disciples did."[53]

As an outgrowth of his spiritualistic leanings, Karlstadt had rejected Christ's bodily presence in the Sacrament in *Dialogue* partly on the basis of John 6:63, the *locus classicus* of all spiritualists: "It is the Spirit who gives life, the flesh is of no avail" (ESV). This was Luther's first skirmish over a passage that the Sacramentarians would use against him repeatedly. Since the Leipzig Debate (1519), Karlstadt had used John 6:63 to argue against the externalization of religion, which was his major concern.[54] Now he used this passage in the Lord's Supper debate. In so doing, Karlstadt was following the example of Erasmus, who used John 6:63 in a similar manner.[55] Because the flesh is of no avail, then Christ's body cannot be in the Sacrament, argued Karlstadt.

Luther responded in a twofold manner in "Against the Heavenly Prophets." If, as Karlstadt asserted, the "flesh" in John 6:63 referred to the flesh of Christ, then it would follow that Christ's flesh was of "no avail" anywhere—in his mother's womb, on the cross, in heaven. Such a view would effectively nullify the incarnation.[56] But all this was beside the point, contested Luther, because the "flesh" in John 6:63 did not refer to Christ's flesh.

> For Christ does not say, "My flesh is of no avail," but thus, "Flesh is of no avail" [John 6:63]. But of his own flesh he says, "My flesh is food indeed" [John 6:55].
>
> . . . So we should not say that the flesh of Christ is of no avail, but flesh is of no avail, as Paul says, "Flesh and blood cannot inherit the kingdom" [1 Cor. 15:50]. Here "flesh" means a carnal mind, will, understanding or self-contrived opinion, as Paul in Rom. 8[:6] says, "To set the mind on the flesh is death." When Christ (John 6) speaks of his flesh and says it is "food indeed," he corrects the Jews who understand him in a carnal manner, by adding that his words are "spirit and life." Flesh is of no avail, that is, to understand his spiritual words in a carnal manner brings only death.[57]

With this argument, which he would use repeatedly against Zwingli and Oecolampadius,[58] Luther rejected an interpretation of John 6:63 that was shaped by a dualistic or Neoplatonic world view that sharply separated the Spirit from matter and, as a consequence, held that what was creature (in this case bread and wine) could not bear the divine. This was the fundamental worldview of the spiritualists. But it also would find its way into the eucharistic theologies of Zwingli and Oecolampadius.[59]

A major advance in "Against the Heavenly Prophets" is the way in which Luther stressed the Lord's Supper as a means of grace. Karlstadt had ridiculed the notion that bread or wine could bring forgiveness or any help to the Christian. The Spirit, he claimed, must do this directly through faith. On the contrary, claimed Luther, God gave the Spirit only through the outward means of grace that he had decreed.

> Now when God sends forth his holy gospel he deals with us in a twofold manner, first outwardly, then inwardly. Outwardly he deals with us through the oral word of the gospel and through material signs, that is, baptism and the sacrament of the altar. Inwardly he deals with us through the Holy Spirit, faith, and other gifts. But whatever their measure or order the outward factors should and must precede. The inward experience follows and is effected by the outward. . . . For he wants to give no one the Spirit or faith outside of the outward Word and sign instituted by him . . . .

> . . . Do you not see here the devil, the enemy of God's order? With all his mouthing of the words, "Spirit, Spirit, Spirit," he tears down the bridge, the path, the way, the ladder, and all the means by which the Spirit might come to you. Instead of the outward order of God in the material sign of baptism and the oral proclamation of the Word of God he wants to teach you, not how the Spirit comes to you but how you come to the Spirit.[60]

In a further response to Karlstadt's criticism, Luther denied that the Wittenbergers had ever taught that bread and wine alone brought forgiveness. But this gave him occasion to clarify for his readers exactly how the Lord's Supper did give forgiveness.

> So that our readers may the better perceive our teaching I shall clearly and broadly describe it. We treat of the forgiveness of sins in two ways. First, how it is achieved and won. Second, how it is distributed and given to us. Christ has achieved it on the cross, it is true. But he has not distributed or given it on the cross. He has not won it in the supper or sacrament. There he has distributed and given it through the Word, as also in the gospel, where it is preached. He has won it once for all on the cross. But the distribution takes place continuously, before and after, from the beginning to the end of the world.

> . . . If now I seek the forgiveness of sins, I do not run to the cross, for I will not find it given there. Nor must I hold to the suffering of Christ, as Dr. Karlstadt trifles, in knowledge or remembrance, for I will not find it there either. But I will find in the sacrament or gospel the word which distributes, presents, offers, and gives to me that forgiveness which was won on the cross. Therefore, Luther has rightly taught that whoever has a bad conscience from his sins should go to the sacrament and obtain comfort, not because of the bread and wine, not because of the body and blood of Christ, but because of the word

which in the sacrament offers, presents, and gives the body and blood of Christ, given and shed for me. Is that not clear enough?[61]

According to Luther, the Lord's Supper was not a source of forgiveness and, therefore, something in competition with the cross. Neither was it a means of receiving forgiveness, which would place it in conflict with faith. The Sacrament was the distribution of the forgiveness that Christ had won on the cross once-for-all and that faith received. This proved to be a distinction that Luther's opponents had difficulty understanding throughout the course of the controversy.

HULDRYCH ZWINGLI

Luther's main combatant in the Eucharistic Controversy was Huldrych Zwingli, the Swiss reformer. Before turning to Zwingli's initial contributions to the controversy, the following offers a brief comment on the background of his theology.[62]

Born January 1, 1484, in Wildhaus, Switzerland, Zwingli earned his bachelor's degree (1504) and master's degree (1506) at the University of Basel. He studied theology, philosophy, and the new humanistic studies. While at the university, he also appears to have studied and embraced the *via antiqua*, especially the theology of Thomas Aquinas, which would prove to have a lasting influence on the Swiss reformer. Aquinas held that reason and revelation do not contradict each other, that God "gives light and he does not lead us into darkness," which, significantly, Zwingli quoted at Marburg.[63] For Zwingli, like Aquinas, that which was not reasonable to faith[64] could not be true, or, as Zwingli put it at Marburg, "[T]he oracles of the demons are obscure, not the words of Christ."[65]

For some time, Zwingli had been a convinced proponent of Erasmian biblical humanism, which appears to have been the dominant influence on his theology. At the heart of this humanism was the slogan *ad fontes*, which in part referred to the conviction that truth (and the reform of the church) was to be found by returning to the sources of earliest Christianity: the Bible (especially the Greek New Testament) and the church fathers. Zwingli enthusiastically studied both, with John, Paul, and Augustine taking prominence.[66] Zwingli also inherited from Erasmus the latter's strong distinction between the spirit and matter.[67] Fritz Büsser went so far as to say that a point-by-point comparison of Erasmus and Zwingli could suggest that Erasmus was the secret reformer of Zurich.[68] These two influences of scholasticism and humanism repeatedly showed up in Zwingli's eucharistic theology.

Did Luther influence Zwingli's theology and, if so, to what extent? Clearly, as Zwingli himself admits, he was impressed by Luther's stand at the Leipzig Debate, which played a role in his development because it inspired him to action.[69] Martin Brecht believed that Luther influenced

Zwingli in his movement from an Erasmian imitation of Christ to a belief in justification.[70] W. P. Stephens posited that Zwingli's theology was arrived at independently of Luther.[71]

THE MAIN PHASE OF THE EUCHARISTIC CONTROVERSY

The main phase of the Eucharistic Controversy began in November 1524 when Zwingli wrote what was to become his first public statement[72] on the figurative view of Christ's presence, the open *Letter to Matthew Alber*.[73] Multiple handwritten copies of this letter were made and distributed before it and *Commentary on True and False Religion* were both published in March 1525. Although Luther had summarily rejected the symbolic argument of Cornelius Hoen in 1523, in the following year the Swiss reformer was thoroughly impressed by it and made several of the arguments his own. Although difference of opinion exists about the extent of Hoen's influence on Zwingli's eucharistic theology, there is little doubt that it did influence it.[74] This becomes obvious by examining the *Letter to Matthew Alber*, which deserves special attention because it contains most of Zwingli's arguments about the Supper.

Zwingli began the letter by telling Matthew Alber, the Lutheran preacher in Reutlingen, that two reasons prompted him to write. The first involved a rumor that Zwingli had heard concerning Alber and his upcoming debate with Conrad Hermann on the topic of the Lord's Supper. The second reason for Zwingli's letter was that he recently had read Karlstadt's *On the Detestable Abuse of the Eucharist*. Although he approved of Karlstadt's figurative view and many things in the pamphlet pleased him, Zwingli did not concur with all of its particulars and maintained that its language fell short of the subject's demands. He was writing Alber to recommend his view of the Sacrament as superior to Karlstadt's.

In the letter, Zwingli set out to prove the figurative view of the Lord's Supper with two primary proofs, proofs that he would bring forth repeatedly throughout the Eucharistic Controversy. The first proof, which was to be a major argument for Zwingli, was that John 6 and especially John 6:63 made the presence of the essential body of Christ in the elements impossible.[75] With this argument, he adopted and developed an argument that Erasmus also had used,[76] as well as Wycliffe, Hoen, and Karlstadt. At the beginning of the body of the letter, Zwingli asserted: "The gist of this matter can easily be gathered from the sixth chapter of John. Do not listen to those who at once cry out, 'Christ is not dealing there with this sacrament at all.' I hold the same view, but he treats there something by which our unsound views about him are most certainly confuted."[77] The sixth chapter of John is "the bravest and best equipped line of troops."[78] After a running commentary on John 6, Zwingli arrived at the climax of his argument, John 6:63: "What could be brought forward more powerful to make us scorn all the theories devised about the physical and essential body of Christ in this sacrament? 'The flesh profits nothing.' . . . All darts are turned aside by this one shield. Someone will say, 'Do you not believe the body of Christ is eaten here?' Reply: 'The flesh profits nothing. Why should I then discuss it?' "[79] The preceding conclusively shows that for Zwingli, John 6:63, interpreted in the context of John 6, was not merely one of many passages that helped one understand the Sacrament. It was *the* passage that interpreted the question of Christ's presence in the Sacrament.[80]

In Zwingli's second proof that Christ could not be present bodily or essentially in the Sacrament, Hoen's influence became obvious. For the first time, Zwingli used the argument that in interpreting the Words of Institution—"This is my body"—the word *is* must mean "signifies." After discussing and dismissing Karlstadt's interpretation of the Words of Institution (though he praised Karlstadt for the effort), Zwingli offered his interpretation: "I think the hinge of the matter is to be found in a very short syllable, namely, in the word 'is,' the meaning of which is not always given by 'is' but sometimes by 'signifies.' "[81] He then quoted Gen. 41:26; John 15:1; Luke 8:11; and other passages where the copula meant "signifies." Next Zwingli turned to the Words of Institution: "The meaning of Christ's words becomes perfectly plain to this effect: 'This feast signifies or is the symbol by which you will recall that my body, mine, the Son of God, your Lord and Master, was given for you' "[82] and "it is clear that it is the sign itself by which those who rely upon the death and blood of Christ mutually prove to their brethren that they have this faith."[83] Zwingli then attempted to bolster his view further by briefly citing passages from the writings of Tertullian and Augustine.

What, then, was the point of the Lord's Supper according to Zwingli? "Behold the end for which he bids them eat, namely, the commemoration of him."[84] The Lord's Supper was a "ceremony of commemoration of his having been savagely slain for us," wrote Zwingli.[85] But the Swiss reformer also wanted Alber to understand clearly what the Lord's Supper did not do. "Hence, we see, in passing, this also: the eating of the Eucharist does not take away sins but is the symbol of those who firmly believe that sin was exhausted and destroyed by the death of Christ and give thanks therefore."[86] For Zwingli, the Lord's Supper could not be a means of grace nor take away sins because this would contradict the scriptural teaching that salvation comes only through faith in Christ who died for us.[87] The Lord's Supper as a means of grace ultimately would lead to idolatry.[88]

After publishing "Against the Heavenly Prophets" in January 1525, Luther wrote no further treatises on the matter for two years. Zwingli, on the other hand, kept the presses rolling. Much of this had to do with differing local situations. Luther was kept busy with the Peasants' War, the ongoing German translation of the Bible, his literary war with Erasmus, and his marriage. Zwingli was powerfully motivated to continue writing on the Lord's Supper precisely because he was being accused of heresy by his Catholic opponents in Zurich, most notably the town secretary, Joachim am Grüt. Thus in March 1525, Zwingli published *Commentary on True and False Religion*. In April, after a debate between Zwingli and am Grüt, the Zurich Council narrowly voted to abolish the Mass and to institute the Lord's Supper according to the apostolic custom (that is, according to Zwingli's view). Because the vote had been close, Zwingli continued to be concerned about his Catholic opposition. Therefore, in his next publication, the August 1525 *Subsidiary Essay on the Eucharist*,[89] Zwingli further attempted to clarify and fortify his view of the Sacrament. *Commentary on True and False Religion* greatly expanded his arguments found in *Letter to Matthew Alber* but did not significantly develop anything he had previously written.

In *Subsidiary Essay on the Eucharist*, however, Zwingli clarified the nature of the figure of speech in the Words of Institution. For the first time, he referred to it as a trope, a figure of speech developed by the rhetoricians of classical antiquity.[90] Zwingli had been motivated to name his interpretation because am Grüt had rejected the Swiss reformer's biblical proof passages for a figurative understanding of the copula (such as Luke 8:11 and Matt. 13:38, 39) because they took place in parables, whereas the Words of Institution did not. Naming the figure of speech as trope allowed Zwingli, at least in part, to dismiss am Grüt's criticism, pointing out that the passages he had cited were examples of tropes that took place within or next to parables, not that they were parables themselves.[91] That am Grüt had hit a nerve, however, can be seen in the way Zwingli desperately tried to find a new trope passage that had no connection to a parable. This hunt was unsuccessful until Exod. 12:11 was suggested to Zwingli in a dream: "[I]t is the Lord's passover." This passage became an important proof for Zwingli of the symbolic understanding of the Lord's Supper.[92] The use of trope also allowed Zwingli to distance himself from Karlstadt's allegorical/grammatical interpretation.[93]

Another significant development in *Subsidiary Essay on the Eucharist* concerned Zwingli's understanding of reason. The Swiss reformer had been criticized for rejecting the bodily eating of Christ on the basis of reason—because it didn't make sense to human intellect. Zwingli responded to the accusation that he rejected anything that was contrary to reason with a qualification: He had not been referring to natural reason but the reason of faith. Only that which was contrary to the reason of faith was to be rejected. For example, Zwingli held that the virgin birth was not contrary to the reason of faith because it was clear. On the other hand, the bodily presence in the Sacrament was absurd to the reason of faith. "Birth from a virgin is so completely manifested to the sense [reason] of all the faithful that no pious person ever doubted it. . . . That the symbolic bread is the flesh of Christ is so opposed to the sense [reason] that no one of us has ever really believed it . . . This word about the tearing of the flesh is so repugnant to the mind that it does not venture to eat it, but casts it out of the mouth."[94] Why the one was absurd and not the other was never made clear. This distinction could hardly have been convincing to Zwingli's opponents. It does, however, clarify why he rejected the bodily eating of Christ on the basis of reason.

A more important development was Zwingli's first use of Christology to deny the bodily presence. He maintained that the New Testament speaks of Christ's body in a threefold sense. There is the natural body, with which Christ was born and died, his resurrected body, and his mystical body, the church. The bread, Zwingli insisted, could be none of these. It could not be Christ's natural body because then we would have to grind his flesh and skin with our teeth, which John 6:63 disallows. It could not be Christ's risen body because it had ascended and sat down at the right hand of God where it will remain until Christ returns.[95] It could not be Christ's body, the church, because the church was not given for us. Therefore, the bread in the Eucharist could not be Christ's body but must be understood in terms of trope.[96]

The next six months saw a marked escalation in the Eucharistic Controversy. In July 1525, the Wittenberg theologian Johannes Bugenhagen[97] attacked Zwingli's position in *Open Letter against the New Error Concerning the Sacrament of the Body and Blood of Our Lord Jesus Christ*.[98] This marked the first time that a Wittenberg publication had personally attacked Zwingli. The Swiss reformer responded to Bugenhagen several months later with *A Reply to Bugenhagen's Letter*. By that time, it was becoming increasingly known that Luther was denouncing Zwingli by letter.[99] In January 1526, Luther's *Letter to Reutlingen*[100] became his first public statement against Zwingli and his party.

Because of this increased opposition to his position (indeed, he had heard that his eucharistic writings were beginning to be proscribed by the learned in certain places), Zwingli decided that a new, comprehensive treatise was needed. He wrote in German so he could address the laity directly so they could draw their own conclusions. *Eine klare Unterrichtung vom Nachtmahl Christi* ("A Clear Briefing [Instruction] on the Supper of Christ") was published in February 1526.[101]

Zwingli's *A Clear Briefing* (often referred to as *The Lord's Supper*) is important for his eucharistic development in several ways. First, Zwingli marshaled his arguments against three specific theological parties that he opposed, each of which held to a literal presence of Christ's body in the Supper. Although he did not mention them by name, it is clear Zwingli had in mind the traditional transubstantiation party, the Lutheran party, and the moderate Erasmian party. In this connection, a new argument against the bodily presence appeared. If *is* in the Words of Institution is taken literally (*substantive*), then, Zwingli stated, Christ's flesh must be literally perceived. For Zwingli, there was no such thing as an invisible or imperceptible literal corporeality: "Therefore, if the "is" is to be taken literally, the body of Christ must be visibly, literally, corporally and perceptibly present."[102] Not that God lacks the power to do the miraculous, but all his known miracles had been perceptibly present and there had never been an imperceptible miracle: "Since, however, we see and perceive bread, it is evident that we are ascribing to God a miracle which he himself neither wills nor approves: for he does not work miracles which cannot be perceived."[103]

Also evident in this argument was Zwingli's theology of the Word. To those who claimed that Christ's Word spoken over the elements had the power to transform those elements, Zwingli objected that "where God speaks literally his words are fulfilled literally, i.e., in such a way as may be seen and touched and known and experienced."[104] Therefore, the argument that said that Christ's body was literally present because God could do the miraculous through his Word was wide of the mark; nothing could be perceived in the Supper except bread and wine.

Of equal importance was Zwingli's use of Christology to disprove the bodily presence of Christ. Whereas he had done this in a rudimentary fashion in *Subsidiary Essay on the Eucharist*, he went beyond this in *A Clear Briefing*. Zwingli began by stating, as he often had before, that the scriptural teaching of Christ's ascension, session at God's right hand, and second coming made Christ's bodily presence in the Eucharist impossible because Christ did and will do these things only according to his human nature. By definition, the human nature cannot be in more than one place at one time. What about a passage such as Matt. 28:20: "And surely I am with you always, to the very end of the age"? Didn't this passage prove that Christ's body could be literally present in the Eucharist? No, said Zwingli, because this passage referred only to Christ's divine nature. Only Christ's divine nature was with Christians at all times and in all places. Furthermore, Zwingli stated that there is no transference of the abilities of one nature to the other.

> If without distinction we were to apply to his human nature everything that refers to the divine, and conversely, if without distinction we were to apply to the divine nature everything that refers to the human, we should overthrow all Scripture and indeed the whole of our faith. . . . [A]lthough I know that by virtue of the fact that the two natures are one Christ, things which are said of only the one nature are often ascribed to the other. Nevertheless, the proper character of each

nature must be left intact, and we ought to refer to it only those things which are proper to it.[105]

For the first time, it became clear that Zwingli so sharply separated the divine and human natures in Christ that he denied the *communicatio idiomatum* (the communication of Christ's attributes from one nature to the other).[106] What pertained to one nature could be ascribed to the other by virtue of Christ's person (such as in the expression "the Son of God died") but only ascribed. No actual transference occurred. Nothing of the divine nature was actually given or exchanged to the human nature and vice versa.

Zwingli's sharp separation between the divine and human natures was greatly expanded in the 1527 *A Friendly Exegesis*, a German work addressed by the Swiss reformer to Luther. Drawing on Plutarch, Zwingli used the figure of speech *alloiosis* to describe the interchange between the human and divine natures in Christ. According to Zwingli, *alloiosis* was a leap or "interchange, by which when, speaking of one of Christ's natures, we use the terms that apply to the other . . . what applies to one of the natures is predicated of the other."[107] Although *alloiosis* predicated what belonged to one nature to the other, there was no actual transference. In fact, Zwingli gave this warning: "But see at the same time how we must not confuse the understanding of the properties, even if we interchange the names."[108] When Scripture attributed something to one nature that properly belonged to the other, this was an interchange of names not substances. Thus when Scripture said that the Son of God died (for example, in 1 Cor. 15:3), what belonged properly to the human nature was being predicated of the divine nature. However, according to Zwingli, no transference occurred.

> As, therefore, even if one says hundreds of times, "The Son of God was slain," or "The Lord of Glory was crucified," we never understand that his Godhead suffered anything, only his humanity. So whenever power over all things and infinity are attributed to Christ, we never understand that his humanity has these things, even though we hear such modes of expression without offense. For as each nature is in him in its entirety, so each nature preserves its own character (as far as their boundaries are concerned). His humanity can no more reign than his divinity die—even though he who reigns is human, and he who dies is God.[109]

This led Zwingli to the conclusion that Christ's human nature, because it received nothing from the union with the divine nature, could only be at one place at one time. Therefore, because Scripture and the Second Article of the Apostles' Creed declared that Christ was at the right hand of God, his human nature had to be there and nowhere else, though his divine nature existed everywhere. Thus Christ's body and blood could not be in the Eucharist.

Surprisingly, Zwingli's eucharistic writings of 1527 and 1528 further refined his eucharistic theology, but there were no major new developments.[110] Instead, these writings were a point-by-point examination and refutation of Luther's eucharistic position. The same arguments that had already been considered repeatedly occurred in these treatises. According to W. P. Stephens, the main issue for Zwingli was Luther's claim that salvation came through the eating of Christ's body in the Eucharist, whereas for Zwingli salvation came only through faith in Christ's crucifixion for humanity.[111] Zwingli understood Luther's position to be a relapse into salvation by works.

> For if it [the physical eating of Christ's body] would strengthen faith and remit sins, who would not return to the vomit of works? I confess clearly, by heaven, that if I were told by the word of the Lord that sins were forgiven through this supper, I would partake of it every time my conscience troubled me. Would not faith in works straightway come back? . . . To have faith in Christ, the Son of God, is the healing remedy against the wounds of sin, not to eat of his body. Salvation is promised to faith, not to eating.[112]

This is why Zwingli, unlike Martin Bucer and the Strasbourg leaders, considered Luther's eucharistic teaching something that undermined the Gospel itself.[113]

Zwingli also considered Luther's position on the Eucharist to be a relapse into the externalization of the Christian faith, which was a serious problem for the Swiss reformer because he believed that nothing physical could help the soul.

> We think, therefore, that faith is very greatly defiled if we return to the husks of externals, as they say. . . . When we speak of bodily things, we do not mean in any way to depreciate Christ's body as a sacrifice offered for us. We only deny that the application of a physical body to the soul does anything towards justification, both because the mind cannot be fed by the flesh of the body, and because Christ himself has most effectively shown us that that which justifies must be the Spirit, while the flesh profits absolutely nothing.[114]

This is yet another example of Zwingli's dualistic and Neoplatonic leanings, to which he adhered consistently throughout this period.[115]

LUTHER RESPONDS

Other than minor writings,[116] Luther had not contributed to the Eucharistic Controversy since his January 1525 "Against the Heavenly Prophets." His publishing silence was noted by both friends and enemies. His friends reported to him with some alarm the spread and success of the

Zwinglian doctrine, and, therefore, implored Luther to write. His enemies wondered in print if perhaps the Spirit had left Luther and that this
fact accounted for his silence.[117] These forces finally prevailed on Luther.
In late 1526 and especially in 1527 and 1528, he produced and published
several major eucharistic tracts.

Luther did not publish personally the first tract, "The Sacrament of
the Body and Blood of Christ—Against the Fanatics," which was disseminated by others in October 1526.[118] The treatise contained sermons that
Luther had preached during Holy Week 1526. The sermons presented in
simple fashion Luther's eucharistic theology as compared to that of the
Swiss reformers. The second treatise was Luther's first major publication
against Zwingli and his party, the March 1527 "That These Words of
Christ 'This Is My Body,' etc., Still Stand Firm against the Fanatics."[119]
Martin Brecht considered this to be the most systematic of Luther's writings on the Lord's Supper. Certainly, Luther devoted much care and effort
to the treatise, as indicated by the printer's manuscript, still extant, which
shows Luther's numerous corrections.[120] The third treatise was the February 1528 "Confession Concerning Christ's Supper."[121] Luther intended
this to be his last word on the Eucharistic Controversy because he thought
at the time that continued dialogue with his opponents was fruitless. He
also believed his death to be imminent.[122] "Confession" is regarded as the
most detailed and profound of Luther's eucharistic tracts. The 1577 Formula of Concord quoted it more than any other treatise of Luther, which
led the editor of the Weimar edition of Luther's Works to refer to "Confession" as "the shibboleth of the genuine Lutherans."[123]

In each of these major treatises, Luther not only refined but also substantially developed his Lord's Supper theology. Because these developments have a direct bearing on his doctrinal hermeneutic, they will be
considered in the next section. The preceding chronology of the
Eucharistic Controversy reveals how Luther and his opponents developed their eucharistic theologies as they reacted to those who disagreed
with them. Without an understanding of the overall controversy and the
competing eucharistic theologies, one cannot properly locate Luther's
insistence on the bodily presence as an article of faith as defined by his
doctrinal hermeneutic. Luther's implacable insistence on Christ's bodily
presence in the Sacrament was largely caused by his opponents' equally
implacable denial of it, especially by Zwingli. Yet Luther's emphasis on the
bodily presence was merely one facet of a multifaceted theology of the
Lord's Supper. Only against this background can Luther's doctrinal
hermeneutic be properly assessed.

EVIDENCE FOR LUTHER'S DOCTRINAL HERMENEUTIC

The Marburg Colloquy and Luther's eucharistic treatises demonstrate the reformer's doctrinal hermeneutic in an ecumenical setting. Specifically, his doctrinal hermeneutic illuminates why Luther took the unyielding stance he did at Marburg. According to Luther, the Lord's Supper, including the bodily presence of Christ in the elements, was an article of faith, a doctrine necessary for salvation and unity. Luther came to this conclusion on the basis of his doctrinal hermeneutic rather than merely on the basis of pride or stubbornness in the heat of battle, as is sometimes implied. This was the same doctrinal hermeneutic the reformer consistently had been applying to church teachings throughout the 1520s.

CHRIST'S BODILY PRESENCE IN THE SACRAMENT WAS AN ARTICLE OF FAITH

For Luther, Christ's bodily presence in the Lord's Supper was not just any church teaching—it was an article of faith. This was true long before the Eucharistic Controversy. Already in his 1520 "To the Christian Nobility of the German Nation," the reformer had made this clear: "For it is not an article of faith that bread and wine are not present in the sacrament in their own essence and nature, but this is an opinion of St. Thomas and the pope. On the other hand, it is an article of faith that the true natural body and blood of Christ are present in the natural bread and wine."[124] Luther had explicitly defined Christ's bodily presence as an article of faith when he stated his position for the *Unitas Fratrum*. Throughout the Eucharistic Controversy, Luther never wavered from this position. Near the end of part two of "Against the Heavenly Prophets," he made this clear when he thanked his opponents "because they have so greatly confirmed me in regard to this article of faith. For now I see that it is not possible to produce anything in opposition to this article."[125] Near the beginning of the 1527 "That These Words of Christ," Luther listed the various ways the "fanatics" denied the bodily presence. He concluded the list by writing: "Besides all these there is the seventh group, who say, 'This is no article of faith, therefore we should not quarrel over it; let whoever will believe what he will.' These even tread this article under foot."[126] This was a reference to the position of the Strasbourgers, especially Capito and Bucer.[127]

In addition to referring plainly to the bodily presence as an "article," Luther used several other methods to indicate that it was necessary. One method compared the presence of Christ in the Supper to the yolk of an egg or the kernel of a nut. Those who denied Christ's bodily presence in the Sacrament and held that only bread and wine were present "suck the egg dry and leave us the shell, that is, remove the body and blood of

Christ from the bread and wine, so that it remains no more than mere bread, such as the baker does." They removed the kernel from the shell and left Christians with an empty nut, with chaff instead of grain.[128] This same thought was echoed in a 1529 Lenten sermon: "So the devil desired to take away the substance where he could not take away the use. He has allowed many fanatics to come teaching that the sacrament is not body and blood of Christ, but only bread and wine. This is to remove entirely the nature of the sacrament, to destroy the kernel and retain the mere husks."[129] By this language, Luther was clearly indicating the necessity of the bodily presence. To deny that Christ's body and blood were present in the Sacrament was to drain the Sacrament of its substance, its treasure, and make it no Sacrament at all.

Another way in which Luther indicated the necessity of the doctrine of the bodily presence of Christ was by plainly calling its denial a heresy or blasphemy. "I have never read of a more shameful heresy," complained the reformer in "That These Words of Christ." "[F]rom the outset [this heresy] has gathered to itself so many heads, so many factions and dissensions, although on the main point, the persecution of Christ, they are united. But he [the devil] will keep on and attack still other articles of faith, as he already declares with flashing eyes that baptism, original sin, and Christ are nothing."[130] Luther regarded it as "one of the greatest blasphemies" of his time that Zwingli and Oecolampadius dared to say that Christ's flesh availed nothing for believers when they ate it physically.[131]

Luther had no more patience for those who considered the question of Christ's presence in the Lord's Supper to be a minor matter, which was the position of the Strasbourg preachers. "Yes indeed, a Judas' peace and a traitor's kiss it is when they would be friendly to us and get us to the point of watching in silence while they ravage with fire and sword, by which they bring so many souls into the everlasting fire of hell, all the while wishing it to be regarded as a minor matter and of no consequence."[132] At Marburg, too, Oecolampadius had made it clear that for himself and his party, the bodily presence was opinion not belief.[133] Luther saw the devil behind the teaching that Christ's bodily presence in the Sacrament was something unnecessary, as he pointedly remarked in another Lenten sermon from 1529.

> I say this because the devil has again sown a new seed. When he sees that he cannot maintain his error, he says: If some people cannot believe that Christ's body and blood are present, certainly they won't be damned just because they can't believe or understand it. Thus, the devil wants to make of the Sacrament something that need not be believed and says: The Lord's Supper is not dealt with in the Apostles' Creed, therefore it's not necessary to believe it! Watch out here![134]

This statement is important evidence that Luther believed articles of faith were not limited to those expressly mentioned in the Apostles' Creed. On this subject, Hermann Sasse aptly observed: "While Zwingli and all Reformed theologians stressed the fact that the Creeds do not contain any article on the Lord's Supper . . . and while they did not regard a divergence of opinion on the Lord's Supper as church-divisive, for Luther the denial of the Real Presence was heresy destructive to the church—closely related to the great heresies that threatened the existence of the church throughout the centuries."[135]

In all these ways, Luther articulated throughout the Eucharistic Controversy his steadfast conviction that Christ's bodily presence in the Sacrament was an article of faith, a teaching necessary to be believed. Yet what exactly was Luther's understanding of the bodily presence?

Luther made no effort to define carefully the "how" of the bodily presence; in fact, he refused to do so. It was enough that a Christian confessed with Scripture that Christ's body and blood were in the Lord's Supper. Scripture did not speak to the "how" of that presence; therefore, neither should a Christian. "On this [the Words of Institution] we take our stand, and we also believe and teach that in the Supper we eat and take to ourselves Christ's body truly and physically. But how this takes place or how he is in the bread, we do not know and are not meant to know. God's Word we should believe without setting bounds or measure to it."[136] Luther made this statement in 1527, but even in 1520, such a refusal to investigate the manner of Christ's presence was basic for the reformer: "Why do we not put aside such curiosity and cling simply to the words of Christ, willing to remain in ignorance of what takes place here and content that the real body of Christ is present by virtue of the words? Or is it necessary to comprehend the manner of the divine working in every detail?"[137] Luther rejected the theory of transubstantiation, in part, because it unnecessarily pried into the how of the bodily presence, something Scripture did not make clear.

As the Eucharistic Controversy progressed, Luther sharpened his teaching on the manner of Christ's presence in the Supper as he reacted to his opponents' caricatures of his position. When they accused Luther and his party of holding to a crassly visible and local presence of Christ's body in the bread, Luther had to object.

> We poor sinners, indeed, are not so foolish as to believe that Christ's body is in the bread in a crude visible manner, like bread in a basket or wine in a cup, a belief with which the fanatics would like to saddle us, to amuse themselves with our folly. But we believe precisely that his body is present, as his words say and indicate: "This is my body." When the fathers and we occasionally say, "Christ's body is in the bread," we do so quite simply because by our faith we wish to confess

that Christ's body is present. Otherwise we may well allow it to be said that it is in the bread, it is the bread, is where the bread is, or whatever you wish. Over words we do not wish to argue, just so the meaning is retained that it is not mere bread that we eat in Christ's Supper, but the body of Christ.[138]

In this case, the controversy led Luther to define more sharply his understanding of the bodily presence. Specifically, the bodily presence did not entail a local or visible presence.

In the course of the controversy, Luther also was forced to clarify the nature of Christ's body in the Sacrament. He had often said that the body and blood in the Sacrament was the same body and blood of Christ that had been born of Mary, crucified, and raised.[139] This led Zwingli to object that if this was so, Christians would be able to see and touch the former body and blood as they did the latter. Luther's solution was to make a distinction between the form or mode of Christ's body, on the one hand, and the essence or nature of that body, on the other.

In plain language, we do not say that Christ's body is present in the Supper in the same form in which he was given for us—who would say that?—but that it is the same body which was given for us, not in the same form or mode but in the same essence and nature. Now a particular essence can very well be visible at one place and invisible at another.

. . . But it is Zwinglian logic to take substance for accident and "which" for "of what kind," as if I should say, "Christ is not present in the Supper in a certain form, therefore he is not present bodily"; "Christ is not with us in a certain form, therefore he is not present with us at all," jumping right from a particular to a universal.

. . . For if they prove anything with their passages, they prove that Christ is not present in the Supper in a visible, mortal, and earthly mode—a thing which it is not in the least necessary to prove, for we acknowledge it all.[140]

This same distinction was used by Luther when he attempted a compromise formula at the end of the Marburg Colloquy. The compromise stated: "We confess, that, by virtue of the words 'This is my body, this is my blood,' the body and blood are truly—*hoc est: substantive et essentialiter, non autem quantitative vel qualitative vel localiter* [that is, substantively and essentially, however not quantitatively nor qualitatively nor locally]—present and distributed in the Lord's Supper."[141] These words affirmed that Christ's body and blood were present in their true essence but not according to the same measurable, local, form that Christ's body had taken during his earthly ministry.

For Luther, the essential presence of Christ's body and blood in the Sacrament was an article of faith that must be believed. But why did he hold it to be an article of faith? His doctrinal hermeneutic answers that question: Christ's bodily presence in the Sacrament satisfied his scriptural and evangelical canons so he considered it a necessary doctrine.

THE SCRIPTURAL CANON

Because all parties in the Eucharistic Controversy based their Lord's Supper arguments on Scripture alone, it is not surprising that Luther did not use the first part of his scriptural canon in his debates and writings. The remaining part of the canon—that a necessary doctrine must be based on the right Scripture—was at the heart of the debate concerning the Lord's Supper. As expected, Luther had much to say on that issue.

The Words of Institution Are Clear

The teaching of the bodily presence qualified as an article of faith for Luther because it was based on the right Scripture, that is, on clear Scripture: The Words of Institution as recorded in the three gospels and in 1 Corinthians 11.[142] At Marburg, Luther stated this pointedly: "I have a clear and powerful text. Do justice to that text!"[143] For Luther, the clarity of the Words of Institution was so obvious that even unbelievers recognized what they meant: "We know, however, that these words, 'This is my body,' etc. are clear and lucid. Whether a Christian or a heathen, a Jew or a Turk hears them, he must acknowledge that they speak of the body of Christ which is in the bread. How otherwise could the heathen and the Jews mock us, saying that the Christians eat their God, if they did not understand this text clearly and distinctly?"[144] Although Luther certainly knew that the Bible contained obscure verses, the Words of Institution were not among these obscure passages. "Here there are no obscure words, but words that are crystal clear: He took the bread, gave thanks, broke it and gave it to them, saying, 'Take and eat. This is my body.' This is an amazingly clear word."[145] Luther was so confident of the lucidity of the words that in the beginning of "That These Words of Christ," he rather naively remarked: "But 'God's word alone endures forever' .... For this reason I am not worried that this fanaticism will last long. It is much too crude and impudent, and it does not attack obscure and uncertain Scripture but clear, plain Scripture, as we shall hear."[146]

Of course, Luther's opponents did not agree that the Words of Institution were clear. It was for this reason that they insisted so strenuously on John 6:63, which they believed to be a clearer passage. At Marburg, Luther's opponents maintained, as they had earlier, that John 6:63 must interpret the Words of Institution. Luther countered that John 6 "did not deal with the matter at hand."[147] Both sides were attempting to base their teaching on clear Scripture. Luther did so because of his conviction that Christ's bodily presence was an article of faith, and, therefore, such an article had to be based on the right Scripture.

The Right Scripture Rightly Interpreted

Luther held that an article of faith had to be based on the right Scripture rightly interpreted. If it was based on suspect interpretation, the Christian could not rely on it with certainty: "For the text must be quite unambiguous and plain, and must have one single, definite interpretation if it is to form the basis of a clear and definite article of faith."[148] At the heart of this aspect of Luther's scriptural canon was the understanding that the plain, natural, grammatical meaning of Scripture must be accepted, unless another Scripture or an article of faith compelled a different meaning. As early as "Babylonian Captivity," Luther stated this principle clearly: "But there are good grounds for my view, and this above all—no violence is to be done to the words of God, whether by man or angel. They are to be retained in their simplest meaning as far as possible. Unless the context manifestly compels it, they are not to be understood apart from their grammatical and proper sense, lest we give our adversaries occasion to make a mockery of all the Scriptures."[149]

Throughout the Eucharistic Controversy, Luther repeated this rule, for example, as he did in "Confession Concerning Christ's Supper": "For our own people, I am sure, I have rendered this text clear enough, and have laid down this rule: In Scripture we should let the words retain their natural force, just as they read, and give no other interpretation unless a clear article of faith compels otherwise."[150] One reason Luther argued so vociferously for the literal meaning of the Words of Institution was that the necessary status of Christ's bodily presence hung in the balance— because an article of faith must be based on the plain, natural meaning of the text. A figurative interpretation, such as the one that Zwingli proposed, would not do.

Luther's opponents attempted to satisfy Luther's scriptural canon both at Marburg and in earlier writings. Because Luther had said that the simple, natural meaning of the text should remain unless another Scripture or article of faith compelled a figurative understanding, they supplied both Scripture and article. The Scripture was John 6:63. The article of faith was the statement of the creed that Christ had "ascended into heaven and sits at the right hand of God, the Father Almighty." This article of faith disqualified Christ's bodily presence in the Sacrament because, as Zwingli put it, "one and the same body can in no way be in several places at the same time."[151]

Luther rejected both the Scripture and the article Zwingli and his followers put forth as insufficient on several grounds. First, in Luther's opinion neither John 6:63 nor the article of Christ's ascension and session at

God's right hand were clearer than the Words of Institution. It was wrong to interpret clear Scripture (that is, the Words of Institution) with an obscure Scripture passage:

> The holy doctors follow the practice, in expounding the Scriptures, of using lucid and clear passages to clarify the obscure and ambiguous passages. It is also the Holy Spirit's practice to illumine the darkness with the light. But our fanatics proceed the other way around . . . . Just so they also regard the obscure sayings, "Flesh is of no avail," and "Christ is seated at the right hand of God," as sun, and try thereby to darken the words of the Supper.[152]

Second, John 6:63 was insufficient because the "flesh" mentioned in the passage did not refer to Christ's flesh but to the sinful flesh.[153] Third, their use of the article of the creed was insufficient, according to Luther, because Zwingli and his camp wrongly understood it to mean that Christ's body could be in only one location and that it was, therefore, impossible for his body also to be in the Supper. In his response, Luther pointed out that even the scholastics had recognized modes of presence other than a local presence.[154] A body could be present locally (in a certain space only, as Christ was during his ministry on earth); definitively or illocally (non-measurably, no longer bound to a certain space, as Christ came to the disciples through a closed door); and repletively (filling all space simultaneously, which applied to God alone). It was in the definitive or uncircumscribed mode that Christ "can be and is in the bread."[155] Luther did not intend for his discussion about modes of presence to be a dogmatic or theological statement: "All this I have related in order to show that there are more modes whereby an object may exist in a place than the one circumscribed, physical mode on which the fanatics insist."[156] Because Zwingli and his party were declaring the bodily presence to be impossible on philosophical grounds, Luther used philosophy to show that it was indeed possible. His aim was to demonstrate that it was possible for the body of Christ to be present at the right hand of God and in the Supper simultaneously.

Of course, Luther suspected that his opponents' refusal to accept Christ's bodily presence was caused by their sinful reason, which was always an impediment to articles of faith. In a 1529 sermon to the Wittenberg congregation, Luther highlighted that human reason was an impediment to interpreting the Words of Institution.

> Here we must separate our reason from God's Word. You must put out the eyes of reason and toss them into the pit of hell. Instead you must let God's Word be true and cling to it with closed eyes and ears. This is the flaw of the fanatical spirits in this matter, that they let their reason advise whether it is possible that bread and wine can be body and blood. Reason cannot understand this and then adorns itself with

a peacock feather and accepts instead this article, "Jesus Christ ascended into heaven," and says: If he ascended, he cannot be in the bread. For these are opposites: that he is in heaven and that he is held in the hand of a scoundrel on earth.[157]

According to Luther, such sinful reason not only rejected the article of the bodily presence but also would not allow any article of faith to remain.[158] Whereas Zwingli held that teachings of God never contradicted the reason of faith, Luther held that articles of faith always contradicted reason.[159]

In a related battle over reason, Zwingli had rebuffed Luther's interpretation of the Words of Institution as an exegetical impossibility. According to the Swiss reformer, the pronoun *this* either had to refer to the bread or to Christ's body sitting at table (*a la* Karlstadt) but not both.

> Nor can you say that the pronoun "this" points to both the bread and the body of Christ, giving the meaning, "this bread is bread and the body of Christ at the same time," . . . Indeed the first of these explanations, according to which some say the bread is at the same time bread and the body of Christ, makes confusion of the Lord's discourse. For if it is bread, it cannot properly be said of it that it is the body of Christ.[160]

Zwingli considered it to be impossible for two substances to be one. "Not so," answered Luther in his "Confession Concerning Christ's Supper." Framing his answer in the context of Wycliffe's doctrine of identical predication, Luther held up the doctrines of the Trinity and of Christ's person as biblical examples of two or more persons or natures becoming one by virtue of their union. If such was possible with God and Christ,

> [w]hy then should we not much more say in the Supper, "This is my body," even though bread and body are two distinct substances, and the word "this" indicates the bread? Here, too, out of two kinds of objects a union has taken place, which I shall call a "sacramental union," because Christ's body and the bread are given to us as a sacrament.
>
> . . . Thus also it is correct to say, "He who takes hold of this bread, takes hold of Christ's body; and he who eats this bread, eats Christ's body; he who crushes this bread with teeth or tongue, crushes with teeth or tongue the body of Christ." And yet it remains absolutely true that no one sees or grasps or eats or chews Christ's body in the way he visibly sees and chews any other flesh. What one does to the bread is rightly and properly attributed to the body of Christ by virtue of the sacramental union.[161]

In proposing the sacramental union, Luther was not attempting to provide a definitive, final answer to the how of the Sacrament that would satisfy the demands of reason. This would have been to base an article of faith on reason, something that would have violated his scriptural canon. As Sasse has said, the *unio sacramentalis* was intentionally contrasted with transubstantiation, on the one hand, and late medieval consubstantiation, on the other. Sacramental union was similar to consubstantiation in that both presupposed that bread and body, wine and blood existed together. But consubstantiation, like transubstantiation, was a philosophical theory that sought to explain in terms satisfactory to reason the how of the bodily presence—it was a word and concept that Luther never used to describe Christ's presence in the Sacrament. Luther's sacramental union was a statement of faith based on the words of Christ that sought to show that the teaching that bread was at the same time Christ's body was not impossible according to Scripture or reason.[162]

Nor was the sacramental union impossible according to the rules of grammar. According to Luther, synecdoche was a form of speech in which the containing vessel was mentioned instead of the content or in which the name of the whole was given for the part. Luther had first brought up this grammatical rule in "Against the Heavenly Prophets."[163] A mother who said, "This is my child," while pointing to a cradle in which her child lay, was an example of synecdoche. In emphasizing the child, the mother certainly was not denying the presence of the cradle. If a person was to point to a purse and say, "This is a hundred gulden," to emphasize the money it held, the person would not be denying the purse that was present with the money. According to Luther, the statement "This is my body"[164] followed the same grammatical pattern. In all this, Luther was simply trying to demonstrate that the bodily presence was not impossible according to the rules of grammar.

When Zwingli in *Friendly Exegesis*[165] and Oecolampadius at Marburg[166] accused Luther of also giving a figurative interpretation of the Words of Institution with his synecdoche, Luther objected: "The metaphor does away with the content, such as when you understand the 'body' as 'figure of the body.' That the synecdoche does not do. . . . Figurative speech removes the core and leaves the shell only. Synecdoche is not a comparison, but it rather says, 'That is there, and it is contained in it.' "[167] Luther believed his opponents' criticism to be beside the point in two ways. First, synecdoche did not do away with either the elements or Christ's body and blood. By contrast, his opponents' metaphorical interpretation did away with the bodily presence. Second, Luther did not consider synecdoche to be a figurative expression like a metaphor because it did not involve a comparison.

Luther had to respond specifically to Zwingli's main argument: that *is* in the Words of Institution was a trope that meant "represents" or "signifies."[168] It was especially this argument that attacked the scriptural basis of the bodily presence as an article of faith. Following the lead of Hoen,

Zwingli bolstered this argument with other passages of Scripture in which the copula allegedly denoted "represents."

Luther first responded to this argument in detail in "That These Words of Christ."[169] He denied that Zwingli had proven that *is* was understood metaphorically in Scripture and challenged the Swiss reformer again to do so: "But since the point at issue here is whether the word 'is' necessarily means the same in Scripture as the word 'represents,' Zwingli is obliged to prove this from Scripture."[170] Luther also insisted that Zwingli (and Oecolampadius) prove that the copula meant "represents" in the Words of Institution. Even if they could produce an example in one passage of Scripture that supported their metaphorical interpretation, they would still be under obligation to prove that it had the same meaning in the words of the Lord's Supper.[171] Luther then proceeded to examine several of Zwingli's proofs[172] and concluded that none of them proved representation. For example, when Christ said that he was the true vine, he actually was a true vine. In Luther's understanding, "[a]ll these sayings are expressed and understood in terms of being, not of representing."[173]

Although Luther wrote nothing more about this in "That These Words of Christ," he further developed the argument a year later in "Confession Concerning Christ's Supper." Not only did Scripture contain no examples of *is* meaning "represents," argued Luther, neither did any human writing. "Indeed, I will go further: If the fanatics, in any one of all the languages on earth, can produce one saying in which 'is' means the same as 'represents,' then they may claim to have won their case."[174] Their basic flaw was that they failed to understand grammar, that words often take on new meanings, depending on the context. Luther cited as an example *flower*, which according to its primary sense means a plant, such as a rose. But if the word is used in the phrase "Christ is a flower," the word *flower* takes on a new meaning. "All grammarians say that 'flower' here has become a new word and has acquired a new meaning, and now no longer means the flower in the field but the child Jesus. They do not say that the word 'is' here has become metaphorical, for Christ does not represent a flower but is a flower, yet a different flower from the natural one."[175] Luther then explained that this was the sense of all the passages that Zwingli cited as metaphorical. Christ did not *represent* a rock or a vine; instead, he *was* a new rock, a new vine, etc. One should only give a word a new meaning, however, if the immediate or remote context compelled it.

In his debate with Zwingli and his party, Luther was guided by the scriptural canon of his doctrinal hermeneutic. At the heart of his debate with the Swiss and South Germans, and the foremost impediment to unity with them, was their differing views of the bodily presence. Luther affirmed the bodily presence while the Swiss and South Germans denied it. Often overlooked, however, is another vital difference. For Luther, Christ's bodily presence in the Sacrament was an article of faith. It did not carry this importance for the other side. Therefore, as he set out to prove the bodily presence, Luther set out to prove not only that it was true but also that it was an article of faith. He used the same argumentation that he had used to demonstrate all other articles of faith—the scriptural canon of his doctrinal hermeneutic. In his writings prior to the Marburg Colloquy and at Marburg itself, Luther repeatedly demonstrated that the bodily presence of Christ in the Sacrament was an article of faith because it was based on the right Scripture (clear) rightly interpreted (the simple not the figurative meaning). This was not a unique argument for the bodily presence; instead, it was one that Luther had been using for many years. In fact, he had previously applied this argument to an ecumenical situation in the dialogue with the *Unitas Fratrum*.

THE EVANGELICAL CANON

For Luther, no teaching could be an article of faith unless it was necessary for salvation or was connected to the gospel of justification by grace for Christ's sake through faith, which is Luther's evangelical canon. The Wittenberg reformer applied his evangelical canon to the teaching of Christ's bodily presence in the Sacrament. In his eucharistic writings and at Marburg, Luther consistently argued that Christ's bodily presence in the Lord's Supper was an article of faith (1) because it was Christ's incarnation in action and (2) because it was the Gospel—it offered forgiveness of sins, life, and salvation.

Christ's Bodily Presence in the Sacrament
Is the Incarnation in Action

Why did Luther regard the Lord's Supper as a necessary article of faith and so stubbornly refuse to budge as he dialogued with Zwingli and his party? One reason was because he believed the bodily presence was Christ's incarnation in action. To deny Christ's presence in the Sacrament was to deny the incarnation, which all parties agreed was a doctrine necessary for salvation. At the end of "That These Words of Christ," Luther sounded a warning that expressed what he believed to be at stake: "Therefore they are not to be trusted. For any spirit that does away with Christ's flesh is not of God, says St. John."[176] Luther added: "Let there be a testing. Now this spirit certainly does away with Christ's flesh, because he makes it a useless, perishable, and altogether common flesh, like beef or veal, as we have heard. Therefore he cannot be honest. I warn, I counsel: Beware, watch out, Satan has come among the children of God!"[177] Luther's reference to 1 John 4:1–3 made it abundantly clear that because his opponents were denying the necessity of the teaching of the bodily presence (they had called it useless), they were denying the incarnation itself. But how did Luther come to this conclusion?

It would be tempting to think, given that Zwingli had injected Christology into the Eucharistic Controversy, that Luther's Lord's Supper Christology was nothing but a reaction. This chronology would be mistaken, however. Long before he had come to blows with Zwingli, Luther had summarized how the incarnation was bound up in the Sacrament: "The body which you receive, the Word which you hear, are the body and Word of him who holds the whole world in his hand and who inhabits it from beginning to end."[178] The Christian received in the Sacrament nothing less than the body of the incarnate Son of God. This was Luther's consistent position. Although Luther did respond to Zwingli's Christology, it is more accurate to say that Zwingli's views motivated Luther to further articulate his long-held Christology.

To attack Christ's bodily presence in the Sacrament was to attack the incarnation. Luther expressed this in a number of different contexts. When Zwingli and his party denied the presence of Christ's body in the Supper on the basis of John 6:63, Luther considered this to be a direct attack on the incarnation. If Christ's flesh could not be in the Sacrament because his flesh was of no avail, then neither could his flesh have been conceived and born. "For if his flesh is not present in the sacrament for the reason that flesh is of no avail, neither is it in his mother's womb, precisely for the same reason that it is of no avail. The reasoning is the same in both instances."[179] Neither could Christ have been bodily present in the manger, in Simeon's arms, at his baptism in the Jordan, at the table at the Last Supper, on the cross, or at the right hand of God.

> You say: Stop, for God's sake, you will buzz yourself to death. In this way you would even buzz Christ right out of the garden, the cross, his whole passion, saying that none of these things happened bodily, because of course he had to be bodily present in them all and yet his flesh is of no avail if it is bodily there.

> Yes, my friend, I shall also buzz him away from the right hand of God, on which our entire interest focuses, and prove that he is not there. For flesh is of no avail. Now although his flesh is seated at the right hand of God, it is still the same flesh of Christ, for it did not become a different flesh at the right hand of God. If it is the same flesh, it is of no avail there either. If it is of no avail, then it is not there either, but is nothing at all, and its fate is the same in this passage as in the Supper.[180]

Luther was pointing out a serious logical inconsistency in the argument of his opponents. More than this, he was emphasizing his conviction that the bodily presence was bound up in Christ's incarnation every bit as much as his conception, birth, life, death, and resurrection. To use John

6:63 to deny the bodily presence was, as Luther saw it, to nullify the incarnation.[181]

Another of the principal arguments of Zwingli and his party was that the article of Christ's ascension and session at the right hand of God precluded his bodily presence in the Sacrament. Although Christ's divine nature was infinite and everywhere, his human nature was finite, limited by time and space, and was only at God's right hand.[182] For Luther, this kind of reasoning betrayed a dangerous misunderstanding of the incarnation and Christ's person. Although at Marburg Luther conceded that Christ's body was finite, as human bodies are finite,[183] he rejected the notion that Christ's human nature was exactly equivalent to ours. This could not be because Christ's human nature was united with divinity. As such, it was different from ours.

> [T]hough his humanity is a created thing, yet since it is the only creature so united with God as to constitute it one person with the divinity, it must be higher than all other creatures and above and beyond them, under God alone. Well, this is our faith. Here we come with a Christ beyond all creatures, both according to his humanity and his divinity; with his humanity we enter a different land from that in which it moved on earth, viz. beyond and above all creatures and purely in the Godhead.[184]

Christ's human nature was like ours, but because it was bound up with the divine nature in the personal union, it was invested with capabilities not possessed by an ordinary human body, such as the ability to be in many places at once.[185] This is why, for Luther, the finite was capable of the infinite.

Here also was the reason that Luther lashed out at Zwingli's *alloiosis* concept. Because the *alloiosis* so stressed the distinction between the two natures of Christ, saying, for example, that only the human nature of Christ died, it threatened to destroy the unity of the person of Christ and the incarnation. Luther, therefore, advised his readers about how to respond to the *alloiosis* argument.

> Now if the old witch, Lady Reason, alloeosis' grandmother, should say that the Deity surely cannot suffer and die, then you must answer and say: That is true, but since the divinity and humanity are one person in Christ, the Scriptures ascribe to the divinity, because of this personal union, all that happens to humanity, and vice versa. And in reality it is so. Indeed, you must say that the person (pointing to Christ) suffers, and dies. But this person is truly God, and therefore it is correct to say: the Son of God suffers.
>
> . . . Thus we should ascribe to the whole person whatever pertains to one part of the person, because both parts constitute one person. This is the way all the ancient teachers speak; so do all modern theolo-

gians, all languages, and the whole Scripture. But this damned alloeo-sis exactly inverts the matter and changes it so that it ascribes to the parts what Scripture assigns to the whole person. He [Zwingli] fash-ions his own tropes to pervert the Scripture and divide the person of Christ, as he has also done with the word "is," just so he may bring to light his new teaching and his foolish ideas.[186]

Whereas for Zwingli no transference occurred between Christ's two natures, Luther said "in reality it was so" because of the personal union. Luther held to the *communicatio idiomatum* and believed that because both natures were united within the person of Christ, his human nature shared the properties of the divine nature,[187] such as omnipresence.[188]

> Wherever this person is, it is the single, indivisible person, and if you can say, "Here is God," then you must also say, "Christ the man is pres-ent too."

> And if you could show me one place where God is and not the man, then the person is already divided and I could at once say truthfully, "Here is God who is not man and has never become man." But no God like that for me! For it would follow from this that space and place had separated the two natures from one another and thus had divided the person, even though death and all the devils had been unable to separate and tear them apart. This would leave me a poor sort of Christ, if he were present only at one single place, as a divine and human person, and if at all other places he had to be nothing more than a mere isolated God and a divine person without the humanity. No, comrade, wherever you place God for me, you must also place the humanity for me. They simply will not let themselves be separated and divided from each other. He has become one person and does not separate the humanity from himself as Master Jack takes off this coat and lays it aside when he goes to bed.[189]

For Luther, the doctrine that Christ's divine nature was many places where his human nature was not separated Christ into two persons and destroyed the incarnation. Luther was accusing Zwingli of the heresy of Nestorianism, just as Zwingli had accused Luther of Monophysitism[190] (of mixing and confusing the natures).[191] Neither charge was true, but Zwingli did come close to Nestorianism because he failed to understand the real unity of the God-man.

Luther went even further in his Christology. On the basis of passages such as Col. 2:9 and John 14:9, he held that God was revealed only in Christ, or, as Luther put it, "apart from Christ there is no God." So when his opponents claimed that Christ's body was bound to one location in heaven, Luther replied:

> From these childish ideas it must follow further that they also bind God himself to one place in heaven, on the same golden throne, since

apart from Christ there is no God, and where Christ is there is the Godhead in all its fulness, as Paul says, "In him the whole Godhead dwells bodily" [2 Cor. 2:9], and John 6 [14:9f.], "Have I been with you so long, and yet you do not know me, Philip? He who has seen me has seen the Father. Do you not believe that the Father is in me and I am in the Father?"[192]

While at Marburg, Oecolampadius admonished Luther not to cling to the humanity and flesh of Christ but to lift up his mind to his divinity. Luther answered that he could hardly put up with such remarks. He did not know or worship any God except him who was made man; nor did he want to have another God besides him. And besides him there was no other God who could save us. Therefore, Luther could not bear to have Christ's humanity curtailed and minimized.[193]

In the course of the Eucharistic Controversy, Luther came to see that the argument over the bodily presence was also an argument over the incarnation. As Hermann Sasse has stated: "If Luther and Zwingli disagreed to such a degree in their understanding of the Incarnation, how could they ever reach an understanding on the Sacrament of the Altar, which for Luther rested completely on the Incarnation, being, as it were, an extension of the Incarnation into our time and into lives?"[194] It is because Luther understood Christ's bodily presence in the Sacrament as "an extension of the Incarnation," which according to the Apostles' Creed was an article of faith, that he also viewed the bodily presence as a necessary article of faith. This, however, was not the only reason that Luther considered Christ's bodily presence in the Lord's Supper an article of faith.

Christ's Bodily Presence in the Sacrament Is the Gospel

Luther's evangelical canon held that only a teaching that was the Gospel or that connected to the Gospel could be an article of faith, a teaching necessary for salvation. For Luther, the Lord's Supper was the Gospel[195] because it proclaimed the forgiveness of sins. Luther stated in 1520: "Now the mass is part of the gospel; indeed, it is the sum and substance of it. For what is the whole gospel but the good tidings of the forgiveness of sins?"[196] The Mass was the "using [of] the gospel and communing at the table of the Lord."[197]

The Lord's Supper was Gospel for Luther not only, or even primarily, because it *proclaimed* the forgiveness of sins. It was Gospel because it *gave* forgiveness to those who believed—it was a means of grace. Luther had stressed this already in his literary joust with Karlstadt. In his eucharistic writings prior to Marburg, Luther continued to emphasize that Christ's body and blood in the Supper was a means of grace through which faith was strengthened and forgiveness was distributed. Zwingli believed that Luther's teaching contradicted the Gospel and the creed, which said that forgiveness came only through faith in the cross. Thus Luther again made the distinction he had made for Karlstadt.

> The blind fool does not know that the *merit of Christ* and the *distribution of the merit* are two different things. . . . Christ has once for all merited and won for us the forgiveness of sins on the cross; but this forgiveness he distributes wherever he is, at all times and in all places, as Luke writes, chapter 24[:46f.], "Thus it is written, that Christ had to suffer and on the third day rise (in this consists his merit), and that repentance and forgiveness of sins should be preached in his name (here the distribution of his merit comes in)." This is why we say there is forgiveness of sins in the Supper, not on account of the eating, nor because Christ merits or achieves forgiveness of sins there, but on account of the word through which he distributes among us this acquired forgiveness, saying, "This is my body which is given for you."[198]

That forgiveness of sins came through the Eucharist could hardly be in competition with the cross. The cross was the source of forgiveness, the Lord's Supper one of the means of its distribution. Although they allegedly agreed on this point at Marburg, Zwingli's subsequent writings showed that he again rejected the Eucharist as a means of grace.[199]

In the passage above, Luther also clarified that he did not believe that forgiveness came because of the eating (which Zwingli had charged) but because of the Words of Institution. It was faith in the words of Christ— "given for you for the forgiveness of sins"—that brought forgiveness. Therefore, the words of Christ in the Supper were far more important than the body and blood.[200] Faith in the words of Christ in the Supper was the spiritual eating—and without this spiritual eating, the physical eating did not avail.

> When have you ever heard from us that we eat Christ's Supper, or teach that it should be eaten, in such a way that there is only an outward, physical eating of the body of Christ? Have we not taught in many books that in the Supper two things are to be kept in mind? One, which is the supreme and most necessary point, consisting of the words, "Take eat, this is my body," etc.; the other is the sacrament or physical eating of the body of Christ. . . . We have said, further, that if anyone physically eats the sacrament without these words or without this spiritual eating, it is not only of no avail to him, but even harmful, as Paul says [1 Cor. 11:27], "Whoever eats the bread in an unworthy manner will be guilty of profaning the body of the Lord."[201]

This did not mean that Christ's bodily presence in the Sacrament did not bring forgiveness. Luther insisted that the Word and Christ's body and blood belonged together and could not be separated. Both were important parts of "one sacramental reality" in which all the parts depended on the others.[202] But when pushed, Luther could declare that Christ's body and blood, even without the Word, could be efficacious by virtue of the incarnation.

> But if again I reply, "I will not let anyone separate the body of Christ from the Word," they would hiss and hoot at me. Well, suppose it is as they dream, that Christ's body is alone in the bread and no Word of God is there with it—though this is not possible; let us see what they gain. . . . For if Christ's body is present without the outward Word of God, it cannot be present there without the inner, eternal Word which is God himself, John 1[:1]. For this is "Word became flesh" [John 1:14] and is in the flesh.
>
> Now I ask, in turn, whether God himself may also be of some avail?[203]

Because of the incarnation, the body of Christ in the Sacrament was "God's flesh, the Spirit's flesh. It is in God and God is in it. Therefore it lives and gives life to all who eat it."[204] Indeed, "we are confronted by the common article of our faith, that Christ's flesh is full of divinity, full of eternal good, life, and salvation, and he who takes a bite of it takes to himself therewith eternal good, life, full salvation, and all that is in this flesh. And if he believed it, he would also have life and salvation from it; but if he did not believe it, this treasure would not help him at all, but would rather harm him."[205] By these repeated statements, Luther insisted on the importance of the bodily presence as the Gospel that distributed salvation and the forgiveness of sins.

Luther could not help but view the position of his opponents as a serious error. Zwingli and Oecolampadius's denial of the Lord's Supper as a means of grace, as Carter Lindberg has put it, "vitiated the gospel by making it dependent upon faith and personal piety . . . The 'because . . . therefore' grammar of God's promise shifted to the 'if . . . then' grammar of human achievement: *if* you have a heartfelt remembrance of Christ's passion, *then* you may participate in the eucharist as an outward and visible sign of an inward and spiritual grace already present."[206] For Luther, the Lord's Supper was Gospel because in it God freely gives forgiveness, life, salvation, and the strengthening of faith.

CONCLUSION

The ecumenical negotiations at the Marburg Colloquy did not result in agreement over the Lord's Supper. Many factors contributed to this outcome, not all of which were theological.[207] The purpose of this chapter was not to ascertain the reasons that unity failed to materialize at Marburg. Rather, the purpose was to demonstrate that throughout the Eucharistic Controversy that culminated at the Marburg Colloquy, Luther insisted that the Lord's Supper, including Christ's bodily pres-

ence, was an article of faith because it satisfied the scriptural and evangelical canons of his doctrinal hermeneutic. Therefore, it was a doctrine
necessary for salvation and unity. In this important moment of ecumenism, Luther used his doctrinal hermeneutic to determine what was
necessary for unity.

In a sense, however, the Swiss and South Germans did the same thing.
Their repeated reference to the Lord's Supper as a minor doctrine
demonstrated that they had a different doctrinal criteriology. They
believed the Eucharist was not confessed in the creed and, therefore,
could not be an article of faith necessary for unity, though it was based on
Scripture. Therefore, the position of the Swiss and South Germans, as
well as that of Luther, were theological opinions,[208] which should not
have been divisive of church fellowship. As Zwingli stated again at Marburg, the spiritual eating of Christ, that is, believing in him, was the main
point. The spiritual eating, on which both parties agreed, should have
been sufficient for unity.[209] Such a call for unity without agreement on
Christ's bodily presence was offensive—and impossible—for Luther.

> In the first place, we begin at the point where they write, produce
> books, and admonish that these subjects ought not be the occasion for
> rending Christian unity, love, and peace. It is a minor matter, say they,
> and an insignificant quarrel, for the sake of which Christian love
> should not be obstructed. They chide us for being so stubborn and
> obstinate about it and for creating disunity.
>
> . . . No, gentlemen, none of this peace and love for me! If I were to
> strangle someone's father and mother, wife and child, and try to choke
> him too, and then say, "Keep the peace, dear friend, we wish to love
> one another, the matter is not so important that we should be divided
> over it!" what should he say to me? O how he should love me! Thus
> the fanatics strangle Christ my Lord, and God the Father in his words,
> and my mother the church too, along with my brethren; moreover,
> they would have me dead too, and then they would say I should be at
> peace, for they would like to cultivate love in their relations with
> me.[210]

These dramatic words only make sense when we realize that Luther
considered Christ's bodily presence in the Eucharist to be an article of
faith, something pivotal to salvation. Denying any article of faith could
only bring terribly devastating consequences for the church. According to
Luther, unity depended on agreement in necessary doctrine, that is, on
being one in faith: "If we are to practice Christian unity with them and
extend Christian love to them, we must also love and be satisfied with, or
at least tolerate, their doctrine and behavior. Let anyone do that if he
wishes. Not I. For Christian unity consists in the Spirit, when we are of
one faith, one mind, one heart, Ephesians 4[:3ff.]."[211]

Unlike the Swiss and South Germans, Luther believed the bodily presence was connected to the creed, though he did not argue that it was explicitly mentioned there. It was connected to the creed through Christ's incarnation because Christ's bodily presence was the incarnation in action. It was also connected to the work of the Holy Spirit in the creed because the Lord's Supper was a means of grace that brought forgiveness, life, and the strengthening of faith.[212] As he had done with the *Unitas Fratrum*, Luther used his doctrinal hermeneutic in an ecumenical context with the Swiss and South Germans at Marburg to determine what was necessary for unity and why.

5

The Schmalkald Articles

Luther's Ecumenical Overture to Rome

One might be puzzled to find an essay on the Schmalkald Articles in a book dedicated to twentieth-century Lutheran-Catholic ecumenical dialogue, especially because the articles appear to be an impediment or even an embarrassment to the modern ecumenical movement. What contribution to unity can Martin Luther's fiery confession possibly make? Yet in *Promoting Unity: Themes in Lutheran-Catholic Dialogue* one finds exactly such an essay. In "Polemicism or Ecumenism: Another Look at the Smalcald Articles," John F. Johnson invites the reader to reexamine this pivotal Lutheran confession to see if, in addition to the polemicism, one might find a "hint" of ecumenism.[1] Johnson argued that the careful reader could find evidence in the confession of ecumenical overtures to the Roman Church.

There is more than a hint of ecumenism in the Schmalkald Articles. In fact, it is actually a thoroughgoing ecumenical document—but not in the conventional sense. The Schmalkald Articles is not ecumenical in tone, that is, it doesn't dialogue in a friendly manner nor is it willing to listen to gain a better understanding of the ecumenical partner.[2] After many years of study and attempted ecumenical dialogue, the author assumes that he knows the theology of his "partner" well. Rather, the Schmalkald Articles is ecumenical because it is written expressly for an upcoming ecumenical council and offers for consideration Luther's doctrinal basis for unity in a consistent and well-reasoned manner. The Schmalkald Articles is a profoundly ecumenical document because in it Luther (1) based unity only on necessary church teachings and (2) offered criteria for defining what makes a church teaching necessary. The criteria were the scriptural and evangelical canons of his doctrinal hermeneutic.

The Schmalkald Articles is an excellent example of the "mature" Luther employing his doctrinal hermeneutic in an ecumenical context, and there is ample evidence for this within the confession. The first part of this chapter explores the origins of the Schmalkald Articles: why it was written and what it was intended to be. The second part examines the Schmalkald Articles to see what evidence for Luther's doctrinal hermeneutic can be found.

THE ORIGIN AND PURPOSE
OF THE SCHMALKALD ARTICLES

Until recently, there was a scholarly consensus concerning the original purpose of and the circumstances surrounding the writing of the Schmalkald Articles. This traditional view held that Luther prepared the articles primarily as a confession of fundamental articles of faith to be used as an ecumenical agenda at the general council in Mantua, Italy. It would give the Protestant Schmalkald League a core confession of faith that delineated what could or could not be compromised with Rome. Second, the Schmalkald Articles was understood to be Luther's personal confession and testimony of faith, which was to stand as an abiding expression of authentic Lutheran theology when compared to the theology of Rome.[3]

In *Luther's Theological Testament*, William Russell challenged this traditional consensus by arguing that the decisive factor shaping the Schmalkald Articles was not the Mantua council but Luther's death struggle, which occurred before, during, and after the writing of the text.[4] Russell maintained that Luther himself and those around him thought he was going to die soon: "The specter of death pervades [the Schmalkald Articles] and makes this document Luther's testament of faith, designed to express clearly the heart of the reformer's theology for seemingly the last time. This document, then, contains what Luther wished to bequeath theologically to posterity."[5]

Russell believed that because Luther perceived his death to be imminent, he wrote and published the articles primarily as his theological last will and testament, that is, as a statement of his theological priorities. In this view, the ecumenical nature of the Schmalkald Articles fades into the background and its testamentary character comes to the fore. Therefore, the historical background of the articles is important. What was the document's intended purpose? Why was it written? What was it supposed to be?

THE LONG-AWAITED GENERAL COUNCIL

Since Luther's appeal for a general council of the church on November 28, 1518,[6] demand for a council had increased steadily throughout the 1520s and 1530s, not only among Luther's followers but also among Roman Catholic leaders. At the end of the Diet of Worms in 1521, Emperor Charles V left Germany and did not return until 1530. During his absence, the German estates, both Catholic and evangelical, repeatedly called for a free and general council to settle religious disputes and to reform the church.[7] The imperial diets of Nuremberg I (1523), Nuremberg II (1524), Speyer I (1526), and Speyer II (1529) called for "free, general councils," each one suggesting a place and a time.[8]

When the emperor returned to Germany and convened the Diet of Augsburg (1530), the evangelicals reminded him in the preface of the Augsburg Confession that the German estates had requested a general and free council "in all the diets of the empire which have been held during your Imperial Majesty's reign."[9] They further reminded Charles of his past promises to work toward such a council and promised him that if unity was not achieved at Augsburg, they would still "participate in such a general, free, Christian council."[10] When meaningful negotiations broke down at the diet, Charles promised in the Recess of Augsburg to urge the pope to call a general council within six months at a suitable location. Such a council was to be dedicated to the reformation of the church and was to convene in no more than one year.[11]

The council did not materialize, largely because of Pope Clement VII's reluctance to call it and because of other political machinations.[12] Not until the election on October 13, 1534, of Cardinal Alessandro Farnese as Pope Paul III was the council seriously considered or pursued. In early 1535, Pope Paul III sent out nuncios to talk to the European rulers about his intention. Pier Paolo Vergerio was sent as papal legate to Germany. On his way to visit the elector of Brandenburg in Berlin, Vergerio stayed in Wittenberg on November 6–7 to meet with Luther and probe his willingness to attend a council. In his colorful conversation with Vergerio, Luther revealed much about his attitude toward a council: (1) He didn't care where the council met. (2) He doubted the council would deal with anything but externals. (3) He suspected the council's real agenda was to condemn him and his theology. (4) Despite all this, he was willing and ready to attend.[13] In Prague on November 30, Vergerio met with Luther's prince, Elector John Frederick of Saxony. The Schmalkald League (a political and military coalition of evangelicals of which John Frederick was a member) subsequently issued a reply on December 21 that rejected the papal proposal but promised to attend a truly free Christian council convened in German lands.[14]

Finally, on June 2, 1536, after nearly twenty years of waiting and (given the preceding developments) to no one's great surprise, Pope Paul III issued the bull *Ad Dominici gregis*,[15] summoning a general council to assemble in Mantua, Italy, beginning May 23, 1537. The bull contained nothing unusual.[16] It stated the traditional reasons for convoking a council, including the restoration of peace to the church by eliminating heresies that had appeared in Christendom. The Lutherans were not explicitly mentioned in this bull. But a later bull, "Concerning the Reforms of the Roman Court," which was dated September 23, greatly concerned the evangelicals because it listed "the pestilential Lutheran heresy" as a heresy to be eliminated.[17]

LUTHER'S ASSIGNMENT

When word of the Mantua council first reached John Frederick in early July 1536,[18] his immediate concern was how to reply to the papal legate who would bring the official invitation to the council.[19] There followed a flurry of discussions and correspondence between John Frederick and the Wittenberg theologians concerning this and other council issues.[20] These discussions confirmed the theologians' willingness and the elector's reluctance to attend the council. It is especially important to note that during these discussions Luther was in full agreement with the theological faculty of Wittenberg. Although he was pessimistic that any good would come from the council, he was committed to attending.

Although the evangelicals' attendance at the council remained undecided and John Frederick held no hope that any good would come from a papal-dominated council, preparations had to be made. Therefore, on December 1, the elector traveled to Wittenberg and personally presented a memorandum to the theologians in Wittenberg that detailed these preparations. At the heart of this memorandum was a pivotal assignment given to Luther.

> Although, in the first place, it may easily be perceived that whatsoever our party may propose in such a council as has been announced will have no weight with the opposition, miserable, blinded, and mad men that they are, no matter how well it is founded on Holy Scripture, moreover everything will have to be Lutheran heresy, and their verdict, which probably has already been decided and agreed upon, must be adopted and immediately followed by their proposed ban and interdict, it will nevertheless be very necessary for Doctor Martin to prepare his foundation and opinion from the Holy Scriptures, namely the articles as hitherto taught, preached, and written by him, and which he is determined to adhere to and abide by at the council, as well as upon his departure from this world and before the judgment of Almighty God, and in which we cannot yield without becoming guilty of treason against God, even though property and life, peace or war, are at stake. Such articles, however, as are not necessary, and in which, for the sake of Christian love, yet without offense against God and His Word, something might be yielded (though, doubtless, they will be few in number) should in this connection also be indicated separately by said Doctor Martin. And when Dr. Martin has completed such work (which, if at all possible for the Doctor, must be done between the present date and that of the Conversion of St. Paul, at the latest) he shall thereupon present it to the other Wittenberg theologians, and likewise to some prominent preachers whose presence he should require, to hear from them, at the same time admonishing them most earnestly, and asking them whether they agreed with him in these articles which he had drawn up, or not.[21]

A close reading of the memorandum and the surrounding correspondence[22] yields several observations about the purpose of the Schmalkald Articles. First, as envisioned by John Frederick, its primary and original purpose was the Mantua council. Luther was to author a document, agreed to and subscribed by all,[23] that separately listed the necessary and unnecessary doctrines of the evangelical faith. Thus those attending the council could present a united front and guide discussions at Mantua. The Schmalkald Articles would show what could be conceded for the sake of unity with Rome and what could not. Second, though there is some indication in the prince's correspondence that this document was to be Luther's testament for posterity,[24] such a purpose clearly was secondary. The context, immediate and remote, points to the council as the purpose for the Schmalkald Articles. For example, if this was to be a testament for posterity would the elector ask Luther to list unnecessary articles that could be conceded? This request makes perfect sense for a primarily ecumenical document but not for a testamentary one.

That the original and primary purpose of the Schmalkald Articles was as an ecumenical/united confession is underscored by Luther within the document itself. In addition to the explicit statements in the title[25] and the Preface[26] of the articles, there is evidence in the text. First, in part I, article 4 of the Schmalkald Articles, Luther shows his understanding of the ecumenical nature of the document when he wrote: "These articles are not matters of dispute or contention, for both sides confess them. Therefore it is not necessary to deal with them at greater length now."[27] For a primarily ecumenical document designed to guide negotiations at the council, this kind of comment makes sense. Second, Luther also explicitly mentioned the council in his text several times, showing that he had it in mind when he composed the articles.[28] Third, Luther's repeated mention of not being able to yield, concede, or give up[29] certain articles is yet another body of evidence that points to the council as the main purpose for the document.[30] Such talk of yielding and conceding, given the historical context described previously, makes the best sense if Luther is giving advice to those on his side who will be deliberating at the council.

This is not to suggest that the Schmalkald Articles was not testamentary in any sense or that Luther's impending death did not influence it at all.[31] Indeed, these issues had a secondary influence on the articles. It seems likely that when the council had been postponed for the second time,[32] and as Luther prepared to publish the document in 1538, the reformer began to view the Schmalkald Articles more as a testament for posterity than as a council document.[33] As a statement of necessary articles of faith, it was not only a statement useful for ecumenical deliberations with Rome but also a concise confession of the core of Luther's evangelical theology and the reasons for his reformation. Because Luther perceived his death to be near, he wished to have the Schmalkald Articles received as an authentic and lasting statement of the essentials of his theology.[34] As originally conceived, however, this document was primarily intended to be a statement of necessary articles of faith for an ecumenical dialogue. As such, it is a rich resource for exploring Luther's doctrinal hermeneutic in such a context.

EVIDENCE OF LUTHER'S DOCTRINAL HERMENEUTIC IN THE SCHMALKALD ARTICLES

Commenting on the Schmalkald Articles, James Schaaf wrote, "The value of the Smalcald Articles today, their chief importance is that they deal with essentials in faith . . . Here is Luther dealing with essentials."[35] The question is, however, essentials according to whom?

At the heart of Luther's struggle with the Roman Church were conflicting doctrinal methodologies. Luther's complaint with Rome was not that it put forth human decrees as church teachings; rather, he objected that Rome insisted on such human teachings as binding articles of faith and damned as heretics those who disagreed.[36] He began to see that Rome's fuzzy definition of necessary doctrine was the problem. The doctrinal hermeneutic of Rome appeared so imprecise that even in 1521 Luther could sarcastically write that because Rome defined every church pronouncement as an article of faith, the whole world was practically drowning in a flood of articles of faith.[37] Rome's fuzzy definition of articles of faith led to damaging consequences. Because doctrine was classified so carelessly, Rome made many doctrines necessary for salvation that had nothing to do with salvation, teachings that contradicted the Gospel and could not be supported by Scripture.

By the time he composed the Schmalkald Articles, Luther certainly knew that any ecumenical discussion with Rome turned on this hinge. Therefore, it was not sufficient merely to include his version of necessary articles of faith. He had to demonstrate why the disputed articles he included were necessary and why the disputed articles that Rome put forth were not. Luther did this by employing the scriptural and evangelical canons of his doctrinal hermeneutic.

Obviously, a detailed theological analysis of each article in the Schmalkald Articles is neither feasible nor desirable.[38] Rather, the remainder of the chapter will focus on demonstrating Luther's doctrinal hermeneutic in action.

SCHMALKALD ARTICLES: PART I

"*The First Part* of the Articles deals with the lofty articles of the divine Majesty"[39] is the title Luther gave to part I of the Schmalkald Articles.

Four brief articles follow that set before the reader the trinitarian and Christological theology confessed in the ecumenical creeds.[40] The skimpiness of this section has been noted frequently. More important, however, is to note the absence of Luther's doctrinal hermeneutic. Why was there no attempt to show that these four articles satisfied Luther's scriptural and evangelical canons?

The answer is found in part I, article 4, where Luther reminds his readers: "These articles are not matters for dispute or contention, for both sides confess them. Therefore it is not necessary to deal with them at greater length now."[41] Both evangelicals and Catholics agreed that these four articles were necessary articles of faith. Because of this, Luther did not need to bring his doctrinal hermeneutic to bear. There was no need to prove that the articles in part I were based on the right Scripture rightly interpreted or to show how they were rooted in and connected to the gospel of justification by faith in Christ.[42] Why include this section at all? Because the purpose of the document is to state those articles of faith that cannot be conceded and that are necessary for unity. Luther rightly understood that the articles contained in the creeds were such.[43]

SCHMALKALD ARTICLES: PART II

The second section of the Schmalkald Articles contains four articles,[44] all of which Luther believed pertained to "the office and work of Jesus Christ, or to our redemption."[45] In this document, Luther was arguing with the Roman Church over what articles were truly necessary for salvation and why. Thus it comes as no surprise that in the first article of part II, Luther set forth the evangelical canon of his doctrinal hermeneutic: justification by faith alone in Christ's redemption alone.

> Here is the first and chief article: That Jesus Christ, our God and Lord, "was handed over to death for our trespasses and raised for our justification" (Rom. 4[:25]); and he alone is "the Lamb of God, who takes away the sin of the world" (John 1[:29]); and "the Lord has laid on him the iniquity of us all" (Isa. 53[:6]); furthermore, "All have sinned," and "they are now justified without merit by his grace, through the redemption that is in Christ Jesus . . . by his blood" (Rom. 3[:23–25]).
>
> Now because this must be believed and may not be obtained or grasped otherwise with any work, law, or merit, it is clear and certain that this faith alone justifies us, as St. Paul says in Romans 3[:28, 26], "For we hold that a person is justified by faith apart from works prescribed by the law"; and also, "that God alone is righteous and justifies the one who has faith in Jesus."[46]

Luther continued by saying that "[n]othing in this article can be conceded or given up, even if heaven and earth or whatever is transitory passed away."[47] He concluded: "On this article stands all that we teach and practice against the pope, the devil, and the world."[48]

When Luther described the article of justification as "the first and chief article,"[49] he did not mean that it was logically or chronologically first. Nor did he mean merely that it was the most important as compared to the other articles. By "first and chief article," Luther meant that justification by grace through faith in Jesus Christ was the heart and norm of all the articles. It was the heart because it is that which created Christians and that which pumped life into the other articles. It was the norm because all other articles could only be articles if they were rooted in or were connected with this one. If they contradicted it in any way, they could not be necessary articles of faith.[50] Of course, as Robert Preus observed, it is obvious that the first chief article included the article of redemption, the article of Christ, and the article of justification by grace through faith interchangeably.[51]

There is also evidence of the scriptural canon in part II, article 1. For Luther, a necessary doctrine must be founded on proper Scripture. It was not by accident, then, that he demonstrated that justification was so founded in part II, 1, 1–5 of the Schmalkald Articles, basing this chief article on eight Scripture passages.[52] This chief article was founded on clear and proper Scripture, not human teachings. Because this article was at the heart of Luther's dispute with Rome, Luther had to show with Scripture that it was a necessary article. Thus in Schmalkald Articles part II, article 1, both the evangelical and scriptural canons of Luther's doctrinal hermeneutic are at work.

Now that his doctrinal criterion was in place, Luther could show why those articles that Rome insisted on as necessary for salvation were not necessary. In part II, articles 2–4, Luther brought his doctrinal hermeneutic to bear in several consistent ways.

First, Luther's scriptural canon is evident in several connections. For example, in Schmalkald Articles part II, article 2, in his "friendly" dialogue with "reasonable" papists about the Mass, Luther asks: "Why do you cling so tenaciously to the Mass? 1. After all, it is nothing but a mere human invention, not commanded by God. And we may discard all human inventions, as Christ says in Matthew 15[:9], 'In vain do they worship me with human precepts.' "[53] Later, when discussing private Masses, Luther pointed out that to commune oneself is "uncertain, unnecessary, and even forbidden. Such people also do not know what they are doing, because they are following a false human notion and innovation without the sanction of God's Word."[54]

The section on the "idolatries" that "this dragon's tail, the Mass" has produced includes additional evidence of the scriptural canon.[55] In fact, a consistent pattern emerges. First, purgatory "is nothing but the human opinions of a few individuals, who can establish no article of faith (something God alone can do). . . . It will not do to formulate articles of faith on the basis of the holy Fathers' works or words. Otherwise, their food, clothes, houses, etc., would also have to be articles of faith—as has been done with relics. This means that[56] the Word of God—and no one else, not even an angel—should establish articles of faith."[57] Concerning pilgrimages: "Now, it is certain that, lacking God's Word, such pilgrimages are neither commanded nor necessary."[58] Fraternities were "a human trifle, without God's Word, totally unnecessary and not commanded."[59] What about relics? "They are also without God's Word, neither commanded nor advised; it is a completely unnecessary and useless thing."[60] "Precious indulgences" were not to be tolerated because they were "without God's Word, without necessity, not commanded."[61] Prayer to the saints was rejected as an article of faith because it "is neither commanded nor recommended, nor does it have any precedent in the Scriptures."[62]

In part II, articles 3 and 4, Luther continued this pattern. Monasteries, "like all other human inventions are not commanded, are not necessary, and are useless."[63] And what of the papacy? "The pope is not the head of all Christendom 'by divine right' or on the basis of God's Word."[64] Further, "[the papacy] is a human fiction. It is not commanded. There is no need for it. And it is useless."[65]

In each of these issues, Luther rejected Roman teachings not only because they contradicted Christ and the Gospel but also because they were not founded on proper Scripture. Apparently, Luther was not satisfied with rejecting them because they conflicted with the Gospel. Their lack of proper scriptural basis was also worthy of mention because it was a fundamental part of Luther's doctrinal hermeneutic, a fundamental part of determining the necessity of a church teaching. Because of this, Luther repeatedly called these flagrant Roman teachings "unnecessary," by which he meant they couldn't be considered essential articles of faith on which salvation and unity depended.

If anything, the evidence for the evangelical canon of Luther's doctrinal hermeneutic in Schmalkald Articles II, articles 2–4 is more abundant. There is no question that for Luther it was the conflict with the chief article that made certain Roman teachings especially damnable. In part II, articles 2–4, Luther measured every supposedly necessary article of Rome by its relationship with the chief article—and found each one lacking. The papacy's version of the Mass "has to be the greatest and most terrible abomination, as it directly and violently opposes this chief article."[66] How so? Because the Mass is

> performed in order that individuals might reconcile themselves and others to God, acquire the forgiveness of sins, and merit grace. . . .
> Thus the Mass should and must be condemned and repudiated,

because it is directly contrary to the chief article, which says that it is not an evil or devout servant of the Mass with his work, but rather the Lamb of God and the Son of God, who takes away our sin [John 1:29].[67]

Similarly, purgatory was also "against the chief article that Christ alone (and not human works) is to help souls."[68] Luther lamented the fact that in pilgrimages "people routinely deserted Christ for their own works and (worst of all!) become idolatrous."[69] Fraternities were "contrary to the first article of redemption"[70] because they claimed to be able to transfer Masses and good works for the benefit of the living and the dead. The worst part of relics was the claim that they "were also to have produced an indulgence and the forgiveness of sin as a good work and act of worship."[71] Speaking of indulgences, they were not to be tolerated because they were "contrary to the first article. Christ's merit is not acquired through our work or pennies, but through faith by grace, without any money or merit—not by the authority of the pope, but rather by preaching a sermon, that is, God's Word."[72] Prayer to saints also was to be rejected because it was "in conflict with the first, chief article and that destroys the knowledge of Christ."[73] In part II, article 3, monasteries were rejected for the same reason: "[A]ll this, too, is contrary to the first and chief article concerning redemption in Jesus Christ."[74]

The reason for Luther's fierce polemic against the pope in Schmalkald Articles part II, article 4 was "that everything the pope has undertaken and done on the basis of such false, offensive, blasphemous, arrogant power . . . negates the first, chief article on redemption by Jesus Christ."[75] How the papacy conflicted with the chief article was immediately explained:

> All his [the pope's] bulls and books are available, in which he roars like a lion . . . that Christians cannot be saved unless they are obedient and submit to him in all things—what he wills, what he says, what he does.[76] This is as much to say: "Even if you believe in Christ and have everything that is necessary for salvation in him, nevertheless it is nothing and all in vain unless you consider me your god and are subject and obedient to me."[77]

For Luther, this was proof that the pope was the Antichrist because he "will not let Christians be saved without his authority."[78]

In Schmalkald Articles part II, Luther amply flexed the evangelical canon of his doctrinal hermeneutic: No article could be necessary for unity if it contradicted the chief article. Interestingly, in most cases he also attempted to demonstrate how the church teaching conflicted with the chief article.

Because the Schmalkald Articles was primarily an ecumenical document in which Luther was discussing which ecclesiastical teachings were truly necessary for unity, his polemic in part II, articles 2–4 becomes understandable. The reformer was reacting to the "articles" that Rome had insisted were essential and was demonstrating why they were not. Further, given Luther's pastoral bent, he was enraged by Rome's false articles of faith because they burdened the consciences of the people by making such teachings necessary for salvation.[79]

SCHMALKALD ARTICLES: PART III

A survey of the scholarly literature reveals many opinions about what Luther was attempting to accomplish in part III of the Schmalkald Articles.[80] The fifteen articles were clearly necessary for Luther, as part III, 15, 3 showed.[81] Why did Luther choose these fifteen articles?[82] Allbeck wrote, "The fifteen articles are not in the order which systematic theology would arrange them. They suggest the order of salvation from sin to fellowship."[83] William Russell echoed this and added:

> Here Luther gives particular attention to the relationship between his central theological concerns and the concrete realities of the Christian life . . . Luther provides posterity with a brief catalog of what he considered to be the most important aspects of the Christian life: word, sacraments, church. These are the various ways by which the catholic evangelism of the Christian church becomes real in anyone's life of faith.[84]

It must be added that as Luther guided his readers along this necessary order of salvation and the concrete realities of the Christian life, he was reminded of still more Roman pretenders to the status of "necessary" articles. That is the reason, for example, for the otherwise strange inclusion of part III, articles 14–15. All this leads to the question: Given its design, what evidence of Luther's doctrinal hermeneutic can be found in part III?

Evidence appears as early as the word *conscience* in the heading. Was it by coincidence that Luther began and ended part III of the Schmalkald Articles by stressing conscience? His heading declared: "We could discuss the following matters or articles with learned, reasonable people or among ourselves. The pope and his kingdom do not value these things very much, because the conscience means nothing to them; money, honor, and power mean everything."[85] The end of part three stated, "These are the articles on which I must stand and on which I intend to stand, God willing, until my death. I can neither change nor concede anything in them. If anyone desires to do so, it is on that person's conscience."[86] These two references to conscience appear to bracket part III and serve as a grammatical clue to the subject matter therein. This would fit not only with the overall purpose of the Schmalkald Articles but also with Luther's evangelical canon. As he stated in "Against the Heavenly Prophets": "[E]verything depends on the conscience."[87] Only articles of faith could "rule the conscience."[88] When the conscience is burdened with unnecessary doctrines as if they were necessary for salvation, Christian freedom is taken away and salvation lost. For Luther, to make concessions on any of the articles in part III of the Schmalkald Articles was to put one's conscience in peril, that is, to threaten one's salvation. Each article was tied to the Gospel either positively or negatively. Thus "conscience" for Luther pointed to his core concern about the chief article.

The structure and order of part III is also evidence of Luther's doctrinal hermeneutic. The article on the Gospel (article 4) played a central and pivotal role. The three articles that preceded article 4 (addressing sin, law, and repentance) were articles of faith because Luther considered them necessary prerequisites to the Gospel, which meant they passed the test of his evangelical canon.[89] Man's original sin and total corruption, the Law that made such original sin manifest, and repentance that confessed one's sinfulness—these three articles were necessary because only they could prepare one to see the need for the forgiveness offered in the Gospel.

The article on the Gospel actually served as a hinge and mapped out the order of the succeeding topics.

> We now want to return to the gospel, which gives guidance and help against sin in more than one way, because God is extravagantly rich in his grace: first, through the spoken word, in which the forgiveness of sins is preached to the whole world (which is the proper function of the gospel); second, through baptism; third, through the holy Sacrament of the Altar; fourth, through the power of the keys and also through the mutual conversation and consolation of brothers and sisters. Matthew 18[:20]: "Where two or three are gathered . . ."[90]

This revealing passage indicates why Luther listed Baptism, the Sacrament of the Altar, the Keys, confession, excommunication, ordination, and the church as articles in part III of the Schmalkald Articles (articles 5–10, 12, respectively). Luther believed each of these was an extension and application of the Gospel. Each distributed the forgiveness of sins to the repentant sinner or at least, in the case of excommunication, had that as its final goal. Luther connected ordination, or the office of preaching, to the Gospel because such an office existed to preach and administer the Gospel in all its forms. All this took place in the church, the assembly of "holy believers and 'the little sheep who hear the voice of their shepherd,' "[91] the place of "the mutual conversation and consolation of brothers and sisters." Article 13, "How a Person Is Justified and Concerning Good Works," reiterates Schmalkald Articles part II, article 1, adding that also the works of believers (sinful and imperfect as these works are) are accounted holy and righteous for Christ's sake. "[T]he human creature should be called and should be completely righteous and holy—according to both the person and his or her works—by the pure grace and mercy that have been poured and spread over us in Christ."[92] Luther wanted to say that the Christian life, that is, the realm of sanctification, was also dependent on, an extension of, and connected to the Gospel of justification by grace for Christ's sake. Therefore, because they were connected to the Gospel as prerequisites or post-applications, the articles of part III satisfied Luther's evangelical canon and were articles of faith.

It appears that Luther included the remaining articles in part III of the Schmalkald Articles because of their negative relationship with his evangelical canon. In article 11, Luther scolded the papacy for prohibiting priests from marrying. As he had done repeatedly in his 1521 treatise "Martin Luther's Judgment against Monastic Vows," the reformer rejected clerical celibacy because it destroyed Christian liberty. It made damnable sin out of something that God had made free. Related to this, Luther rejected monastic vows (part III, article 14) because they "are in direct conflict with the first and chief article" and, therefore, "should simply be done away with."[93] Luther held this position because those who entered the monastic life believed they could enter heaven by their holy life, a belief that denied Christ.[94] Human traditions (part III, article 15)—teachings based only on human words—were obviously in conflict with Luther's scriptural canon. Luther quoted Matt. 15:9 ("They worship me in vain; their teachings are but rules taught by men") to emphasize that necessary doctrines must be founded only on God's Word. Human traditions were also in conflict with Luther's evangelical canon because they claimed to be necessary for salvation. "That the papists say human regulations help attain the forgiveness of sins or merit salvation is unchristian and damnable."[95]

There is further evidence of Luther's doctrinal hermeneutic in part III of the Schmalkald Articles, though it is not as frequent or as obvious as in part II. One possible explanation is that Luther suffered apparent heart attacks on or about December 18–20. After these attacks, he was forced to dictate the rest of the Schmalkald Articles, from part III, article 4 to the end. It is striking that not only did the size of the remaining articles decrease but also the clear references to Luther's doctrinal hermeneutic, which can be found in several places in earlier articles.

In the article on sin, Luther affirmed that his doctrine of hereditary sin passed the test of his scriptural canon because it was founded on Scripture. "This inherited sin has caused such a deep, evil corruption of nature that reason does not comprehend it; rather, it must be believed on the basis of the revelation in the Scriptures (Ps. 51[:5] and Rom. 5[:12]; Exod. 33[:20]; Gen. 3[:6ff.])."[96] By these words, Luther showed that his doctrine of original sin was an article of faith because it was based on Scripture rather than reason. The scholastic theologians' doctrine of original sin (Luther listed seven of their errors), by contrast, failed the scriptural canon because they based it on Scripture wrongly interpreted by reason. Their doctrine of sin also was rejected because it conflicted with Luther's evangelical canon:

> These and many similar things have arisen from a lack of understanding and ignorance about both sin and Christ our Savior. We cannot tolerate these purely pagan teachings, because, if these teachings were right, then Christ has died in vain. For there would be no defect or sin in humankind for which he had to die—or else he would have died only for the body and not for the soul, because the soul would be healthy and only the body would be subject to death.[97]

In part III, article 3, in a section entitled "Concerning the False Penance of the Papists," Luther's doctrinal hermeneutic also comes into view. The sophists' doctrine of penance was divided into three parts—contrition, confession, and satisfaction—and Luther added, "[W]ith this comfort and pledge: that the person who is truly contrite, goes to confession, and makes satisfaction by these actions merits forgiveness and pays for sins before God."[98] This clearly rejected Luther's evangelical canon because "[h]ere there was no Christ. Nothing was mentioned about faith, but instead people hoped to overcome and blot out sin before God with their own works."[99] Because the papal doctrine of penance contradicted the Gospel of justification through faith for Christ's sake, it was rejected as a necessary article of faith.

CONCLUSION

One yet unanswered question is why Elector John Frederick asked Luther to compose the document that would become the Schmalkald Articles. Why didn't he ask Philipp Melanchthon, who had authored the two previous major Lutheran confessions, the Augsburg Confession and the Apology of the Augsburg Confession? The conventional answer is that the elector wanted a definitive statement of Luther's reformation theology—and who better than Luther to draft such a statement?

The Schmalkald Articles began as an assignment for a general council of the church. It was to be a statement of necessary articles of faith that could not be conceded in ecumenical negotiations with Rome. Perhaps the elector knew that it had to be written by someone who was practiced in distinguishing what was a necessary doctrine and what was not. Perhaps the elector knew that such an assignment fit Luther perfectly. Luther had developed a doctrinal hermeneutic: a truly evangelical and scriptural method of determining which articles were necessary for salvation and unity.

The Schmalkald Articles is an excellent example of the mature Luther using this doctrinal hermeneutic in an ecumenical setting. It is more than a statement of what Luther considered to be the essential Christian faith. It is Luther openly defining essential doctrine, openly telling both sides of the ecumenical discussion not only *what* was necessary doctrine but also *why* such doctrine was necessary.

6

IMPLICATIONS OF LUTHER'S DOCTRINAL HERMENEUTIC FOR THE CHURCH

The focus of this book has been a methodological pattern observed in Luther's writings and ecumenical dialogues, a pattern defined in this study as Luther's doctrinal hermeneutic. This doctrinal hermeneutic was the reformer's method of judging which church teachings were articles of faith that all Christians were obligated to believe. Luther developed this method as he pondered the nature of Scripture and the Gospel and as he reacted to competing definitions of doctrine. What resulted was a rigorous pair of interpretive canons—one scriptural and the other evangelical—that the reformer consistently used to assess whether a teaching was necessary for salvation. Far from being a mere historical curiosity, Luther's doctrinal hermeneutic has far-reaching implications for the contemporary church, implications both pastoral and ecumenical.

Luther's doctrinal hermeneutic has profoundly relevant implications for pastoral care because of its emphasis on Christian freedom. It was the overarching question of salvation—"What must I do to be saved?"—that drove Luther to apply his canons to the church teachings of his day. Excoriated as heretic and threatened with excommunication because he questioned and rejected certain church teachings, Luther personally knew the angst of a wrongly burdened conscience. Did one's salvation really depend on belief in and obedience to every church teaching, as certain of Luther's contemporaries were claiming? If every teaching did not need to be believed, then which ones were necessary? Luther's doctrinal hermeneutic provided the answer to these salvific questions: Only those teachings that are based on the right Scripture rightly interpreted and that are necessary for salvation—connected to the gospel of justification—can be necessary articles of faith. If believing a particular doctrine did not make one a Christian, then disbelieving it did not make one a non-Christian. Thus Luther's doctrinal hermeneutic liberated the conscience by demonstrating that one's salvation depended only on believing necessary articles of faith. Unfortunately, the full unfolding of the implications this has for pastoral care will have to wait for a more complete treatment.

It is what Luther's doctrinal hermeneutic contributes to the contemporary Ecumenical Movement, however, that is the subject of this chapter. Because Luther's doctrinal hermeneutic served him well in several ecumenical dialogues in the sixteenth century, it has much to recommend it now. Obviously, Luther's ecumenical context was quite different from that of the present day. His efforts were aimed at preserving or salvaging unity among groups in the Western church threatened with disunity. By contrast, the efforts of the current Ecumenical Movement focus on restoring unity among hundreds of (in most cases) long-separated denominations. That caveat aside, the remainder of the chapter will show that Luther's doctrinal hermeneutic is a much-needed reforming word for the Ecumenical Movement.

THE MODERN ECUMENICAL MOVEMENT

Unity in the holy Christian church is a given, both in the sense that it already exists and in the sense that it is a gift of God, given in Christ. This inner or spiritual unity in the *Una Sancta* consists in faith that trusts in Christ alone as Savior. Such inner unity exists among all who have this faith in Christ, wherever they may be throughout the world (John 10:16; 17:20–21; Eph. 4:4–6; Rom. 12:4–5; 1 Corinthians 12–14).

Just as the one church can be considered inwardly or outwardly,[1] so also can church unity. There exists not only an inner unity but also an outer or external unity. This external unity or church fellowship consists in fellowship in Word and Sacraments. Its basis is agreement in doctrine and a common confession of faith. Unlike inner unity, which cannot fail, outer unity can be divided and often has been. It is the will of God that Christians strive to preserve or restore external unity in the visible church, thereby manifesting the unity in the *Una Sancta* (Rom. 15:5–6; 1 Cor. 1:10–12; Eph. 4:1–3). This bears repeating: Such striving for and preserving of external unity is not optional but is commanded by God. It is this external unity that is the domain of ecumenism[2] (the work of uniting the external church) and the Ecumenical Movement.

The birthplace of the modern Ecumenical Movement is usually said to have been the 1910 World Missionary Conference in Edinburgh. This conference, chaired by John R. Mott, had gathered to plan mission strategy to avoid the scandal of the competing claims of different churches.[3] Because discussing doctrinal differences was forbidden at the Edinburgh Conference, attendee Episcopal Bishop Charles H. Brent decided to work toward an organization that would examine the causes of the divisions among the churches. It was largely through his efforts that the first Faith and Order Conference was held in Lausanne, Switzerland, in 1927 to discuss these matters.[4] Two years earlier, under the leadership of Nathan

Söderblom, the first World Life and Work Conference was held in Stock-holm. Whereas the Faith and Order movement concerned itself with doc-trine, the Life and Work Conference focused on addressing economic and social needs throughout the world.[5] These two movements eventually became part of the World Council of Churches (WCC) when it was formed in Amsterdam in 1948.[6] One year earlier, the Lutheran World Federation (LWF) had become a reality in Lund, Sweden.[7]

After the creation of the WCC, there was an accelerated push for vis-ible unity among the churches. Many mergers among Protestant churches occurred. A major and somewhat surprising development was that the Vatican, which previously had forbidden members of the Roman Catholic Church from participating in the Ecumenical Movement,[8] reversed course at the Second Vatican Council (1962–1965). As articulated in the 1964 Vatican II decree *Unitatis Redintegratio*, the restoration of external unity among the churches was said to be the will of Christ and, therefore, was to be of the highest priority for all faithful Catholics.[9] Beginning especially in the 1960s, there were hundreds of national and international bilateral and multilateral dialogues held among the churches for the purpose of even-tually achieving visible unity. Many blessings from God resulted from these dialogues. Churches came to understand one another's histories and doctrinal beliefs more clearly; cooperation in social causes helped millions of people around the globe. True progress was made in many ways.

THE FORM AND BASIS OF UNITY

All parties in the Ecumenical Movement have agreed that the current divisions in the external church are unacceptable and that restoration of unity among the churches is the indisputable goal.[10] All parties in the Ecumenical Movement have not agreed, however, on the form such unity should take or the basis of such unity.

For example, the WCC has favored conciliarity as the model for unity. Conciliarity, as defined by the 1973 Salamanca Assembly of the WCC, was based on the use of church councils in the undivided church of the first centuries.[11] Although there was diversity in the ancient church, and though the local churches were separated by distance and cultural differ-ences, they considered one another fully catholic because they confessed the same apostolic faith. When problems arose that threatened that faith, councils were held to preserve unity. It later was made clear, however, that this conciliar fellowship model of unity was an organic unity[12] in which unique confessional identities might have to give way to a transconfes-sional union.[13] What was the doctrinal basis for conciliarity according to the WCC? This was spelled out at the 1975 Assembly in Nairobi as "a common understanding of the apostolic faith, a common ministry, and a common Eucharist."[14]

Another proposed model for unity has been reconciled diversity, the favored model of the LWF. This unity was summarized at the 1984 Seventh Assembly of the LWF in Budapest.

> The true unity of the church . . . is given in and through proclamation of the gospel in Word and sacrament. This unity is expressed as a communion in the common and, at the same time, multiform confession of the one and the same apostolic faith. It is a communion in holy baptism and in the eucharistic meal, a communion in which the ministries are recognized by all as expressions of the ministry instituted by Christ in his church.
>
> . . . The diversity present in this communion rises out of the different cultural and ethnic contexts in which the one church of Christ lives out its mission and out of the number of church traditions in which the apostolic faith has been maintained, transmitted, and lived throughout the centuries. In recognizing these diversities as expressions of the one apostolic faith and the one catholic church, traditions are changed, antagonisms overcome, and mutual condemnations lifted. The diversities are reconciled and transformed into a legitimate and indispensable multiformity within the one body of Christ.[15]

In reconciled diversity, as is the case within the LWF, each member church body retains its organizational identity. No merger or organic unity needs to occur. In addition, as long as all member churches proclaim the same Gospel in Word and Sacraments and hold to the common but multiform apostolic faith (whatever that is!), no further doctrinal consensus is needed. Strictly understood, all other differences, including different formulations (confessions) of faith (for example, the Lutheran Confessions) and different ministries, are of secondary value and in no way impede unity. Such differences are considered to be legitimate diversity that is reconciled and no longer divisive of church fellowship. Thus one can only presume that the LWF is hardly serious about the doctrinal basis listed in its constitution: "[T]he Holy Scriptures of the Old and New Testaments to be [are] the only source and norm of its doctrine, life and service. It sees in the three Ecumenical Creeds and in the Confessions of the Lutheran Church, especially in the unaltered Augsburg Confession and the Small Catechism of Martin Luther, a pure exposition of the Word of God." According to the LWF's reconciled diversity model of unity, historic confessions of faith such as the Lutheran Confessions need not be a real basis for unity; instead, they are part of the diversity to be reconciled. If confessional formulations aren't church divisive in ecumenical relations with non-Lutherans, why should such formulations be divisive in ecumenical relations among Lutherans?

The most recent form of church unity proposed by the WCC is worth mentioning. "The Unity of the Church as Koinonia: Gift and Calling" was produced at the Seventh Assembly of the WCC in Canberra, Australia, in 1991. *Koinonia* is the New Testament Greek word for "communion" or "fellowship." Although drawing on the biblical concept of communion (in itself nothing new), koinonia unity is, in reality, the model of reconciled diversity in a new package. The same emphasis on reconciled diversity is present,[16] as well as the same doctrinal basis for unity.[17]

The ultimate goal of the reconciled diversity approach is "full communion," also referred to as pulpit and altar fellowship. The definition of full communion in the ecumenical policy statement of the Evangelical Lutheran Church in America (ELCA) is representative. Full communion, according to the statement, "is rooted in agreement in essentials and allows diversity in nonessentials." It includes at least six points: (1) a common confession of the Christian faith; (2) a mutual recognition of Baptism and a sharing of the Lord's Supper, allowing for joint worship and transfer of members; (3) a mutual recognition and availability of ordained ministers to the service of all members of churches in full communion; (4) a common commitment to evangelism, witness, and service; (5) a means of common decision making on critical issues of faith and life; and (6) the lifting of any mutual condemnations. Moreover, according to the ELCA,

> We hold this definition and description of full communion to be consistent with Article VII of the Augsburg Confession, which says, "for the true unity of the church it is enough to agree concerning the teaching of the Gospel and the administration of the sacraments." Agreement in the Gospel can be reached and stated without adopting Lutheran confessional formulations as such. It allows for flexible, situation-oriented decisions about order and decision making structures. It does not demand organic union, though it does not rule it out. This definition is also in agreement with the understanding of unity adopted by the Seventh Assembly of the Lutheran World Federation in 1984, "The Unity We Seek."[18]

Note that in keeping with the reconciled diversity model of unity, the ELCA statement declares that agreement in the Gospel can be reached and stated "without adopting Lutheran confessional formulations as such." In other words, church bodies that enter into full communion with the ELCA, including their ministers, are not required to subscribe to the Lutheran Confessions. Thus the Lutheran Confessions, including the Augsburg Confession, are eliminated as a doctrinal basis for unity. Agreement in "essentials" or "agreement in the Gospel" or "a common confession of the Christian faith" will suffice for unity.

THE ECUMENICAL IMPASSE

During the 1960s and 1970s, a heady optimism pervaded the Ecumenical Movement. The churches involved in bilateral and multilateral dialogues experienced real progress in better understanding the theology of their ecumenical partners. Convergence and, in some cases, consensus occurred on specific doctrines that previously had divided the churches. Extensive visible unity among the churches seemed to be within grasp.

Then the Ecumenical Movement hit a wall. Little further progress occurred. Although the churches admitted that real consensus had happened, they also admitted that serious differences remained. There was *recognition* of convergence and piecemeal consensus but not the official *reception* that leads to full communion. In the literature of the 1980s and 1990s, frustration and impatience became the new themes. In the words of one author: "Now, however, these dialogues seem halted. Our time has been called an 'ecumenical winter.' The hopes and enthusiasms that sprang up in the wake of Roman Catholicism's embrace of the ecumenical movement at Vatican II have faded. In some quarters they have completely died out."[19] Many who had long participated in various dialogues—often for twenty years or more—repeatedly were heard lamenting this new impasse. It was suspected that despite agreement on this or that doctrine, a deeper fundamental difference still existed, a difference that was the real reason division persisted.

In an article entitled "Fundamental Difference—Fundamental Consensus," Harding Meyer reflected on the impasse. He noted how, beginning in the early 1970s, theologians involved in the dialogues had argued that doctrinal differences justifying the separation of the churches no longer existed because of successes in the dialogues. This optimism of the 1970s gave way to the pessimism of the 1980s.

> At present, coinciding almost exactly with the beginning of the 1980s, a growing number of very different voices is being raised. They say something like this: all the mutual agreements reached in inter-church theological dialogues, particularly in the dialogues between the Protestant churches and the Roman Catholic church . . . are to a certain extent merely the cure for individual symptoms rather than overcoming the real cause of the disease. Thus the ecumenical "root causes," the more deeply submerged and really divisive divergences, the so-called "fundamental divergences" or "fundamental dissents," are still neither comprehended nor abolished but instead continue to exist and remain effective.[20]

The literature of the period was replete with scholarly opinions of just what the fundamental difference or consensus was.[21] An especially honest appraisal of the impasse that has continued to mark the Ecumenical Movement, and the accompanying frustration, is found in an article by Gerhard O. Forde. Forde was reflecting on the impasse in the Catholic-Lutheran dialogue, but what he said applies to the Ecumenical Movement in general and is worthy of quoting at length.

One of the major hindrances in ecumenical discussion is the apparent difficulty in isolating, not to say understanding and expressing, fundamental differences, or knowing what to do with them when we find them. . . . We seem somehow to be afraid that serious investigation of differences will impede or even throw the movement into reverse, perhaps foster a return to the era of hostile polemics. One who wants to talk about such differences is usually regarded as something of a pariah.

. . . I am of the opinion that the ecumenical movement will not make much more meaningful progress until it tries to put its finger on fundamental differences, and then faces anew the question of what to do about them. Reluctance on the part of many Christians to join or support the movement wholeheartedly stems from the suspicion that differences have not really been faced, but rather just "papered over."

. . . The nagging question before the ecumenical movement is why, after all the effort, time, and money spent on the dialogues, and the convergences and the agreements, we still do not appear to be much closer together. Participation in one such dialogue for some fifteen years now has suggested to me that we need a different strategy. We have likely done about as much as we can in pursuing agreements and convergences on discrete topics. Results tend to be more or less predictable and for that reason disappointing because they don't seem to light any fires or bring us closer together.[22]

A different strategy, one that seeks to uncover a fundamental difference, is needed, says Forde. Luther's doctrinal hermeneutic is just such a strategy. Luther's doctrinal hermeneutic uncovers the fundamental difference and points the way to its resolution. The fundamental difference is that the churches define essential doctrine differently; they define the irreducible content of the apostolic faith in conflicting ways. From its beginning, the Ecumenical Movement has adopted as its the slogan, "Unity in essentials, in nonessentials charity." But what are the essentials? Who or what decides? Behind many an ecumenical impasse are competing methods of defining essential doctrine or dogma, methods that often operate on an unconscious level. George Lindbeck has made a similar observation:

It has become apparent to me, during twenty-five years of involvement in ecumenical discussions and in teaching about the history and present status of doctrines, that those of us who are engaged in these activities lack adequate categories for conceptualizing the problems that arise. We are often unable, for example, to specify the criteria we implicitly employ when we say that some changes are faithful to a doctrinal tradition and others unfaithful, or some doctrinal differences are church-dividing and others not.[23]

Luther's doctrinal hermeneutic provides such criteria by openly defining essential articles of faith in a compelling and forthright manner. It
does so in a way that honors both the Gospel of Jesus Christ and the
Scriptures as absolutely authoritative. Luther's doctrinal hermeneutic says,
"Unity in essentials," then offers a persuasive definition of what makes a
church teaching or practice essential.

Luther's Doctrinal Hermeneutic: A Reforming Contribution to the Ecumenical Movement

In naming this book *The Ecumenical Luther*, I am aware of the delicious
irony of the title. After all, Luther, and the Reformation that sprang from
him, has often been accused of single-handedly dividing Western Christendom, a charge that the evangelical Lutheran Church has taken seriously but, ultimately, has refuted.[24] Therefore, it is ironic (as well as
seemingly quite cheeky) to suggest that a methodology in Luther, of all
people, can be an important contribution to restoring unity among the
churches. That, however, is precisely the thesis of this chapter. Moreover, by claiming that a theological method from the sixteenth century is
of relevance to this postmodern, postliberal, ecumenical world, one runs
the risk of being accused of the monstrous crime of repristination, or at
least of being anachronistic. Such an accusation would be wide of the
mark in this case—unless claiming that a methodology from the past
church can have great and lasting relevance for the present church is
repristination, which, of course, it isn't.

Luther's Doctrinal Hermeneutic Defines an Article of Faith That Is Necessary for Unity

Both in the sixteenth century and in ours, it has been assumed that
unity is not dependent on agreement in every church teaching. Separated
Christians need only agree on "essential" or "necessary" or "fundamental"
doctrines. The previous chapters have shown that all parties in the Reformation disputes or unity dialogues considered this to be a given. All would
have agreed with the well-known words of Ireneaus of Lyons that were
recorded in Eusebius's *Church History* that disagreement in regard to the
Fast does not destroy but confirms the agreement in faith.[25] Therefore,
when Luther insisted that only necessary doctrines were necessary for
unity, he was not introducing anything unique or novel. That unity
requires agreement in doctrine but not agreement in every doctrine continues to be assumed in the Ecumenical Movement. In his encyclical *Ut
Unum Sint* ("That They May Be One"), Pope John Paul II reaffirmed

what had been decreed in the Vatican II "Decree on Ecumenism": In unity, nothing should be required beyond what is necessary. "From this basic but partial unity it is now necessary to advance towards the visible unity which is required and sufficient (*id quod requiritur et sufficit*) . . . In this process, one must not impose any burden beyond that which is strictly necessary (cf. Acts 15:28)."[26]

But the problem, concisely stated by Gerard Kelly, is that "[t]he churches do not yet agree on what is necessary (the *id quod requiritur et sufficit*) for the unity of the church."[27] Adding to the significance of this statement is that it comes at the very end of Kelly's book, which traced the entire history of the Faith and Order Commission of the WCC. According to Kelly, after seventy years of meetings and dialogues, though real progress occurred on many fronts, this one thing was still standing in the way of the churches attaining full communion: They did not yet agree on what is necessary for unity. The churches, often unknowingly, define essential doctrine by different sets of criteria.

This disagreement over what is necessary for unity also stems in part from the inability (or refusal) of the churches to clearly articulate a definitive list of doctrines that are necessary. This problem concerns especially the Roman Catholic Church, but to a lesser extent it involves the entire Ecumenical Movement. When the question is asked, "On what core teachings and practices do we need to agree to have full communion?" incredible vagueness of expression abounds. Phrases such as "the apostolic faith"[28] or "the faith of the Church through the ages"[29] are frequently recycled with little specificity as to what they mean.

It is never quite clear, for example, what doctrinal agreement the Catholic Church is insisting on for unity. Certain phrases are presented, the content of which is never explained. In Roman Catholic ecumenical literature, the phrases "deposit of faith,"[30] "the content of revealed faith in its entirety,"[31] "the whole body of doctrine,"[32] "the whole truth,"[33] and "hierarchy of truths"[34] are examples of expressions that name the minimum doctrinal basis needed for full communion with Rome. But the doctrines and practices to which these phrases point are never fully and clearly explicated. For example, John Paul II writes: "The unity willed by God can be attained only by the adherence of all to the content of revealed truth in its entirety. In matters of faith, compromise is in contradiction with God who is Truth."[35] What exactly is "the content of revealed truth in all its entirety"? This is never explained or defined. Again, what is the meaning of this statement: "Full communion of course will have to come about through the acceptance of the whole truth into which the Holy Spirit guides Christ's disciples. Hence all forms of reductionism or facile 'agreement' must be absolutely avoided"?[36] Unfortunately, the meaning of "the whole truth" is not elucidated. Such evasiveness and murkiness is akin to attempting to hit a target that one cannot see and it does nothing to advance the cause of unity.

When Roman Catholic theologians occasionally have dared to delineate clearly the minimum doctrinal content that is necessary and sufficient for unity, other Catholics have rejected their proposals as wholly insufficient. For example, in *Unity of the Churches: An Actual Possibility*, Heinrich Fries and Karl Rahner proposed eight theses that, if followed, could lead to swift unity among the churches. The first thesis of the Fries-Rahner proposal stated the doctrinal agreement needed for unity: "The fundamental truths of Christianity, as they are expressed in Holy Scripture, in the Apostles' Creed, and that of Nicaea and Constantinople are binding on all partner churches of the one Church to be."[37] Rejection of this proposal was swift. Among those dissenting was Avery Dulles. Dulles agreed that the fundamental truths in the Scriptures and the Apostles' and Nicene-Constantinopolitan Creeds were necessary—but such fundamental truths fell far short of the doctrinal agreement needed for full, visible unity. Dulles proceeded to mention the procession of the Spirit and the papal and Marian dogmas as examples of additional necessary doctrines, but he did not articulate what the full doctrinal agreement that was needed might be. Once again the precise bare minimum necessary for unity was left frustratingly vague.[38] Jon Nilson (himself a Roman Catholic scholar) has captured the problem succinctly:

> Without clarity on what is indispensable, there can be no assurance that we are not imposing unjustifiable obligations and demands on partner churches. The only obligations and demands that are justifiable are the ones we hold before God as integral to the gospel. If they include more than the scriptures and the two creeds, we must explain how far they do extend—and why they do so—to our partners.[39]

What Nilson is missing in the Catholic Church's ecumenical methodology can be found in Luther's doctrinal hermeneutic. The reformer's hermeneutic clearly defines what is indispensable—namely, what doctrinal agreement is necessary for unity—by clearly defining what makes something a necessary doctrine. Only those teachings that are based on the right Scripture rightly interpreted and/or are necessary for salvation and integral to the Gospel of grace in Christ Jesus are doctrines that must be agreed on for unity among the churches. On the basis of his scriptural and evangelical canons, Luther could then draft a statement that proposed the irreducible doctrinal basis for unity, such as the Schmalkald Articles (discussed in chapter 5) or the treatise "The Adoration of the Sacrament" (discussed in chapter 3). It is precisely this kind of doctrinal hermeneutic that could, if embraced, help to bring about agreement on what is necessary for unity and why.

LUTHER'S DOCTRINAL HERMENEUTIC JUDGES
ALL DOCTRINE ON THE BASIS OF SCRIPTURE ALONE
(THE SCRIPTURAL CANON)

Luther's doctrinal hermeneutic makes an important contribution to the Ecumenical Movement because it judges what is essential doctrine on the basis of what is the highest norm and authority in the church—the canonical Scriptures—rather than on some lesser authority.

Chapter 2 detailed the scriptural canon of Luther's doctrinal hermeneutic. According to that canon, a church teaching could be considered an essential doctrine only if it was based on the right Scripture, rightly interpreted. For Luther, the Bible was the highest authority in the church, and it was the only critical authority when it came to defining necessary doctrine. Chapter 2 described how Luther gradually rejected the consensus of authorities that late Catholic medieval theology had assumed to be self-evident. Although the medieval tradition considered the Bible as primary, it was merely one authority among others: canon law, papal decrees, church councils, reason, church fathers, and scholastic doctors (sacred tradition). In addition, it was assumed (by the Catholic controversialists, for example) that these authorities were a unified whole and could never really contradict one another. As Luther discovered teachings in the tradition that either had no support in Scripture or were contradicted by Scripture, he eventually came to hold that Scripture alone had the authority to determine doctrine.[40]

Already in his 1518 "Proceedings at Augsburg," Luther had made this clear: "The truth of Scripture comes first. After that is accepted, one may determine whether the words of men can be accepted as true."[41] Although human writings could be of real benefit to the church, only the Scriptures could be the basis of an essential doctrine. "Nothing should be asserted in questions of faith without scriptural precedent."[42] "Scripture alone is the true lord and master of all writings and doctrine on earth. If that is not granted what is Scripture good for?"[43] "Scripture is our court of appeal and bulwark."[44] "We should have a pure faith that believes nothing without a foundation in Scripture. Everything we are to believe is abundantly contained in Scripture."[45] About purgatory, Luther wrote, "I have discussed all this in order to show that no one is bound to believe more than what is based on Scripture."[46]

Luther gave such preferential authority to the canonical Scripture because he believed it to be the living Word of God. The reformer demonstrated this when responding to the argument that the Scriptures were obscure and needed to be illuminated by the church fathers: "If the

Spirit spoke in the fathers, he spoke even more in his own Scripture. And whoever does not understand the Spirit in his own Scripture—who will believe that he understands him in the writings of someone else?"[47] For Luther, because the Scriptures were the Spirit-inspired Word of God, they were without error and therefore more trustworthy than any other authority. "This is my answer to those also who accuse me of rejecting all the holy teachers of the church. I do not reject them. But everyone, indeed, knows that at times they have erred, as men will; therefore I am ready to trust them only when they give me evidence for their opinions from Scripture, which has never erred."[48] The Scriptures were superior and prior to whatever the church decreed because it was the word of promise that gives birth to the church and not vice versa; the Word was the creator and the church was creature. "For the Word of God is incomparably superior to the church, and in this Word the church, being a creature, has nothing to decree, ordain, or make, but only to be decreed, ordained, and made. For who begets his own parent? Who first brings forth his own maker?"[49] This is not to suggest that Luther conceived of no authoritative role for the church. Quite to the contrary, "all spirits are to be tested in the presence of the Church at the bar of Scripture."[50] The community of faith, especially those who filled the preaching office, had an important role in refuting opponents and comforting sinners. Unquestionably, therefore, the canonical Scriptures alone were authoritative in determining essential doctrine.

Yet it is precisely on the question of the authority of Scripture that the churches involved in ecumenism disagree. Realizing this fact is of the utmost importance. The Ecumenical Movement's view of Scripture and its authority, more than any other factor, is at the heart of its participating churches' inability to agree on what is truly necessary for unity. In fact, according to Norvald Yri, the word that best captures the Ecumenical Movement's view of Scripture's authority is *uncertainty*. Yri did an exhaustive study of the attempts between 1910 and 1974 in the Ecumenical Movement to articulate an understanding of the authority of the Bible. His conclusion is that during those years nothing that even remotely resembled the Reformation view of the authority of Scripture was dominant at any time.[51] That the Ecumenical Movement is confused about the authority of Scripture comes as no surprise. It is a direct result of the dismantling of biblical authority begun in the eighteenth-century Enlightenment.

The Enlightenment and Biblical Criticism

The Enlightenment was an intellectual and academic (and in certain places political) movement that celebrated the autonomy, all-sufficiency, and perfect objectivity of human reason. Its watchword was *freedom*, freedom from anything that threatened personal autonomy, especially the church and her authority. As reason was exalted, revelation was debased. The Bible came to be viewed as merely human literature, a book no different than any other. A new way of critically analyzing Scripture arose that saw it merely as an object of historical inquiry (historical-criticism). The Bible's inspiration and divine authority were ridiculed. It was no longer considered to be "God's Word," or at best it was considered to be so in an extremely limited sense. As for the Bible's contents, only that which could be proven by scientific inquiry was retained, and an antisupernatural presupposition reigned.

These critics considered it self-evident that the biblical books were not written by those who claimed to be the divinely inspired authors. In the nineteenth century, source criticism labored to discover the sources of the biblical books, especially targeting the Pentateuch and the Gospels. After World War I, form criticism arose, which believed the Gospels to be comprised of units of oral tradition that needed to be classified into forms or categories. Each of these forms (such as parables, legends, myths, proverbs, etc.) was then assigned to a *Sitz im Leben* (life setting) of the early church, such as preaching or the baptismal ceremony. Rudolf Bultmann was the most famous proponent of this approach. Out of form criticism came redaction criticism, which claimed that the author of each Gospel was a single individual who took the disparate units of tradition passed on by the early church and interwove them into a cohesive whole. But in all these critical approaches, the Bible was seen merely as a window through which to see the communities that created it. Practically nothing was taken at historical face value. Little or nothing could be known about the historic Jesus, for example. All that was revealed in the Gospels was truth about the Christ of faith, the Jesus that the first generations of Christians had invented for their own purposes.

What could be revealed, claimed the biblical critics, were the theologies of "Matthew" and "Luke" and "John." Each of these redactors and their communities (for example, the Matthean community) had its own agendas and situations that led to the creation of the theology. In addition, the theologies of Paul and Peter and James and John in their epistles were understood to be competing theologies that reflected the conflicting theologies found in the early church. In short, given the way they assumed the Bible had been assembled, the critics came to view the unity of the Bible and its theology, both in the Old and the New Testament, as untenable. If the Bible no longer had a single author (the Holy Spirit), how could it have the same theology throughout?

Concurrent with these critical approaches, neoorthodoxy, championed by Karl Barth, sought to call the church back to the Bible. Neoorthodoxy taught that God truly had revealed himself in Jesus Christ and truly did communicate to humankind through the Bible. The Bible itself was not the Word of God, but it was a vehicle through which one could have a "divine encounter" with the Word of God. According to neoorthodoxy, what is important is not the words of Scripture themselves but the Word of God behind and beyond the Scriptures. Therefore, though neoorthodoxy returned the Bible to a place of relative importance in the church, it did not restore the Bible's authority.

Beginning in the late 1970s, influenced by secular literary criticism, scholars began to study the text of Scripture for its own sake, rather than for the sake of learning something about its historical background. Narrative criticism is concerned about the coherence and integrity of the author's "story world." For example, the Gospels are studied to discover plot, characters, setting, and events. The narrator (or implied author) and the implied reader are analyzed. In more recent years, reader-response criticism spun off from narrative criticism. In reader-response, it is not the author's intention that determines the meaning of the text. Nor does the text itself contain objective meaning. The reader injects meaning into the text or cocreates meaning with the text. Deconstructionism is a criticism that looks for hidden meanings behind the text. Feminist criticism critiques the androcentric and patriarchal character of the Bible, as well as the androcentric character of past and present biblical scholarship. None of these criticisms, however, study the Bible as the inspired and authoritative Word of God. The Bible is read as human literature and nothing more. It is not even reliable history. Such a dismal result is unsurprising because the interpretive methods and presuppositions of these critics have been profoundly shaped by secular literary criticism and the behavioral/social sciences, rather than by the historic teaching of the church.

Another interpretive approach to the Bible, and one of more recent coinage, is social criticism. The goal of social criticism in its various forms is to understand the first-century Mediterranean world and how the first listeners might have heard (or read) the New Testament writings. Social criticism analyzes the New Testament documents, as well as other ancient literature and archaeological material, to gain a better understanding of the cultures, rhetoric, groups, and everyday life of the biblical world. Rhetorical criticism benefits from social criticism by applying what is known about the use of rhetoric in the Greco-Roman world to the texts of the New Testament (especially Pauline literature).[52]

It would be rash to reject summarily all these critical approaches as worthless. Through some of them, the church has profited and continues to profit because it has learned about the history and culture of the Mediterranean world, the background of the first-century church communities, and Greco-Roman literary genres. However, these approaches have taken a heavy toll on the church's belief in the divine inspiration and authority of the Scriptures. Therefore, is it any wonder that the Bible has ceased to be authoritative in some churches, given the historical-critical presupposition that it is a mere human production, a patchwork compilation of texts? Is it any wonder the Bible has lost prominence in some circles given the presupposition that, though it may contain truth, it is historically untrustworthy and is a divided mishmash of competing and conflicting theologies? Is it any wonder the Bible is being pushed aside when the Gospels are studied only as narrative "story worlds" or as platforms for radical feminist bromides or as texts that contain little or no objective meaning in and of themselves? Can such a Bible be an authoritative source and norm for the church's doctrine? The churches that have uncritically embraced such critical approaches have reaped what they have sown.

Some theologians are finally awakening to this sobering reality. In *Reclaiming the Bible for the Church*, Lutheran, Roman Catholic, and Orthodox scholars argue that the Bible as authoritative Scripture needs to be reclaimed for the church and by the church. A noticeable and alarming gap has opened between the historical-critical method of biblical studies and the church's dogmatic interpretation of the Bible. In a somewhat understated way, Carl Braaten and Robert Jenson summarize the problem in the introduction to *Reclaiming the Bible for the Church*:

> The historical-critical method was originally devised and welcomed as the great emancipator of the Bible from ecclesiastical dogma and blind faith. Some practitioners of the method now sense that the Bible may have meanwhile become its victim.
>
> . . . The methods of critical reason have tended to take over the entire operation of biblical interpretation, marginalizing the faith of the church and dissolving the unity of the Bible as a whole into a multiplicity of unrelated fragments. The academy has replaced the church as the home of biblical interpretation. Biblical critics frequently claim that their use of the historical-critical method is free of confessional assumptions and theological motivations, that their approach enjoys the status of objective historical science. Upon closer scrutiny, however, it is possible to show the historical critics approach the texts with their own set of prior commitments, sometimes hiddenly linked to ideologies alien or hostile to the faith of the Christian church.[53]

Because of such a critical approach to the Bible, many ecclesiastical circles believe the Bible may provide guidance on questions of doctrine and ethics, but it cannot speak an authoritative word (though the Bible may still be used to "build a case"). Who or what, then, can speak an authoritative word? Ultimately, only the autonomous self that exercises reason—reason that has been informed by the latest learning the culture has to offer. Or a group of autonomous selves using their culture-informed reason to arrive at a "consensus" are often considered as qualified to speak an authoritative word.[54]

The way to "reclaim the Bible for the church" is for the church to return to the historic belief that the Bible is the divinely inspired Word of God in everything it says. Therefore, Scripture is absolutely authoritative in all that it says—for doctrine and life. To "reclaim the Bible for the church" means to return to Luther's scriptural canon, which assumed that when it communicates essential teaching, the Bible is clear, timeless, and should be grasped according to its plain meaning. But this is not the whole solution.

It was stated previously that, more than any other factor, the Ecumenical Movement's view of Scripture and its authority is at the heart of the inability to agree on what is truly necessary for unity. Historical criticism in all its forms has been a major influence on the Ecumenical Movement's eroding confidence in Scripture's authority. It is not the only negative influence, however.

The Problem of Sacred Tradition

In its most basic form, the scriptural canon of Luther's doctrinal hermeneutic states that an article of faith must be based on Scripture alone, not on human writings or traditions. This canon was presented against the tendency in late medieval theology to equate all ecclesial authorities as a consistent and harmonized whole. The word *tradition* was often used in the late Middle Ages to refer to all nonbiblical Catholic authorities, including, but not limited to, papal or conciliar decrees, teachings of the church fathers, opinions of the scholastics, the prescriptions of canon law, or even custom. In a sense, even in the early sixteenth century, the papal church had two authoritative sources of doctrine—Scripture and tradition. This "two authorities" theory of church teaching was declared to be essential Catholic doctrine at the Council of Trent[55] (1546–1563) and was reaffirmed in the "Dogmatic Constitution on Revelation" at the Second Vatican Council:

> Hence there exist a close connection and communication between sacred tradition and sacred Scripture. For both of them, flowing from the same divine wellspring, in a certain way merge into a unity and tend toward the same end. For sacred Scripture is the word of God inasmuch as it is consigned to writing under the inspiration of the divine Spirit. To the successors of the apostles, sacred tradition hands on in its full purity God's word, which was entrusted to the apostles by Christ the Lord and the Holy Spirit. . . . Consequently, it is not from sacred Scripture alone that the Church draws her certainty about everything which has been revealed. Therefore both sacred tradition and sacred Scripture are to be accepted and venerated with the same sense of devotion and reverence.

> Sacred tradition and sacred Scripture form one sacred deposit of the word of God, which is committed to the Church . . . She [the Church] has always regarded the Scriptures together with sacred tradition as the supreme rule of faith, and will ever do so.[56]

To this one deposit of truth of Scripture and tradition Vatican II linked "the living teaching office of the Church" (the Latin word is *magisterum*),[57] which alone has the authority to authentically interpret the one deposit. "It is clear therefore, that sacred tradition, sacred Scripture, and the teaching authority of the Church, in accord with God's most wise design, are so linked and joined together that one cannot stand without the others."[58]

By God's grace, and to its credit, the Roman Catholic Church has managed to do what many Protestant and Lutheran churches were not able to do: to use the tools of historical and literary criticism profitably without compromising belief in the inspired and authoritative Scriptures as the rule of faith. Having dodged one attack on the authority of Scripture, however, the Roman Catholic Church succumbed to another. By elevating sacred tradition to an authority equal with Scripture, saying it springs from the same source and that both Scripture and tradition are all God's Word, categorically erodes the authority of the Scriptures—not to mention that there is nothing in the canonical Scriptures that encourages or commands Christians to look to an ongoing authoritative sacred tradition.[59] To justify the necessity of such sacred tradition by making reference to Scripture's alleged insufficiency or obscurity is not only to denigrate the authority of Scripture but also to place sacred tradition above Scripture in terms of authority. According to this view, other churches that do not have the authority of sacred tradition cannot and do not have the entire "deposit of faith" or all that is essential for the fullness of salvation or the fullness of unity. Luther's scriptural canon will not allow this. A completely different doctrinal hermeneutic is at work in the Catholic Church's "two authorities" methodology. This is the heart of the disunity between Rome and the churches of the Reformation. To pretend that sacred tradition—filled as it is with almost countless writings, laws, decrees, and customs over hundreds of years—only explicates and agrees with but never contradicts the Bible beggars the imagination! It is historically disingenuous to claim that the sacred tradition never contradicts itself, let alone the Scriptures.

It is for good reason that John Paul II, when speaking in *Ut Unum Sint* of "areas in need of fuller study before a true consensus of faith can be achieved," listed as the first area: "(1) the relationship between Sacred Scripture, as the highest authority in matters of faith, and Sacred Tradition, as indispensable to the interpretation of the Word of God."[60] It is appropriate to list this first because so much that divides the Protestant churches from the Roman Catholic Church comes out of and depends on the sacred tradition. Again, it is not the Catholic Church's sacred tradition itself that violates Luther's scriptural canon. Tremendous good has come from the church fathers and the various ecumenical councils, useful teaching that has confessed the faith clearly, edified the faithful, and defended the faith. All of this is to be treasured and used wisely. What is problematic is to claim that a teaching based *only* or *primarily* on sacred tradition is necessary for salvation or required for "necessary and sufficient" visible unity. This begs the question: In what sense is sacred Scripture "the highest authority in matters of faith" if there is so much necessary for the church that is not contained in the sacred Scriptures? Or in what sense is sacred Scripture the highest authority when its clear teachings can be effectively overruled by sacred tradition?

Consider the following examples, which unfortunately can be sketched only briefly here.

1. The immaculate conception[61] and assumption[62] of Mary are, for the Catholic Church, essential truth. They insist that believing such teachings in common with them is necessary to achieve a full consensus. Yet the Scriptures are entirely silent concerning both teachings. These Marian doctrines are based entirely on and articulated by the sacred tradition and papal decrees. Of course, it is well known that an essential doctrine can be implied by the Scriptures though such a doctrine is not explicitly spelled out there. Infant Baptism is an example of such a doctrine. The two Marian doctrines under consideration, however, can in no way be considered true by biblical implication. The few references to Mary in the Scriptures never even hint at such teachings. To base unity on anything other than what is essential doctrine is to lay unnecessary burdens on one's brethren in Christ. Only that which is founded on the Spirit-inspired and authoritative Scriptures can be an essential doctrine.

2. Of equal significance is the primacy of the pope. This was declared to be dogma at the First Vatican Council; therefore, it is a teaching that must be accepted before full communion with Rome can occur. Pope John Paul II hints at this in *Ut Unum Sint*: "The Catholic Church, both in her praxis and in her solemn documents, holds that the communion of the particular Churches with the Church of Rome, and of their Bishops with the Bishop of Rome, is—in God's plan—an essential requisite of full and visible communion."[63]

The pope's primacy has been nuanced in various ways. It has been described in terms of power and jurisdiction, as in the words of the Vatican I Constitution *Pastor Aeternus*, in which it was decreed that the Roman pontiff had "full and supreme power of jurisdiction over the whole Church" concerning faith and morals but also discipline and government over "each and every Church" and over "each and every shepherd and faithful."[64] Or as John Paul II has more recently done, it can be described as a loving service of mercy established by Christ on behalf of the churches to preserve unity while not denying that it is a primacy of power and jurisdiction.[65]

Despite the winsome rhetoric of servanthood framed within the theme of unity, there is no question that the pope's primacy includes power and jurisdiction over all the churches. In the words of *Ut Unum Sint:* "With the power and the authority without which such an office would be illusory, the Bishop of Rome must ensure the communion of all the Churches."[66] There is no question that, according to the Catholic Church, the Bishop of Rome, because of his primacy by divine law, has jurisdiction over all other churches and bishops. Therefore, he would require obedience in some sense from churches that entered full communion with him.[67]

Numerous dialogues have wrestled with the pope's primacy because it has been seen as one of the great obstacles to unity. The best possible construction has been placed on the extreme statements made about papal primacy at Vatican I and elsewhere.[68] Yet a lingering question remains: Why should the churches consider the pope's primacy as an essential doctrine necessary for unity when it is not based on Scripture? Where can we find the pope's primacy taught in Scripture? Matt. 16:18–19[69] has long been claimed as scriptural proof (and elsewhere where Peter takes a leading role). Yet as is well known, this passage says nothing about papal primacy, though it possibly might be saying something about Peter's primacy, though even this is disputed. The tortured argument states: Christ gave primacy to Peter. Peter went to Rome and was the first bishop of Rome. Every bishop of Rome since then has been the successor of Peter, exercising the same primacy that he exercised, by the will of Christ.[70] If the office of the pope was presented merely as something that developed historically by human law and, as such, might be helpful for the church today, such a lack of biblical support would not be so troublesome. But because the papacy is presented as a divine office that is an essential doctrine that all Christians must believe and with which they must agree for unity, a much stronger foundation is needed. An essential teaching must be based on Scripture that is clear—if Scripture truly is the highest authority in the church. Luther's words still ring true:

> First, since everything that is done in the church is proclaimed in clear and plain passages of Scripture, it is surely amazing that nothing is openly said in the whole Bible about the papacy. This

is especially strange since my opponents consider the papacy the most important, most necessary, and most unique feature in the church. It is a suspicious situation and makes a bad impression that so many matters of lesser importance are based upon a multitude of reliable and clear passages of Scripture, while for this one doctrine no one has been able to produce a single clear reason.[71]

Unity should not be made to depend on a teaching that is not based on clear canonical Scripture.

3. Another example will illustrate the sacred tradition contradicting and subsequently overruling a clear teaching of Scripture. As shown in chapter 2, a second aspect of Luther's scriptural canon is that a necessary article of faith must be based on the right Scripture—not just any Scripture will do. According to Luther, the Scripture had to be clear and it had to be teaching, not example. When he argued against the necessity of monastic celibacy, for example, he wrote, "I am not arguing whether Paul lived a life of celibacy, but whether his example should be made into a law or a matter of doctrine."[72] The fact that Paul remained celibate could not, by itself, establish an essential doctrine or practice that obligated all priests or monks. Nowhere does Scripture forbid Christian leaders from marrying. It is well known that Peter, the apostles, and the brothers of Jesus were married.[73] 1 Timothy 3 clearly tells us that an *episkopos* (overseer, bishop, pastor) should be the husband of one wife.[74] Scripture calls forbidding to marry a doctrine of demons.[75] Christ Jesus and Paul explicitly say that not everyone has the gift to remain celibate.[76] On the basis of Scripture, celibacy can be recommended, but it can never be made into a law that binds Christians. Yet in the case of clerical celibacy, this is precisely what the Catholic Church has done. They forbid what God has made free[77] and make it an essential teaching. On what basis do they do this? Not on the basis of clear Scripture, which permits clerical marriage, but on the basis of sacred tradition and several passages that recommend virginity but never command it as necessary.[78] Thus, at least in this case, when sacred tradition and clear Scripture conflict, tradition wins out and clear Scripture is rejected. Doesn't this mean that sacred tradition has a higher authority than sacred Scripture?

The purpose of the preceding exercise is to demonstrate that Luther's doctrinal hermeneutic is a needed word of reformation to the churches, especially in the context of the Ecumenical Movement. It is to be recommended because it bases necessary doctrine only on the highest of authorities: sacred Scripture, the right Scripture, rightly interpreted.

Full Communion between the ELCA and the ECUSA

Another case study that illustrates the contribution that Luther's doctrinal hermeneutic can make to the Ecumenical Movement is the full communion announced between the ELCA and the Episcopal Church in the United States of America (ECUSA), which became official on January 1, 2001. The recommendation for and the basis of this full communion was detailed in "Call for Common Mission," which in turn was a revision of an earlier recommendation for full communion between the churches, the 1991 "Concordat of Agreement."

The "Concordat of Agreement" was the culmination of more than twenty years of ecumenical dialogue between the two church bodies. Three rounds of bilateral dialogue between Lutherans and Episcopalians—called Lutheran-Episcopal Dialogue—were held between 1969 and 1991, with each round discussing various doctrinal topics. The most difficult topic was saved for last. From 1988–1991, Lutheran-Episcopal Dialogue III took up the question of ministry and the historic episcopate and published its findings in 1991 in *Toward Full Communion*.[79] The doctrine of the historic episcopate[80] had become known as "the historic impasse"[81] in Lutheran-Episcopal dialogue. The problem, simply stated, is this: Since the adoption of the Chicago-Lambeth Quadrilateral of 1886–1888, the Episcopal Church has viewed the historic episcopate as one of four elements[82] necessary for the reunion of the churches.[83]

Meanwhile, the Lutherans refused to accept the historic episcopate as a necessary condition for full communion. Often citing Augsburg Confession XXVIII, they argued that the form of *episkope* (ministry) was an adiaphoron, though the one *episkope* (ministry) of Word and Sacrament was not. Although open to adopting the historic episcopate and the threefold ordering (bishops, presbyters, and deacons) as a guardian of unity, the Lutherans refused to recognize it as an essential teaching necessary for unity.[84]

The "Concordat of Agreement" appeared to break through this historic impasse. In paragraph 5 of subsection B, "Actions of the Episcopal Church," the Episcopal Church

> hereby pledges, at the same time that this Concordat of Agreement is accepted . . . to begin the process for enacting a temporary suspension, in this case only, of the 17th century restriction that "no persons are allowed to exercise the offices of bishop, priest, or deacon in this Church unless they are so ordained, or have already received such ordination with the laying on of hands by bishops who are themselves duly qualified to confer Holy Orders." The purpose of this action will be to permit the full interchangeability and reciprocity of all Evangelical Lutheran Church in America pastors as priests or presbyters and all Evangelical Lutheran Church in America deacons as deacons in the

Episcopal Church without any further ordination or re-ordination or supplemental ordination whatsoever.[85]

This unique concession by the ECUSA was certainly a breakthrough in its dialogue with the ELCA and an important step toward full communion. However, what the right hand gave, the left seemed to take away. Paragraph 5 continued:

> The purpose of temporarily suspending this restriction, which has been a constant requirement in Anglican polity since the Ordinal of 1662, is precisely in order to secure the future implementation of the ordinals' same principle within the eventually fully integrated ministries. It is for this reason that the Episcopal Church can feel confident in taking this unprecedented step with regard to the Evangelical Lutheran Church in America.[86]

This wording shows that the purpose for temporarily suspending the Ordinal of 1662 was to fully implement it later. Paragraph 14 made it more clear that full communion would not be complete until all ELCA bishops were incorporated into the historic episcopate.[87] In other words, full communion depended on the introduction of the historic episcopate. From the ECUSA side, the historic episcopate was clearly a doctrine necessary for unity.

Edward D. Schneider, a Lutheran participant in Lutheran-Episcopal Dialogue III, dissented for this very reason. After remarking that the text of the "Concordat" in paragraph 14 makes the historic episcopate a condition for full communion, he continues,

> Moreover, it was very clear throughout the dialogue process that the bottom line would be that there could be no agreement for full communion if the ELCA did not agree to adopt the historic episcopate. If that does not mean that adopting the historic episcopate is a condition for full communion . . . then language has lost its plain meaning. All the circumlocution in the world will not change that simple fact.[88]

When the 1997 ELCA Worldwide Assembly voted down the "Concordat" by six votes, the assembly requested that a new proposal for full communion be submitted to the next assembly. "Call for Common Mission," a revision of the "Concordat," was the result of that request.

Did "Call for Common Mission" change anything regarding the necessity of the historic episcopate? Linguistic changes, yes—substantive change, no. The ELCA again agreed to submit itself to the historic episcopate of the Episcopal Church, which would happen gradually, as before. A new paragraph about the necessity of the historic episcopate for full communion responded to the main criticism that had come from the Lutheran side.

The Episcopal Church is free to maintain that sharing in the historic catholic episcopate, while not necessary for salvation or for recognition of another church as a church, is nonetheless necessary when Anglicans enter the relationship of full communion in order to link the local churches for mutual responsibility in the communion of the larger church. The Evangelical Lutheran Church in America is free to maintain that this same episcopate, although pastorally desirable when exercised in personal, collegial, and communal ways, is nonetheless not necessary for the relationship of full communion.[89]

The Episcopal Church admitted that though the historic episcopate was not necessary for salvation, it was necessary for full communion. The ELCA stressed that the historic episcopate was desirable but was necessary neither for salvation nor unity. From the ECUSA side, full communion would not happen unless the ELCA agreed to submit itself to the historic episcopate.[90] Thus the ELCA was being pressured to base unity on a doctrine that was not necessary—something that clearly violated Luther's doctrinal hermeneutic. Despite the ELCA's rhetoric, in reality submission to the historic episcopate was necessary. There would have been no full communion without it. The ELCA's claim that it is free to maintain the historic episcopate is self-deception. Only if such a decision had been made apart from the pressures of an ecumenical relationship that demanded it would this have been a free choice that did not violate Luther's doctrinal hermeneutic.

Since full communion was declared, a lively debate has been raging within the ELCA over the appropriateness of the accord with the ECUSA.[91] On one side are those who hold that the unity agreement has precipitated a confessional crisis. The problem, they say, is that the agreement with the ECUSA scuttled Augsburg Confession VII by making something other than consensus (agreement) in the teaching of the Gospel and the administration of the sacraments necessary for unity.[92] The "something" in this case is the historic episcopate, a clear example of a human tradition or rite, they say. The other side argues that Augsburg Confession VII is not relevant or applicable to the modern ecumenical situation. For example, Carl Braaten asks, "Is it really sufficient for church unity that churches agree on the preaching of the gospel and the administration of the sacraments? Will such a minimal condition suffice as an ecumenical principle to achieve a true community of divided churches?" His answer is no. "It should be clear that Article VII is not sufficient as an ecumenical principle for inter-church agreement and fellowship."[93] But this is a terribly superficial reading of Augsburg Confession VII—as well as a betrayal of the Reformation and the Gospel. The thesis of this book should make clear that, given Luther's doctrinal hermeneutic, it is incredible to claim that Augsburg Confession VII can be understood to say that only preaching of the Word and administrating the sacraments should be necessary for unity.[94]

Vitor Westhelle is close to the truth when he writes:

> Melanchthon's "marks" of the church in AC VII are really neither marks nor innovations, but only pointers to what properly grounds the sufficient and necessary unity of the church: the gospel of Jesus Christ as it is conveyed to the church by the apostolic witness registered in the Scriptures. . . . Article VII is the *sola scriptura* principle at work. And the *sola scriptura* at work is called the church (*ubi verbum, ibi ecclesia*).[95]

The intent of Augsburg Confession VII is to show that the basis of unity can only be the *doctrina evangelii* ("doctrine of the Gospel," both preaching and doctrinal content),[96] that is, necessary doctrine that conveys or is connected to the Gospel and grounded in the Scriptures alone: Luther's evangelical and scriptural canons. The same teaching is echoed in Formula of Concord, Solid Declaration X, 31: "For this reason the churches are not to condemn one another because of differences in ceremonies when in Christian freedom one has fewer or more than the other, as long as these churches are otherwise united in teaching and in all the articles of the faith as well as in the proper use of the holy sacraments."[97] The authors of this marvelous paragraph showed themselves to be excellent students of Luther, his doctrinal hermeneutic, and his reformation. Agreement in necessary articles of faith, both believed and used, is the only necessary basis for unity among the churches; nothing more or nothing less will suffice for unity.

LUTHER'S DOCTRINAL HERMENEUTIC BASES THE DEFINITION OF ESSENTIAL DOCTRINE ON THE GOSPEL (THE EVANGELICAL CANON)

Chapter 2 also made the case for the evangelical canon of Luther's doctrinal hermeneutic. Just as the essential nature of a doctrine was tested by asking, "Is it based on the right Scripture, rightly interpreted?" so it also was tested by asking the questions, "Is it necessary for salvation? Does it save one if believed or damn one if not believed? Is it connected to the gospel of justification by grace for Christ's sake through faith?"

This canon of Luther's doctrinal hermeneutic is the better known of the two, in the sense that whenever Lutherans speak about justification as the article by which the church stands or falls, they are speaking about what I am calling Luther's evangelical canon. Whenever Lutherans speak of justification as the criterion that determines all articles, as "the integrative center of all faith and theology," or as "the 'plumb line' by which all doctrine and practice is to be judged," they are speaking of the evangelical canon.[98]

It is well known that an unresolved difference in the 1997 "Joint Declaration on the Doctrine of Justification"[99] concerns the question of whether justification is *the* criterion (the Lutheran position) or merely "an indispensable criterion" (the Roman Catholic position and the wording adopted in the final text) for judging all doctrine and practice. Roman Catholics freely admitted in the "Joint Declaration" that they are "bound by several criteria."[100] These "several criteria" are not elucidated in the document. However, when Cardinal Edward Cassidy later offered the official Roman Catholic response to the "Joint Declaration" on June 25, 1998, he further elaborated on what the "several criteria" are: "[F]or the Catholic Church the message of justification, according to Scripture and already from the time of the Fathers, has to be organically integrated into the fundamental criterion of the '*regula fidei*', that is, the confession of the one God in three persons, christologically centred and rooted in the living Church and its sacramental life."[101] This quote betrays some confusion over the Lutheran position. Luther's evangelical canon of justification *is* organically integrated into "the confession of the one God in three persons, christologically centred and rooted in the living Church and its sacramental life." In the evangelical canon, the Gospel is the interpretive lens—the good news that the triune God has justified the world freely through faith in Jesus Christ—and this justification is delivered through Word and Sacraments and lived in the church. Justification is organically integrated into the rule of faith! It is this that makes Luther's evangelical canon such an important contribution to the Ecumenical Movement.[102] The evangelical canon is no mere peripheral criterion; it is the criterion that tests whether something is an essential doctrine by the very heart of the Christian faith.

The reality, however, is that the Catholic Church has a very different doctrinal hermeneutic, as we have already seen. In the final analysis, it is the rule of faith—which for them is everything that the Catholic Church has declared to be dogma, including their doctrines of sin, grace, Christ, faith, the church, human nature, etc. It is this expansive view of the *regula fidei* that guides the teaching office of the church (*magisterium*) in its determination of whether a teaching in the Scriptures or in the sacred tradition is essential doctrine. Thus, for the Catholic Church, it is not justification that ultimately decides whether something is a doctrine that must be believed, as it is for Lutherans.

A correct understanding of justification preserves the truth of the other articles of faith. For example, justification, when properly understood, gives all credit for salvation to God and to what he has done in Christ. If this is true, then it follows that nothing that anyone else has done or ever can do—and nothing in us, about us, or by us—can ever contribute anything to salvation. How could we contribute anything, given that, apart from us and outside of us, God in Christ already did everything needed to save us, namely, suffering and dying on the cross? Because of Christ's atoning sacrifice, neither sin nor guilt is counted against us and all punishment has been borne by Christ. The gift of salvation is complete and paid for fully—and nothing can be contributed toward a gift already purchased. It either can be received (which faith does) or rejected (which unbelief does). It is this that leads Lutherans to confess that we are justified *sola fidei* (by faith alone), *sola gratia* (by grace alone), *solus Christus* (by Christ alone). When justification is the ultimate criterion of essential doctrine, God receives all the glory.

Thus a correct understanding of justification leads to a correct understanding of theology, Christology, soteriology, atonement, grace, faith, and all other articles. Any explanation of these articles of faith that conflicts with the correct view of justification is to be rejected as false. And any church teaching that does not involve this view of justification is not an article of faith that is necessary for salvation or unity. This is the methodology of Luther's evangelical canon.

This is exactly what Luther did in the Schmalkald Articles, as demonstrated in chapter 5. Any teaching or practice that Rome presented as necessary for salvation and/or unity that contradicted "the chief article" was considered to be unnecessary. This is exactly what Lutherans must continue to do in all ecumenical dialogues. If the Catholic Church truly agrees with Lutherans on "the basic truths" of justification, then it would no longer base unity with Lutherans on doctrines that contradict justification—such as the sacrament of penance, purgatory, or the doctrine of indulgences, which all teach that though God forgives us in Christ, there is still temporal punishment that we have to endure. The thought is that though Christ bore our eternal punishment, we still have to atone for our own temporal punishment—either in this life or in the next—before we can enter heaven. This contradicts justification by misunderstanding the atonement, robs Christ of his glory, and tempts Christians to rely on their own works or the works of others to be saved. Edward Yarnold states it simply:

> The problem is this. Roman Catholics believe that a person may die in a state of grace but still need to pass through the purifying experience of purgatory before being admitted to heaven. They also believe that the prayers and good works of the Church can assist the dead in this process of purification, and that the Church has the power to attach to these pious acts an indulgence or declaration that they are of benefit to the departed who are undergoing the purifying process of purgatory. How then can Roman Catholics maintain at the same time that the

restoration of the sinner to grace is wholly the work of God through the merits of Jesus Christ? Do the Roman Catholic doctrines of purgatory and indulgences not imply that Christ did not do everything needed to be done on our behalf, leaving something for the Church to add to his redeeming work?[103]

The obvious answer is yes. The Roman Catholic doctrines of penance, purgatory, and indulgences do imply that Christ didn't do everything needed to save us and that the church, therefore, must complete Christ's work. Thus Luther's evangelical canon disqualifies these doctrines as being necessary for salvation or for unity.

In ecumenical dialogue, Luther's evangelical canon refuses those who want to base unity on too much. It also refuses to base unity on too little. If anything, in today's ecumenical climate, which tends toward reductionism, the latter is the more prevalent problem. For example, the LCMS does not ordain women to the pastoral ministry. The ELCA does. The LCMS considers this difference to be a church-dividing issue. The ELCA does not. In other words, the LCMS considers the ordination of women to be an essential doctrine, but the ELCA does not. Why?

First, let's note that there are clear passages of Scripture that prohibit women from being pastors, such as 1 Cor. 14:34 and 1 Tim. 2:12.[104] The second passage is grounded in the order of creation. The only way to overcome these clear passages of Scripture is to use a method of biblical criticism that erodes the Bible's authority and trustworthiness, as was discussed in the first part of this chapter. Such criticism, for example, could say that Paul didn't really write 1 Timothy (or the other pastoral letters), that 1 Cor. 14:34 is a later interpolation added by someone other than Paul, or that these passages lack authority because they reflect Paul's first-century Jewish cultural biases. Even if the faulty premise is granted that either Paul didn't write the passages or that a culturally warped Paul did write them, these arguments are ultimately impotent because the passages are part of the biblical canon. All parties involved believe that the biblical canon is authoritative, the source and norm of all Christian theology. If we randomly dismiss teachings of Paul because they don't fit current cultural wisdom, what will we have left?

But the foregoing doesn't answer why the LCMS believes the ordination of women to be an essential doctrine. Such a position isn't merely the result of the fact that the Scriptures forbid it. It is primarily because the doctrine of the holy ministry *is* an essential article of faith. Why? Because the one preaching office is grounded on clear Scriptures and primarily because the one holy ministry of Word and Sacrament is connected to and bound up in the Gospel. It is connected to the Gospel because, by the will of God, it conveys salvation (cf. Rom. 10:14–15: "And how can they hear without someone preaching to them? And how can they preach unless they are sent? As it is written, 'How beautiful are the feet of those who bring good news!' ").[105] It was for this reason that Luther included ordination and call as an essential doctrine in part III of the Schmalkald Articles, as seen in chapter 5. Therefore, it is because the holy ministry is a necessary doctrine that the question of the ordination of women, by derivation, becomes essential.

The LCMS's position on ecumenism is "confessional agreement among *all* Christians that extends to *all* the articles of faith revealed in the Sacred Scriptures and comprised in the Lutheran Symbols [Book of Concord of 1580]."[106] To unite with another church that does not agree in all the articles would be unionism and would be to countenance falsehood. However, are the articles of faith limited to the doctrines that are specifically addressed in the Book of Concord? Certainly not. It is not only those teachings that already have been understood to be essential (such as the doctrinal content of the Book of Concord) that are essential—such a position would be ridiculously static. Luther would hold that any teaching that satisfies his doctrinal hermeneutic is an article of faith—a much more dynamic approach. Just as the Lutherans of the sixteenth century saw the need to articulate further the scriptural articles of faith because of the controversies through which they passed, though they already had the ecumenical creeds, so may we see a similar need. In fact, this is what the church has always done. Every doctrine should be tested rigorously by Luther's evangelical and scriptural canons to determine whether the doctrine is essential and required for unity. The doctrine of creation vs. evolution; the doctrine of the Word; ethical teachings such as the teaching of sexuality, marriage and divorce, and abortion; and whatever else is questioned or in controversy should be tested accoring to the doctrinal hermeneutic.

Seeking Agreement or Accommodation?

Those who are familiar with Luther's method of overcoming doctrinal differences (as seen in chapters 3–5) and with the methodology of contemporary ecumenical dialogues to accomplish the same goal cannot help but notice a real difference. Luther (and also those who framed the Lutheran Confessions) refused to extend the right hand of fellowship until genuine agreement existed on the precise point of controversy or difference (for example, the bodily presence of Christ). Painstaking and rigorous analysis and debate on the basis of Scripture was carried out by both sides to convince the other side of the rightness of one position over the other. Unity was achieved by discovering which position was right and rejecting the other—or perhaps by discovering that both were wrong.

This also was the way of the ecumenical councils. When the first council at Jerusalem (Acts 15) met to discuss the matter of justification, it was understood that both sides could not be right. Either the Gentiles were justified by faith apart from works of the Law (Paul's position) or they were justified by faith and the keeping of circumcision and the Mosaic Law. Unity was achieved at the Jerusalem Council not by accommodating both viewpoints, but by deciding, on the basis of the apostolic faith, which position was right and which was wrong. The same was true at Nicaea in A.D. 325. The council strove to preserve unity in the church not by finding a way that accommodated both Arianism and the Orthodox party, but by discovering the truth and being faithful to it. Arianism was declared to be wrong and outside the pale of normative Christianity. For Luther and the ecumenical councils, unity was achieved only by a genuine agreement in doctrine—only by acknowledging the truth and rejecting the error.

In contemporary ecumenical dialogue, a completely different methodology is at work. Accommodation rather than agreement is the goal. Consensus rather than correct confession of faith is the desired outcome. Consider two examples. In 1997, the ELCA, the Presbyterian Church U.S.A., the Reformed Church in America, and the United Church of Christ entered into full communion with one another. They signed "A Formula of Agreement," which declared that each recognized the others as churches in which the Gospel was rightly preached and the sacraments administered according to the Word of God. The denominations also withdrew all historic condemnations, declaring them to be inappropriate. Full communion was said to rest on the doctrinal consensus recorded in *A Common Calling: The Report of the Lutheran-Reformed Committee for Theological Conversations 1988–1992*.[107] But listen to the conclusion of *A Common Calling*:

> In discovering our agreement on the essential matters of the gospel, we have also recognized the important theological differences that remain between our churches in questions such as the understanding of the Lord's Supper and christology. These theological differences are, we believe, crucial for the ongoing ecumenical relations between these traditions. We view them not as disagreements that need to be overcome but as diverse witnesses to the one gospel that we confess in common. Rather than being church-dividing, the varying theological emphases among, and even within, these communities provide complementary expressions of the church's faith in the triune God.[108]

On the one hand, we are told that agreement in the essentials of the Gospel has been discovered. On the other hand, it is admitted that important theological differences remain among the church bodies in the doctrine of the Lord's Supper and Christology. Yet these were the essential doctrines over which the original divisions had occurred! Instead of overcoming the differences, the whole discussion is recast into accommodation: "We view them not as disagreements that need to be overcome but as diverse witnesses to the one gospel that we confess in common." Not agreement in doctrine but accommodation of differing doctrines is achieved. And this diversity is said to be sufficient for full communion!

A second example involves the Roman Catholic-Lutheran dialogue and the "Joint Declaration on the Doctrine of Justification." We already have seen that the "Joint Declaration" declared that "consensus in the basic truths" of justification had been achieved and the mutual condemnations dropped. Yet an analysis of the document shows that, paragraph after paragraph, there is accommodation far more often than agreement. Contradictory positions simply are put side by side and said to be no longer contradictory. Differences are admitted, but it is claimed that they do not destroy the consensus that has been achieved. Neither side is wrong or ever was wrong. Instead, because of new insights, the differences can now be seen in a new light.

> Like the dialogues themselves, this Joint Declaration rests on the conviction that in overcoming the earlier controversial questions and doctrinal condemnations, the churches neither take the condemnations lightly nor do they disavow their own past. On the contrary, this Declaration is shaped by the conviction that in their respective histories our churches have come to new insights. Developments have taken place, which not only make possible, but also require the churches to examine the divisive questions and condemnations and see them in a new light.[109]

In other words, neither Lutherans nor Catholics say they have changed their positions. They refuse to disavow their past. What they said in the past was not wrong. What has changed, we are told, is that "new developments" have enabled the dialogue participants to see the divisive questions in a new light. This means that differences have not been overcome; instead, they have been transcended or accommodated. Longstanding differences are no longer divisive because the participants don't want them to be divisive. As Robert Preus wrote in 1995:

> But there has been a settlement of a different kind. The settlement [on justification] is an amalgam of the old Lutheran and Roman Catholic definitions, or rather, a pasting together of the two disparate sets of definitions—sort of like a treaty. Neither side gives up its sets of definitions and meanings. The treaty provides that the Lutheran and the Roman Catholic will no longer battle over words, meanings, and definitions, but each will keep his own. And this is the agreement, the settlement, the consensus.[110]

It needs to be said again: Accommodation is not agreement. Accommodation means that differences in doctrine remain, but the parties agree to a peaceful coexistence. This is not, however, the way the ancient church sought to preserve or to restore unity, nor is it the way Luther, with his doctrinal hermeneutic, approached it. The difference was rigorously studied, debate occurred, treatises were written. In many cases one side was considered to be in the right, the other side in the wrong. It is sad to say that in today's ecumenical climate communion often has been achieved not by overcoming doctrinal differences, but by the churches deciding that they don't want to fight anymore. The truth, however, is something worth fighting for. Better to have the truth of God's Word and its essential doctrine than a false and accommodating unity at the expense of the truth.

The contention of this chapter has been that Luther's doctrinal hermeneutic has much to contribute to the Ecumenical Movement. It speaks to a fundamental difference among the churches involved in that movement. The fundamental difference is conflicting doctrinal criteriologies, which often exist on an unconscious level. Because of the conflicting definitions of essential doctrine, the churches struggle to agree on what is required and sufficient for unity.

Luther's doctrinal hermeneutic provides a valuable service and speaks a reforming word to the Ecumenical Movement. His hermeneutic does this by encouraging the churches to think more clearly about the defining of doctrine and by calling them back to criteria that are based on the church's highest authority (the canonical Scriptures) and the heart of its theology (the justifying gospel of Jesus Christ). Luther's doctrinal hermeneutic is a reforming word because it asks the churches to examine rigorously every alleged necessary doctrine, no matter how ancient, treasured, or popular, to ensure that such doctrines are truly essential. Such an approach requires hard work and patience from a movement whose patience is already strained. The work, however, is well worth it because false unity is as displeasing to God as unnecessary disunity. May the one Shepherd of the church manifest visibly the unity of his one flock.

ABBREVIATIONS

AC   Augsburg Confession

ARG   *Archiv für Reformationsgeschichte*

BSLK   *Die Bekenntnisschriften der evangelisch-utherischen Kirche*. 11th ed. Göttingen: Vandenhoeck & Ruprecht, 1992.

CCath   Corpus Catholicorum. Münster: Aschendorff, 1919–.

CR   Corpus Reformatorum. Vols. 1–28. Halle: C. A. Schwetschke, 1834–60.

ELCA   Evangelical Lutheran Church in America

ECUSA   Episcopal Church in the United States of America

K-W   Kolb, Robert, and Timothy J. Wengert, eds. *The Book of Concord*. Translated by Charles Arand et al. Minneapolis: Fortress, 2000.

LCMS   The Lutheran Church—Missouri Synod

LWF   Lutheran World Federation

LQ   *Lutheran Quarterly*

LW   Luther, Martin. *Luther's Works*. American Edition. General editors Jaroslav Pelikan and Helmut T. Lehmann. 56 vols. St. Louis: Concordia, and Philadelphia: Muhlenberg and Fortress, 1955–86.

SA   Schmalkald Articles

StL   Luther, Martin. *Dr. Martin Luthers Sämmtliche Schriften*. 2d ed. 23 vols. in 24. Edited by Johann Georg Walch. St. Louis: Concordia, 1881–1910.

UuA   Volz, Hans, and Heinrich Ulbrich, eds. *Urkunden und Aktenstücke zur Geschichte von Martin Luthers Scmalkaldischen Artikeln (1536–1574)*. Berlin: De Gruyter, 1957.

WA   Luther, Martin. *D. Martin Luthers Werke. Kritische Gesamtausabe. Schriften*. 68 vols. Weimar: Hermann Böhlaus Nachfolger, 1883–1999.

WABr   Luther, Martin. *D. Martin Luthers Werke. Kritische Gesamtausabe. Briefwechsel*. 18 vols. Weimar: Hermann Böhlaus Nachfolger, 1930–85.

WATr   Luther, Martin. *D. Martin Luthers Werke. Kritische Gesamtausabe. Tischreden*. 6 vols. Weimar: Hermann Böhlaus Nachfolger, 1912–21. Reprinted in 2000.

WCC   World Council of Churches

Z   Zwingli. Ulrich. *Huldreich Zwinglis sämtliche Werke*. Edited by Emil Egli and Georg Finsler. Corpus Reformatorum, vols. 88–101 (I–XIV). Reprint, Zurich: Theologischer Verlag Zurich, 1983.

ZKG   *Zeitschrift für Kirchengeschichte*

NOTES

FOREWORD

1. See Harding Meyer, " 'Delectari assertionibus' On the Issue of the Authority of Christian Testimony," in *Piety, Politics, and Ethics: Reformation Studies in Honor of George W. Forell*, ed. Carter Lindberg, Sixteenth Century Essays & Studies 3 (Kirksville: Sixteenth Century Journal Publishers, 1984), 1–14.

2. LW 27:41f. (= WA 40/2:51.13ff.).

3. WA 10/1.2:430.30–32.

4. James Kittelson, "Luther on Being 'Lutheran,' " *Lutheran Quarterly* 12:1 (Spring 2003): 99–110, here 106 with citation from "Luther's Warning to His Dear German People" (LW 47:27–28, 30).

PREFACE

1. Werner Elert, *Eucharist and Church Fellowship in the First Four Centuries*, trans. N. E. Nagel (St. Louis: Concordia, 1966), 109.

CHAPTER 1

1. Bernhard Lohse, *Martin Luther's Theology*, trans. and ed. Roy A. Harrisville (Minneapolis: Fortress, 1999), 9.

2. See, for example, Carter Lindberg, "Luther's Critique of the Ecumenical Assumption That Doctrine Divides but Service Unites," *Journal of Ecumenical Studies* 27 (Fall 1990): 679–96.

3. LW 54:110 (= WATr 1:294–95, no. 624).

4. Gerhard Ebeling, "The Significance of Doctrinal Differences for the Division of the Church," in *Word and Faith*, trans. James W. Leitch (Philadelphia: Fortress, 1963), 164.

5. Ebeling, "Significance of Doctrinal Differences," 166. It was this same observation that motivated George Lindbeck to formulate his "cultural-linguistic" definition of doctrine. "It has become apparent to me, during twenty-five years of involvement in ecumenical discussions and in teaching about the history and present status of doctrines, that those of us who are engaged in these activities lack adequate categories for conceptualizing the problems that arise. We are often unable, for example, to specify the criteria we implicitly employ when we say that some changes are faithful to a doctrinal tradition and others unfaithful, or some doctrinal differences are church-dividing and others not" (George A. Lindbeck, *The Nature of Doctrine* [Philadelphia: Westminster, 1984], 7).

6. Eeva Martikainen, "Future Emphases in Ecumenical Research," *Lutheran World Federation Documentation* 32 (March 1993): 102–3.

7. I have chosen to use *hermeneutic* in this simple sense, despite the fact that the word has a long history with varied usage and has been employed by both theologians and philosophers. In theology, *hermeneutic* has been applied to both the meaning of Scripture and doctrine. In philosophy, it has been applied to questions of epistemological method. For a summary of the various ways *hermeneutic* has been used in theology and philosophy, see Thomas B. Ommen, *The Hermeneutic of Dogma*, AAR Dissertation 11 (Missoula: Scholars Press, 1975), 1–60, 105–65.

8. To call the dialogues in which Luther was involved "ecumenical" is, admittedly, anachronistic. Neither Luther nor the other participants in the dialogues used the late nineteenth-century word *ecumenical* to describe their discussions. Furthermore, Luther's method of dialoguing was a far cry from the ecumenical dialogues of the late twentieth century, which involved face-to-face meetings among representatives of organizationally distinct church bodies. Despite this disclaimer, Luther's dialogues were ecumenical in the sense that they were conversations (either in person or in writing) for the purpose of achieving unity among Christians.

9. An exception to this silence is Martin Brecht's definitive three-volume biography of Luther. Brecht does not articulate Luther's view of doctrine in a substantial manner, but he does occasionally call attention to writings of Luther in which the reformer takes up the topic of doctrine. See Brecht, *Martin Luther: His Road to Reformation, 1483–1521*, trans. James L. Schaaf (Minneapolis: Fortress, 1985); *Martin Luther: Shaping and Defining the Reformation, 1521–1532*, trans. James L. Schaaf (Minneapolis: Fortress, 1990); and *Martin Luther: The Preservation of the Church, 1532–1546*, trans. James L. Schaaf (Minneapolis: Fortress, 1993).

10. Julius Köstlin, *The Theology of Luther in Its Historical Development and Inner Harmony*, trans. Charles E. Hay (Philadelphia: Lutheran Publication Society, 1897), 2:270–73.

11. Gerhard Ebeling, *Luther*, trans. R. A. Wilson (Philadelphia: Fortress, 1964), 68, 172.

12. Gerhard Ebeling, "Doctrine and the Word of God," in *Word and Faith*, trans. James W. Leitch (Philadelphia: Fortress, 1963), 173–81.

13. Philip S. Watson, *Let God Be God!* (London: Epworth, 1947), 9–15.

14. Paul Althaus, *The Theology of Martin Luther*, trans. Robert C. Schultz (Philadelphia: Fortress, 1966), 3–8, 224–25.

15. Gerhard O. Forde, *Where God Meets Man* (Minneapolis: Augsburg, 1973), 120–23.

16. Robert D. Preus, *The Theology of Post-Reformation Lutheranism* (St. Louis: Concordia, 1970), 1:138–39.

17. Kurt E. Marquart, *The Church and Her Fellowship, Ministry, and Governance*, ed. Robert Preus, vol. 9 of Confessional Lutheran Dogmatics (Ft. Wayne, Ind.: International Foundation for Lutheran Confessional Research, 1990), 50–77.

18. Eugene F. A. Klug, *Church and Ministry* (St. Louis: Concordia, 1993), 123–30.

19. Robert D. Preus, *Justification and Rome* (St. Louis: Concordia Academic Press, 1997), 15–20, citing LW 54:157. Gritsch and Jenson have also called attention to the hermeneutical role of justification when they referred to it as having "metalinguistic character" that defines what "kind of talking" is properly "proclamation and word of the church" (Eric W. Gritsch and Robert W. Jenson, *Lutheranism* [Philadelphia: Fortress, 1976]).

20. Francis Pieper, *Christian Dogmatics* (St. Louis: Concordia, 1951), 2:512–16.

21. Eeva Martikainen, *Doctrina* (Helsinki: Luther-Agricola-Gesellschaft, 1992), 29–44, 45–50, 65–71, 83–88.

22. Carl S. Meyer, ed., *Luther for an Ecumenical Age* (St. Louis: Concordia, 1967).

23. Mark Edwards and George Tavard, *Luther, Reformer for the Churches* (Philadelphia: Fortress, 1983).

24. Peter Manns, Harding Meyer, Carter Lindberg, and Harry McSorley, eds., *Luther's Ecumenical Significance* (Philadelphia: Fortress, and New York: Paulist, 1984).

25. Two writings in particular have been popular with Luther scholars: Luther's remarks on Gal. 5:9 in his 1531 Galatians commentary (LW 27:35–39) and Luther's statement concerning justification in the 1537 Schmalkald Articles (SA II, 1, 1–4). Bold statements in the scholarly literature about Luther's understanding of doctrine are often based on only one or two quotes from either of these writings. Why the obsession with these two writings? Probably because they are among the best known of Luther's writings. The Galatians commentary has long been cherished as devotional literature by generations of Christians. The Schmalkald Articles became one of the confessional documents of the Lutheran Church and is especially important because of its treatment of the doctrine of justification by grace for Christ's sake through faith.

26. The primary source of Luther's writings is the Weimar Edition of Luther's Works, but references also are made to the American Edition of Luther's Works. Literature that contributes to an understanding of Luther's use of concepts such as "doctrine" or "article of faith" is also explored. Finally, secondary sources that specifically treat Luther's ecumenical contributions are evaluated.

27. See, for example, William R. Russell, *Luther's Theological Testament* (Minneapolis: Fortress, 1995). Russell's thesis is that the Schmalkald Articles was primarily Luther's last will and testament.

CHAPTER 2

1. Norman Cantor, *Inventing the Middle Ages* (New York: William Morrow, 1991), 367.

2. For example, James Kittelson complains about motif scholars who "drag Luther into the twentieth century with scarcely a bow toward the world in which he actually worked" and end up constructing "an arguably artificial or at least highly derivative version of 'a' theology that may in fact never have existed save at particular places and particular times" (Kittelson, "Luther the Theologian," in *Reformation Europe: A Guide to Research II*, ed. William S. Maltby [St. Louis: Center for Reformation Research, 1992], 3:26, 27). Heiko Oberman also warns against Luther's interpreters who, "intent on mining his riches, have been given to present him as 'relevant' and hence 'modern.' Thus they have been inclined to bypass or remove medieval 'remnants.' " For Oberman, "the Reformer can only be understood as a late medieval man" (Oberman, *Luther: Man between God and the Devil*, trans. Eileen Walliser-Schwarzbart [New Haven: Yale University Press, 1989], xv).

3. Vatican I defined *dogma* in these words: "Morever, by divine and Catholic faith are to be believed all those things which are contained in the written or handed-on word of God and which are also put forth by the Church, whether by her solemn declaration or by her ordinary and universal teaching authority, to be believed as divinely revealed" (as quoted in Karl Rahner and Karl Lehmann, *Kerygma and Dogma*, Mysterium salutis [New York: Herder & Herder, 1969], 38). The original statement is in H. Denzinger and A. Schönmetzer, eds., *Enchiridion Symbolorum definitionum et Declarationuim de rebus fidei et morum* (Freiberg: Herder, 1965), 3011. The word *dogma* apparently was used for the first time in the Vatican I sense in the 1792 polemical tract *Regulus fidei catholicae* by P. N. Chrisman, who used *dogma* to distinguish formal church doctrine from theological opinion. See Alister E. McGrath, *The Genesis of Doctrine* (Oxford: Basil Blackwell, 1990), 8–9.

4. For example, Thomas Ommen reinterprets the Vatican I notion of dogma in reaction to the critique of Gerhard Ebeling. See Ommen, *The Hermeneutic of Dogma*, AAR Dissertation 11 (Missoula: Scholars Press, 1975). Gerald O'Collins summarizes the recent infallibility debate among Roman Catholic theologians and suggests that the concept of dogma will remain valid only if limited and

reinterpreted. See O'Collins, *The Case against Dogma* (New York: Paulist, 1975). See also Rahner and Lehmann, *Kerygma and Dogma*.

5. Albert Lange, "Der Bedeutungswandel der Begriffen 'fides' und 'hairesis' und die dogmatische Wertungen der Konzilentscheidungen von Vienne und Trient," *Münchener Theologische Zeitschrift* 4 (1953): 133–46. See also Rahner, who writes: "[M]edieval theology uses in a far more fundamental sense the word 'articulus' when it wants to refer to what we today generally call 'dogma' " (Rahner and Lehmann, *Kerygma and Dogma*, 28–29).

6. Jaroslav Pelikan, *Reformation of Church and Dogma 1300–1700*, vol. 4 of *The Christian Tradition* (Chicago: University of Chicago Press, 1984), 60–61.

7. Alister McGrath has made a similar observation: "Many, on both sides of the Reformation debates of the first three decades of the sixteenth century, found themselves unable to ascertain what doctrines were officially acknowledged and recognized by the church, and which were merely the private, if publicly expressed, views of theologians" (McGrath, *Genesis of Doctrine*, 8).

8. William of Ockham, *Treatise against Pope Benedict XII*, cited in Pelikan, *Reformation of Church and Dogma*, 61.

9. In addition to using the Latin *articulus*, Luther routinely employed several German words to indicate articles of faith: *Artikel*, *Stück*, *Heubstuck*, and *Hauptartikel*. Ultimately, the context must decide whether Luther was using these words in the sense of "articles of faith."

10. "A Discussion on How Confession Should Be Made, 1520," LW 39:36 (= WA 6:163). The phrase "the twelve articles of faith" referenced the Apostles' Creed, which had long been divided into twelve articles, legend having it that each of the twelve disciples contributed an article. The creed was occasionally referred to as "the faith."

11. "The Bondage of the Will, 1525," LW 33:105 (= WA 18:663).

12. "To the Christian Nobility of the German Nation Concerning the Reform of the Christian Estate, 1520," LW 44:199 (= WA 6:456).

13. "The Babylonian Captivity of the Church, 1520," LW 36:111 (= WA 6:562–63).

14. "Against the Heavenly Prophets in the Matter of Images and Sacraments, 1525," LW 40:83–84 (= WA 18:66–67).

15. "The Freedom of a Christian, 1520," LW 31:335 (= WA 7:43–44).

16. "Concerning the Answer of the Goat in Leipzig, 1521," LW 39:130 (= WA 7:278–79).

17. On the life and writings of Thomas Müntzer (ca. 1489–1525), see Hans-Jürgen Goertz, *Thomas Müntzer* (Edinburgh: T & T Clark, 1993); Michael G. Baylor, ed. and trans., *The Radical Reformation* (Cambridge: Cambridge University Press, 1991); Peter Blickle, *Communal Reformation* (Atlantic Highlands: Humanities Press, 1992); and Tom Scott and Bob Scribner, eds., *The German Peasants' War* (Atlantic Highlands: Humanities Press, 1990). For a summary, see Carter Lindberg, *The European Reformations* (Cambridge, Mass.: Blackwell, 1996), 143–68.

18. "Letter to the Princes of Saxony Concerning the Rebellious Spirit, 1524," LW 40:57 (= WA 15:218).

19. "We start with the churchyard. It is preaching or teaching [doctrine] which is concerned only with outward works which are bound up with time and place. These matters are the ceremonies, the outward performances and techniques in matters of dress or food . . ." ("A Sermon on the Three Kinds of Good Life for the Instruction of Consciences, 1521," LW 44:235 [= WA 7:795]). Significantly, later in the sermon Luther contrasted churchyard doctrine with "sanctuary" doctrine, which was the Gospel. Of this sanctuary doctrine, Luther said, "Look! Here is really sound doctrine! . . . This is the road to heaven. No

man remains wicked; on the contrary, all become righteous" (LW 44:242 [= WA 7:801]).

20. *Exsurge Domine* was issued by Pope Leo X on June 15, 1520, and published in Germany in September 1520. This bull condemned forty-one theses taken from Luther's writings and gave him sixty days to recant or face excommunication.

21. "Defense and Explanation of All the Articles, 1521," LW 32:80 (= WA 7:429).

22. "An Order of Mass and Communion for the Church at Wittenberg, 1523," LW 53:34 (= WA 12:216).

23. Bernhard Lohse, *Martin Luther's Theology*, trans. and ed. Roy A. Harrisville (Minneapolis: Fortress, 1999), 9.

24. "Catholic controversialists" is the most common name in modern Reformation scholarship assigned to the defenders of the Catholic faith. They referred to themselves most frequently as *docti*; Luther called them *Rominstae* and *papistae*. Although the phrase is anachronistic because members of the Church of Rome were not called "Roman Catholic" until after the Council of Trent (1545–1563), the phrases "Catholic controversialists" and "Roman polemicists" are used in this book. On the controversialists, see David V. N. Bagchi, *Luther's Earliest Opponents* (Minneapolis: Fortress, 1991); P. Fraenkel, "John Eck's Enchiridion of 1525 and Luther's Earliest Arguments against Papal Primacy," *Studia theologica* 21 (1967): 110–63; P. Fraenkel, "An der Grenze vor Luthers Einfluss," *ZKG* 89 (1978): 21–30; Mark U. Edwards Jr., "Catholic Controversialist Literature, 1518–1555," *ARG* 79 (1988): 189–204; and J. M. Headley, "The Reformation as Crisis in the Understanding of Tradition," *ARG* 78 (1987): 5–22.

25. This was understood by at least some of Luther's contemporaries. Only months before the publication of the "Ninety-five Theses," Cardinal Cajetan had prepared a memorandum for Rome in which he insisted that there was a need for a clearer definition of indulgences. In May 1518, the theological faculty at the Sorbonne took issue with relating the release of a soul in purgatory with the payment of money. See Heiko Oberman, *Werden und Wertung der Reformation*, Spätscholastik und Reformation 2 (Tübingen: J. C. B. Mohr, 1979), 192 n. 90. That the two papal bulls had not decided the question of indulgences in a binding way is also recognized by modern Roman Catholic scholars. For example, Nicolaus Paulus, *Geschichte des Ablasses im Mittelalter vom Ursprunge bis zur Mitte des 14. Jahrhunderts* (Paderbon: F. Schöningh, 1923), 3:88.

26. The Dominican Tetzel, in addition to being the indulgence salesman that drew Luther's ire, held the office of inquisitor of heretical depravity for the province of Saxony. Cajetan appointed Tetzel to this position in 1509. It was in this capacity that Tetzel published against Luther. See Bagchi, *Luther's Earliest Opponents*, 22.

27. Silvestro Mazzolini, usually called Prierias (he was from Prierio), was also a Dominican. He was the master of the sacred palace, and the pope had appointed Prierias to the Roman commission tasked with introducing canonical proceedings against Luther.

28. Eck served as professor of theology in Ingolstadt from 1510 to 1543. Until Eck died, he was a vigorous opponent of Luther.

29. Konrad Wimpina, also a Dominican, was rector of the University of Frankfurt an der Oder.

30. In Thesis 105 (against Luther's Thesis 78); see CCath 41:337.

31. WA 1:243–46.

32. Valentin Gröne, *Tetzel und Luther*, 2d ed. (Soest: Nasse, 1860), 234–37, cited in Martin Brecht, *Martin Luther: His Road to Reformation, 1483–1521*, trans. James L. Schaaf (Minneapolis: Fortress, 1985), 209.

33. The 50 theses (*Subscriptas positiones*) are found in V. E. Löscher, ed., *Vollständige*

Reformations—Acta und Documenta, 3 vols. (Leipzig: J. G. Erben, 1720–1729), 1:517–22.

34. "Obelisks," along with "Asterisks," Luther's written reply to Eck, can be found in WA 1:281–314.

35. See Brecht, *Road to Reformation*, 211.

36. See Bagchi, *Luther's Earliest Opponents*, 26–35, 79–85.

37. LW 31:5–16 (= WA 1:221–28).

38. WA 1:294, 302, cited in Bagchi, *Luther's Earliest Opponents*, 32.

39. CCath 41:33–107.

40. CCath 41:54.

41. Bagchi, *Luther's Earliest Opponents*, 80, 81.

42. Bagchi, *Luther's Earliest Opponents*, 82.

43. This is exactly what Prierias had maintained in the fourth *fundamentum* of his *Dialogue*: "The Roman Church can decide on faith and custom as much by deeds as by words. And there is no difference between them save that words are more convenient for this purpose than are deeds. Custom attains the force of law. Consequently, as he is a heretic who dissents from the authority of Scripture, so also is he a heretic who dissents from the teaching and practice of the Church in respect of faith and morals." This led to the *Corollary*: "Whoever says of indulgences that the Roman Church cannot do what it has *de facto* already done is a heretic" (cited in Bagchi, *Luther's Earliest Opponents*, 28; original text in CCath 41:55–56). In other words, according to Prierias, the rule of faith included whatever practices the church had adopted through custom.

44. Bagchi, *Luther's Earliest Opponents*, 84–85.

45. "Explanations of the Ninety-five Theses, 1518," LW 31:83 (= WA 1:529–30).

46. "Explanations," LW 31:94 (= WA 1:536–37).

47. "Letter to Elector Frederick, January 13?, 1519," LW 48:105 (= WABr 1:307).

48. "Explanations," LW 31:83 (= WA 1:530).

49. One scholar has argued that these four men frequently misrepresented Thomas Aquinas in this controversy. See D. R. Janz, *Luther on Thomas Aquinas*, Veröffentlichungen des Instituts für europaïsche Geschichte Mainz 140 (Stuttgart: Franz Steiner, 1989), 32–45.

50. Antoninus (1389–1459), archbishop of Florence and a Dominican scholar, wrote *Summary of Moral Theology*; Peter de Palude (1275?–1342), a teacher in Paris, wrote a commentary on Peter Lombard's *Sentences*; Augustine of Ancona (d. 1328), an Augustinian Eremite, wrote *Summary of the Power of the Church*; and John Capreolus (d. 1444), a Dominican scholar, was considered one of the greatest students of Thomas Aquinas in the fifteenth century.

51. "Explanations," LW 31:146, 147 (= WA 1:568).

52. In 1483, on pain of excommunication, Pope Sixtus IV forbade the Dominicans (who rejected it) and the Franciscans (who affirmed it) from accusing each other of heresy over the question of the immaculate conception of Mary because "it has not yet been decided by the Roman Church or the apostolic see." See Carl Mirbt, *Quellen zur Geschichte des Papsttums und des römischen Katholizismus*, 4th ed. (Tübingen: J. C. B. Mohr, 1924), 243. The immaculate conception was proclaimed dogma by Pope Pius IX in 1854.

53. "Explanations," LW 31:172 (= WA 1:582–83).

54. "Explanations," LW 31:172 (= WA 1:582–83).

55. "Explanations," LW 31:108 (= WA 1:545). Luther is commenting on Thesis 8: "The penitential canons are imposed only on the living, and according to the

canons themselves, nothing should be imposed on the dying" ("Ninety-five Theses, 1517," LW 31:26).

56. Thomas de Vio (1469–1534) was from Gaeta, thus he was called Cajetan. He was probably the most famous theologian of his day. As a Dominican, he had studied Aquinas intensively, even writing a commentary on Aquinas's *Summa Theologiae* that was still in use in the twentieth century. Cajetan, a longtime supporter of papal infallibility, became cardinal of S. Sisto in 1517.

57. This was Luther's second summons and was dated August 23. Luther had received the first summons on August 7. The second summons accused Luther not only of heresy but also of heresy that was notorious and public. See Brecht, *Road to Reformation*, 247–48.

58. On Luther's hearing before Cajetan, see Jared Wicks, "Thomism between Renaissance and Reformation," *ARG* 68 (1977): 9–32; Bernhard Lohse, "Cajetan und Luther," in *Evangelium in der Geschichte* (Göttingen: Vandenhoeck & Ruprecht, 1988), 44–63; and Brecht, *Road to Reformation*, 246–65.

59. The *Extravagantes Communes* was a section of canon law comprised of papal decrees made between 1261 and 1471.

60. "Proceedings at Augsburg, 1518," LW 31:261–62 (= WA 2:7).

61. "Proceedings at Augsburg," LW 31:262 (= WA 2:8).

62. "Proceedings at Augsburg," LW 31:266–67 (= WA 2:10–11).

63. "Proceedings at Augsburg," LW 31:282 (= WA 2:21) (*author's emphasis*).

64. Jacobus Latomus (ca. 1475–1544), professor at the University of Louvain in Belgium, was another Catholic controversialist that engaged Luther. The University of Louvain had condemned Luther's writings in 1519. In March 1520, Luther published this condemnation along with a biting response (WA 6:181–95). Latomus then published a defense of the original condemnation in May 1521. It was to this document that Luther was responding in "Against Latomus, 1521," LW 32:135–260 (= WA 8:43–128).

65. "Against Latomus," LW 32:154 (= WA 8:54).

66. "Against Latomus," LW 32:230 (= WA 8:108).

67. "Defense and Explanation," LW 32:11–12 (= WA 7:317).

68. This bull threatened Luther with excommunication in sixty days unless he recanted. The actual bull of excommunication, *Decet Romanum Pontificem*, was issued on January 3, 1521, and was executed on January 28. "Defense and Explanation" was actually the last of four treatises that Luther wrote in response to *Exsurge Domine*: "Adversus execrabilem Antichrisi bullam, November 1520"; "Wider die Bulle des Endchrists, November 1520"; "Assertio omnium articulorum M. Lutheri per bullam Leonis X. novissium damnatorum, December 1520"; and "Grund und Ursach aller Artikel D. Martin Luthers so durch römische Bulle unrechtlich verdammt sind, March 1521." For a summary of Luther's excommunication, see Brecht, *Road to Reformation*, 389–432.

69. "Defense and Explanation," LW 32:81 (= WA 7:429–30).

70. "The Gospel for the Sunday after Christmas, Luke 2," LW 52:146 (= WA 10/1:446).

71. "Defense and Explanation," LW 32:96 (= WA 7:453).

72. Germane to the discussion is Luther's concluding advice on purgatory: "My advice is that no one allow the pope to invent new articles of faith, but be willing to remain in ignorance, with St. Augustine, about what the souls in purgatory are doing and what their condition is. . . . But if you wish to discuss this question then you must leave room for surmise and differences of opinion, as I do. Do not make your own ideas into articles of faith as that abomination at Rome does.

For then your faith may become a nightmare. Hold to Scripture and the Word of God. There you will find truth and security—assurance and a faith that is complete, pure, sufficient, and abiding" ("Defense and Explanation," LW 32:98 [= WA 7:455]).

73. "Answer to the HyperChristian, Hyperspiritual, and Hyperlearned Book by Goat Emser in Leipzig—Including Some Thoughts Regarding His Companion, the Fool Murner, 1521," LW 39:205 (= WA 7:673).

74. "Defense and Explanation," LW 32:11 (= WA 7:315). The Augustine quote is from "Letter 82 (to St. Jerome)," *MPL* 33.286–87.

75. "Answer to the HyperChristian, Hyperspiritual, and Hyperlearned Book," LW 39:165 (= WA 7:640).

76. "Avoiding the Doctrines of Men *and* A Reply to the Texts Cited in Defense of the Doctrines of Men, 1522," LW 35:142 (= WA 10/2:82).

77. Between 1519 and 1521, Hieronymus Emser (1478–1527) became one of Luther's most bitter Catholic controversialist opponents. Luther wrote four treatises against him alone. Like Luther, Emser had studied at the University of Erfurt, where he also lectured on humanism. Before 1510, Emser was in Leipzig as court chaplain and secretary to Duke George of Ducal Saxony. Emser received a degree in theology from the University of Leipzig. For background on Emser's literary battle with Luther in 1521, see Ernst Ludwig Enders, ed., *Luther und Emser*, 2 vols. (Halle: Niemeyer, 1890–1892).

78. "Dr. Luther's Retraction of the Error Forced upon Him by the Most Highly Learned Priest of God, Sir Jerome Emser, Vicar in Meissen, 1521," LW 39:230 (= WA 8:248).

79. Augustine Alveld (b. 1480) was a monk in Leipzig. In May 1520, he published a Latin work entitled "Concerning the Apostolic See, Whether It Is a Divine Law or Not." By the end of May, he published a German revision entitled "A Very Fruitful and Useful Little Book." Of all the controversialists who wrote against Luther to defend the divine right of the papacy (Bagchi lists nine), Luther responded only to Alveld. Undoubtedly, this was because Alveld wrote in German, and Luther was concerned that such teaching would harm the people. See Bagchi, *Luther's Earliest Opponents*, 45–53. On Alveld's life and writings, see Kurt Galling, ed., *Die Religion in Geschichte und Gegenwart*, 3d. ed., 7 vols. (Tübingen: J. C. B. Mohr, 1957–1965), 1:301.

80. "On the Papacy in Rome, against the Most Celebrated Romanist in Leipzig, 1520," LW 39:101–2 (= WA 6:322).

81. "Defense and Explanation," LW 32:80–81 (= WA 7:429). Luther was referring to Article 29.

82. See Rahner and Lehmann, *Kerygma and Dogma*, 35.

83. "Babylonian Captivity of the Church," LW 36:28 (= WA 6:508). Luther held this position for practical reasons, which he explained later in the same treatise in a discussion about ordination: "For who knows which is the church that has the Spirit? For when such decisions are made there are usually only a few bishops or scholars present; and it is possible that these may not be really of the church. All may err, as councils have repeatedly erred, particularly the Council of Constance, which erred most wickedly of all. Only that which has the approval of the church universal, and not of the Roman church alone, rests on a trustworthy foundation" (LW 36:108 [= WA 6:561]). Because councils could err and had often done so, they could not be trusted, though Luther suggested that something decided by a truly ecumenical council (made up of members beyond the Roman Church) could define doctrine.

84. "Answer to the HyperChristian, Hyperspiritual, and Hyperlearned Book," LW 39:157 (= WA 7:633). This same idea was echoed in Luther's 1523 "Concerning

the Ministry": "For such an assertion has no support in the Word of God and is based only on human opinions, on ancient usage, or on the opinions of the majority, any one of which is ineffectual to establish an article of faith without sacrilege and offense, as I have sufficiently shown elsewhere" (LW 40:19 [= WA 12:178]).

85. "Lectures on Joel," LW 18:108.

86. For a helpful summary of the individual proponents and their arguments, see Bagchi, *Luther's Earliest Opponents*, 163–68.

87. The literature on Luther's understanding of Scripture's clarity is vast. See Rul-doph Hermann, *Von der Klarheit der Heiligen Schrift* (Berlin: Evangelische Ver-lagsanstalt, 1958); Friedrich Beisser, *Claritas scripturae bei Martin Luther* (Göttingen: Vandenhoeck & Ruprecht, 1966); and Bernhard Rothen, *Die Klarheit der Schrift*, 2 vols. (Göttingen: Vandenhoeck & Ruprecht, 1990–1992).

88. Responding to Hieronymus Emser's argument in "Answer to the HyperChrist-ian, Hyperspiritual, and Hyperlearned Book," LW 39:164 (= WA 7:638–39).

89. "Against Latomus," LW 32:217 (= WA 8:99).

90. On Luther's "De servo arbitrio," see Harry McSorley, *Luther: Right or Wrong?* (New York: Newman, and Minneapolis: Augsburg, 1969).

91. Desiderius Erasmus (ca. 1469–1536) was known as the prince of the humanists. On Erasmus's life and work, see Roland H. Bainton, *Erasmus of Christendom* (New York: Scribner's, 1969); Robert Stupperich, *Erasmus von Rotterdam und seine Welt*, De Gruyter Studienbuch (Berlin: De Gruyter, 1977); and Ernst Wil-helm Kohls, *Die Theologie des Erasmus*, 2 vols. (Basel: Friedrich Reinhardt, 1966).

92. "Bondage of the Will," LW 33:25 (= WA 18:606–7). Luther made the same point in "To the Councilmen of All Cities of Germany That They Establish and Maintain Christian Schools, 1524": "For even the holy fathers (as we have said) frequently erred. And because of their ignorance of the languages they seldom agree; one says this, another that. . . . This is also why the sophists have con-tended that Scripture is obscure; they have held that God's word by its very nature is obscure and employs a peculiar style of speech. But they fail to realize that the whole trouble lies in the languages. If we understood the languages nothing clearer would ever have been spoken than God's word" (LW 45:363–64 [= WA 15:40–41]).

93. "Bondage of the Will," LW 33:25 (= WA 18:606–7).

94. "Bondage of the Will," LW 33:25–26 (= WA 18:606–7).

95. "Bondage of the Will," LW 33:28 (= WA 18:609).

96. E. Gordon Rupp and Philip S. Watson, eds. and trans., *Luther and Erasmus*, Library of Christian Classics 17 (Philadelphia: Westminister, 1969), 44–46.

97. "Bondage of the Will," LW 33:90–91 (= WA 18:652).

98. "Nor do I approve of those who have recourse to boasting of the Spirit; for I have had this year and am still having, a sharp enough fight with those fanatics who subject the Scriptures to the interpretation of their own spirit" ("Bondage of the Will," LW 33:90 [= WA 18:652]).

99. "Babylonian Captivity of the Church," LW 36:107 (= WA 6:560–61).

100. John 14:26: "But the Counselor, the Holy Spirit, whom the Father will send in my name, will teach you all things and will remind you of everything I have said to you." John 21:25: "Jesus did many other things as well. If every one of them were written down, I suppose that even the whole world would not have room for the books that would be written."

101. "Answer to the HyperChristian, Hyperspiritual, and Hyperlearned Book," LW 39:170 (= WA 7:644).

102. *Contra epistulam Manichaei, MPL* 42:176.6.

103. "Avoiding the Doctrines of Men," LW 35:150 (= WA 10/2:89).

104. "Avoiding the Doctrines of Men," LW 35:150 (= WA 10/2:89). For example, *Contra Faustum Manichaeum*, xi.5, *MPL* 42:248–49.

105. "Avoiding the Doctrines of Men," LW 35:152 (= WA 10/2:91).

106. "Avoiding the Doctrines of Men," LW 35:152–53 (= WA 10/2:91).

107. Behind this assertion, of course, was the assumption that some passages of Scripture were not clear, something Luther freely acknowledged.

108. "Against Latomus," LW 32:199 (= WA 8:86).

109. "Against Latomus," LW 32:167 (= WA 8:63)

110. "Babylonian Captivity of the Church," LW 36:107 (= WA 6:560).

111. "Bondage of the Will," LW 33:95 (= WA 18:656).

112. Luther stressed the same point in "The Gospel for Christmas Eve, Luke 2" as he discussed Luke 2:1–14 and the birth of Christ: "Although this statement is assuredly based on several passages of Scripture, yet nowhere is it set forth as clearly and abundantly as here. . . . This article possesses much importance and we must never permit it to be taken away in time of tribulation; the evil spirit does not attack anything so violently as our faith. For this reason we must be prepared and know where in Holy Scripture this faith is set forth, so that we can point whatever attacks our faith to these places" (LW 52:30, 31 [= WA 10/1:93, 95]).

113. "Defense and Explanation," LW 32:67–68 (= WA 7:409). Luther was commenting on Article 25.

114. "That there is a purgatory cannot be proved by those Scriptures which are in the canon, which are authentic and trustworthy" ("Disputation of Johann Eck and Martin Luther," WA 2:324). See also Lohse, *Martin Luther's Theology*, 124–25.

115. "Defense and Explanation," LW 32:96 (= WA 7:453).

116. "The Judgment of Martin Luther on Monastic Vows, 1521," LW 44:317 (= WA 8:617).

117. On Karlstadt, see Hermann Barge, *Andreas Bodenstein von Karlstadt*, 2 vols. (1905; repr., Nieuwkoop: De Graaf, 1968); Ronald J. Sider, *Andreas Bodenstein von Karlstadt* (Leiden: Brill, 1974); Mark U. Edwards Jr., *Luther and the False Brethren* (Stanford: Stanford University Press, 1975); James S. Preus, *Carlstadt's "Ordinaciones" and Luther's Liberty*, Harvard Theological Studies 26 (Cambridge: Harvard University Press, 1974); Ronald J. Sider, *Karlstadt's Battle with Luther* (Philadelphia: Fortress, 1978); Calvin Pater, *Karlstadt as the Father of the Baptist Movements* (Toronto: University of Toronto Press, 1984); Ulrich Bubenheimer, *Consonantia Theologia et Jurisprudentiae* (Tübingen: J. C. B. Mohr, 1977); and Hans J. Hillerbrand, "Andreas Bodenstein of Carlstadt, Prodigal Reformer," *Church History* 35 (1966).

118. "Against the Heavenly Prophets," LW 40:79–223 (= WA 18:62–125, 134–214).

119. "Eight Sermons at Wittenberg, 1522," LW 51:70ff. (= WA 10/3:1–64). For more on these sermons, see Neil R. Leroux, *Luther's Rhetoric: Strategies and Style from the Invocavit Sermons* (St. Louis: Concordia Academic Press, 2002).

120. On this and on what follows, see the helpful chapter "Luther and the Spiritualists" in Carter Lindberg, *The Third Reformation* (Macon, Ga.: Mercer University Press, 1983), 55–130.

121. "Against the Heavenly Prophets," LW 40:131–32 (= WA 18:114).

122. "Against the Heavenly Prophets," LW 40:134–35 (= WA 18:116–17).

123. "And observe carefully please that he has the courage to call the Law of Moses

human doctrines, even though it was delivered through angels" ("Lectures on Galatians," LW 27:180). Luther was commenting on Gal. 1:10.

124. "Against the Heavenly Prophets," LW 40:92 (= WA 18:75–76).

125. "How Christians Should Regard Moses, 1525," LW 35:172–73 (= WA 16:390).

126. "How Christians Should Regard Moses," LW 35:172 (= WA 16:390).

127. "How Christians Should Regard Moses," LW 35:170 (= WA 16:384).

128. "How Christians Should Regard Moses," LW 35:170 (= WA 16:385).

129. "Proceedings at Augsburg," LW 31:276 (= WA 2:17).

130. Luther's remark about the second wall the Romanists had built to protect themselves from criticism is representative: "Therefore, their claim that only the pope may interpret Scripture is an outrageous fancied fable. They cannot produce a single letter [of Scripture] to maintain that the interpretation of Scripture or confirmation of its interpretation belongs to the pope alone. They themselves have usurped this power" ("To the Christian Nobility," LW 44:134 [= WA 6:411]).

131. "Answer to the HyperChristian, Hyperspiritual, and Hyperlearned Book," LW 39:164–65 (= WA 7:639).

132. "Sermons on the Second Epistle of St. Peter," LW 30:166 (= WA 14:31).

133. "Sermons on the Second Epistle of St. Peter," LW 30:167 (= WA 14:32).

134. See, for example, Oberman, *Luther: Man between God and the Devil*, 250–53.

135. Commenting on Gal. 4:24 in "Lectures on Galatians," LW 27:311.

136. Commenting on Gal. 4:24 in "Lectures on Galatians," LW 27:311.

137. "Against the Heavenly Prophets," LW 40:190 (= WA 18:180).

138. "Babylonian Captivity of the Church," LW 36:30 (= WA 6:509). Luther had written to Hieronymus Emser: "That is why Origen received his due reward a long time ago when his books were prohibited, for he relied too much on this spiritual meaning, which was unnecessary, and he let the necessary literal meaning go. When that happens Scripture perishes and really good theologians are no longer produced. Only the true principal meaning which is provided by the letters can produce good theologians" ("Answer to the HyperChristian, Hyperspiritual, and Hyperlearned Book," LW 39:178 [= WA 7:650]).

139. "Against Latomus," LW 32:167 (= WA 8:63).

140. "Lectures on Deuteronomy," LW 9:24, 25 (= WA 14:560, 561).

141. "Against the Heavenly Prophets," LW 40:153 (= WA 18:143).

142. "The Gospel for the Main Christmas Service, John 2," LW 52:49 (= WA 10/1:191): "[N]atural reason creates heresy and error, while faith teaches the truth and clings to it; for it clings to Scripture, which neither deceives nor lies."

143. "Lectures on Hebrews," LW 29:119 (= WA 57/3:109).

144. "On the Papacy in Rome," LW 39:67 (= WA 6:294).

145. "Answer to the HyperChristian, Hyperspiritual, and Hyperlearned Book," LW 39:171 (= WA 7:644).

146. "Letter to the Christians at Strassburg in Opposition to the Fanatic Spirit, 1524," LW 40:67–68 (= WA 15:394).

147. "Babylonian Captivity of the Church," LW 36:111 (= WA 6:562–63).

148. "Defense and Explanation," LW 32:79–80 (= WA 7:429).

149. See *The Ecumenical Luther*, chapter 2 n. 52.

150. See Robert D. Preus, *The Theology of Post-Reformation Lutheranism*, vol. 1, *A Study of Theological Prolegomena* (St. Louis: Concordia, 1970), 143–54.

151. "Even among the articles of faith, not all were of equal importance with the fundamental doctrines of the Trinity and the person of Christ" (Pelikan, *Reformation of Church and Dogma*, 61).

152. "Against the Heavenly Prophets," LW 40:207 (= WA 18:197).

153. "The Abomination of the Secret Mass, 1525," LW 36:313 (= WA 18:23–24).

154. "Defense and Explanation," LW 32:19 (= WA 7:329).

155. Commenting on 1 Pet. 4:1–3 in "Sermons on the First Epistle of St. Peter," LW 30:117 (= WA 12:372). Similar to this is an earlier statement in "A Brief Instruction on What to Look for and Expect in the Gospels, 1521": "The chief article and foundation of the gospel is that before you take Christ as an example, you accept and recognize him as a gift, as a present that God has given you and that is your own. . . . See, when you lay hold of Christ as a gift which is given you for your very own and have no doubt about it, you are a Christian. Faith redeems you from sin, death, and hell and enables you to overcome all things" (LW 35:119, 120 [= WA 10/1:11, 12]).

156. "Preface to the Epistle of St. Paul to the Romans, 1522," LW 35:370.

157. "Judgment of Martin Luther on Monastic Vows," LW 44:286 (= WA 8:599).

158. "Judgment of Martin Luther on Monastic Vows," LW 44:289 (= WA 8:600).

159. "Judgment of Martin Luther on Monastic Vows," LW 44:287 (= WA 8:599).

160. Paragraph 18 of the 1997 *Joint Declaration on the Doctrine of Justification* (JDDJ) comes close to noting this emphasis but falls short. It refers to justification as "an indispensable criterion which constantly serves to orient all the teaching and practice of our churches to Christ." However, it is important to note some textual history behind this paragraph. In 1996, the German contingent of the Lutheran World Federation had proposed that justification be recognized "as criterion" that "constantly serves to orient all the teaching and practice of our churches to Christ." After much discussion, this change was officially adopted into paragraph 18 of the June 1996 version of JDDJ. Soon afterward, however, this wording was vetoed by the Roman Sacred Congregation for Doctrine of the Faith. The Pontifical Council for Promoting Christian Unity was told that it could only concede that the doctrine of justification was "an" indispensable criterion. With the addition of *an*, the article of justification became merely one criterion among several, thus it was acceptable to the Roman Catholic definition of doctrine. See Eberhard Jüngel, "Um Gottes willen—Klarheit!" *Zeitschrift für Theologie und Kirche* 94 (1997): 394–406.

161. "Judgment of Martin Luther on Monastic Vows," LW 44:289 (= WA 8:600).

162. "Lectures on Galatians," LW 27:179.

163. "Luther to the Christians of Riga, Reval and Dorpat, August 1523," in Preserved Smith and Charles M. Jacobs, eds. and trans., *Luther's Correspondence and Other Contemporary Letters* (Philadelphia: Lutheran Publication Society, 1918), 2:200–201. Cf. WA 12:149.

164. "Against the Heavenly Prophets," LW 40:82.

165. "Against the Heavenly Prophets," LW 40:82.

166. Rupp and Watson, *Luther and Erasmus*, 1.

167. Already in the 1518 Heidelberg Disputation, Luther had made his position on free will unequivocal in Theses 13–18. In Thesis 13, Luther stated that "[f]ree will, after the fall, exists in name only, and as long as it does what it is able to do, it commits a mortal sin" (LW 31:40, 48–52).

168. Rupp and Watson, *Luther and Erasmus*, 39. In a letter that he had written to Zwingli eighteen months earlier, Erasmus revealed more clearly how far removed he was from Luther's theology, referring to the teaching of justification

by faith alone as an absurd riddle: "Luther proposes some riddles that are absurd on the face of them: all the works of the saints are sins, which are forgiven by the undeserved mercy of God; free will is an empty name; a man is justified by faith alone, and works have nothing to do with it. I do not see that it does any good to dispute about the way Luther wishes these things to be understood. . . . [F]or I think I have taught almost everything that Luther teaches, only I have not done it so fiercely and have abstained from certain riddles and paradoxes" ("Erasmus to Zwingli, August 31, 1523," in Smith and Jacobs, *Luther's Correspondence*, 196–97, 198).

169. "Bondage of the Will," LW 33:35 (= WA 18:613).

170. McSorley takes up the question of whether Erasmus was a semi-Pelagianist and how he differed from the mainstream Catholic view. See McSorely, *Luther: Right or Wrong?* 288ff.

171. "Bondage of the Will," LW 33:266–67, 268–69 (= WA 18:769, 770).

172. This a reference to the scholastic phrase *facere quod in se est* ("do what is in you"), which was used by Thomas Aquinas and others. According to Carter Lindberg, the concept originated with Aristotle's idea of *habitus* (by being good, one becomes good) and was adapted by medieval theologians, such as Aquinas. Aquinas stated that grace does not do away with nature but completes it. Thus the phrase "do what is in you" meant that salvation is a process inside us as we strive to perfect ourselves. We become righteous as we do righteous works. See Lindberg, *European Reformations*, 60–63, 68–69. Luther clearly condemned this Aristotelian notion: "But in particular it is the Parisian school that is condemned in this connection, that impure and foul whore which has declared that Aristotle's teachings on morals are not in conflict with the teachings of Christ, since he teaches nothing other than that virtue is acquired by works, saying, 'By doing good we become good.' The Christian conscience curses this statement as bilge water of hell and says, 'By believing in a Christ who is good, I, even I, am made good: his goodness is mine also, for it is a gift from him and is not my work' " ("Judgment of Martin Luther on Monastic Vows," LW 44:300 [= WA 8:607–8]).

173. Lindberg, *European Reformations*, 70.

174. "Bondage of the Will," LW 33:42, 43 (= WA 18:618).

175. "Judgment of Martin Luther on Monastic Vows," LW 44:296 (= WA 8:606).

176. "Against the Heavenly Prophets," LW 40:134 (= WA 18:116).

177. "Judgment of Martin Luther on Monastic Vows," LW 44:298 (= WA 8:606).

178. "Judgment of Martin Luther on Monastic Vows," LW 44:299 (= WA 8:607): "It is this knowledge of freedom and this health of conscience that is assailed by every device of human and ungodly doctrines."

179. "Lectures on Hosea," LW 18:35: "Wicked doctrines destroy both in conscience and in substance."

180. "Against the Heavenly Prophets," LW 40:122 (= WA 18:105).

181. "Avoiding the Doctrines of Men," LW 35:141 (= WA 10/2:81).

182. "Avoiding the Doctrines of Men," LW 35:153 (= WA 10/2:91).

183. "Judgment of Martin Luther on Monastic Vows," LW 44:300 (= WA 8:607).

184. "Against the Heavenly Prophets," LW 40:90–91 (= WA 18:73).

185. "Against the Heavenly Prophets," LW 40:131, 137–38 (= WA 18:114, 120).

186. "Order of Mass and Communion," LW 53:31 (= WA 12:214).

187. Luther still held the same position in 1525: "In the first place, I would kindly and for God's sake request all those who see this order of service or desire to follow it: Do not make it a rigid law to bind or entangle anyone's conscience, but use it in Christian liberty as long, when, where, and how you find it to be practi-

cal and useful" ("The German Mass and Order of Service, 1525," LW 53:61)
[= WA 19:72]).

188. "German Mass," LW 53:62 (= WA 19:73). Was the liturgy of the Mass a source
of doctrine for Luther? Certainly he considered the liturgy of the Mass an
important medium of doctrine. For example, in the 1525 "German Mass,"
Luther declared that the "first" thing that any good German service should
include is catechesis. Although it certainly influenced doctrinal development,
Luther did not consider the ancient liturgy to be a source of doctrine—only
Scripture could fulfill that role. During the years 1518 to 1525, Luther does not
appear ever to have referred to *lex orandi, lex credendi* or the concept behind it.
Whereas Luther considered the Lord's Supper to be a necessary doctrine, a particular liturgy of the Lord's Supper was not necessary doctrine. In *The Ecumenical Luther*, chapter 4, Luther's key eucharistic texts related to the Marburg
Colloquy are addressed, as well as the colloquy itself. In all these treatises
(including the 1523 "Order of Mass and Communion" and the 1525 "German
Mass"), Luther does not insist on any particular liturgy as necessary. In fact, he
insists on freedom in "external forms." The only exception to this freedom is if
the liturgy contradicts the Gospel, Scripture, and the Words of Institution (that
is, the bodily presence). The claim cannot be made that Luther was completely
consistent in this regard. For example, though Zwingli had radically altered the
eucharistic liturgy in Zurich to correspond to his figurative/memorial view of
the Lord's Supper, Luther never addressed this liturgical change at Marburg nor
did he take it up in any of his key eucharistic treatises prior to Marburg. Yet in
the 1525 "Abomination of the Secret Mass," Luther rejected the Roman Canon
of the Mass in a sort of running commentary that critiqued it point by point,
and he rejected it precisely because the Canon of the Mass contradicted his two
canons. Why did Luther critique the one eucharistic liturgy but not the other?
Perhaps the answer is that by so clearly rejecting Zwingli's eucharistic theology,
Luther considered it self-evident that Zurich's eucharistic liturgy was also to be
rejected.

189. See *The Ecumenical Luther*, pp. 33–37.

190. An example of this is Luther's comments to the Livonians. See *The Ecumenical
Luther*, p. 51–52.

191. "At this point I would like to have it understood that I do not propose this article because I wish to repudiate the pope. Let him have as much power as he will,
it makes no difference to me, and he is welcome to it. But there are two things I
can neither tolerate nor keep silent about. First, he and his supporters torture,
violate, and blaspheme the holy Word of God in order to establish their power.
Second, they revile, slander, and anathematize the Greeks, and all others who do
not submit to the pope, as though these were not Christians. They act as if
being a Christian meant being bound to the pope and to Rome, while St. Paul
and Christ have bound it only to faith and to God's Word . . ." ("Defense and
Explanation," LW 32:68). In other words, Luther objected to the doctrine of the
divine origin of the papacy because it was not based on the right Scripture
rightly interpreted (scriptural canon) and because the proponents of this doctrine made it necessary for salvation (Luther's evangelical canon).

192. "Letter to the Christians at Strassburg," LW 40:67–68 (= WA 15:394).

193. Two examples will suffice. In his "Sermon for the First Sunday in Advent,"
Luther wrote: "Therefore the church is a mouth-house, not a pen-house, for
since Christ's advent that Gospel is preached orally which before was hidden in
written books. It is the way of the Gospel and of the New Testament that it is to
be preached and discussed orally with a living voice. Christ himself wrote nothing, nor did he give command to write, but to preach orally" (John Nicholas
Lenker, ed., *Sermons of Martin Luther*, trans. John Nicholas Lenker et al [repr.,
Grand Rapids: Baker, 1983], 1:44). Similar to this was the reformer's strong

statement in his lectures on Malachi: "The Word is the channel through which the Holy Spirit is given. This is a passage against those who hold the spoken Word in contempt. The lips are the public reservoirs of the church. In them alone is kept the Word of God. You see, unless the Word is preached publicly, it slips away. The more it is preached, the more firmly it is retained. Reading it is not as profitable as hearing it, for the live voice teaches, exhorts, defends, and resists the spirit of error. Satan does not care a hoot for the written Word of God, but He flees at the speaking of the Word. You see, this penetrates hearts and leads back those who stray" ("Lectures on Malachi," LW 18:401). Not placing a passage such as this in the context of everything that Luther said about the Scriptures (see examples throughout *The Ecumenical Luther*, chapter 2) could lead to a distorted understanding of Luther's doctrine of the Word.

CHAPTER 3

1. Held from November 28 to December 4, the meeting was the sequel to three previous consultations held in Prague in 1986, 1987, and 1989 (Prague I, II, and III) that brought together representatives of the churches related to the first and to the radical reformations. The churches represented in these meetings were the Church of the Brethren, Czechoslovak Hussite Church, Evangelical Church of Czech Brethren, Hutterian Brethren, Mennonites, Society of Friends, and Waldensians. The objective of these meetings was to explore the traditions of these churches and their potential for contemporary ecumenical dialogue. The Consultation in Geneva was different. It was organized by the World Alliance of Reformed Churches in cooperation with the Lutheran World Federation and the Mennonite World Conference. Reformed and Lutheran World Federation theologians were invited to join this discussion.

2. The term "first reformation" was coined by Czech Brethren scholars as a name for what they considered to be reforming movements within late medieval Catholicism from the twelfth through the sixteenth centuries. The leading bodies to come from these movements were the Waldensians, Unity of Brethren, and other Hussite bodies. The impetus to coin this phrase seems to have been the felt need that these bodies were significant in their own right, not merely "forerunners." Cf. Amedeo Molnár, "The First Reformation," *Moravian Theological Seminary Bulletin* (1972–1977): 103–7; and the discussion in Jarold Knox Zeman, *The Anabaptists and the Czech Brethren in Moravia 1526–1628*, Studies in European History 20 (The Hague: Mouton, 1969), 41–45. Also see Carter Lindberg, "A Specific Contribution of the Second Reformation," in *Towards a Renewed Dialogue*, ed. Milan Opocensky, Studies from the World Alliance of Reformed Churches 30 (Geneva: World Alliance of Reformed Churches, 1996), 39–62, who argues that Luther's reformation was theologically discontinuous with the late medieval Catholic renewal movements.

3. See, for example, Jaroslav Pelikan, "Luther and the Confessio Bohemica of 1535," (Ph.D. thesis, University of Chicago, n.d.); Jaroslav Pelikan, "Luther's Negotiations with the Hussites," *Concordia Theological Monthly* 20 (July 1949): 496–517; Jaroslav Pelikan, "Luther's Endorsement of the Confessio Bohemica," *Concordia Theological Monthly* 20 (November 1949): 829–43; and Jaroslav Pelikan, *Obedient Rebels* (New York: Harper & Row, 1964), 105–46.

4. "The Adoration of the Sacrament, 1523," LW 36:275–305 (= WA 11:431–56).

5. For an excellent discussion of the definitive research done on the *Unitas Fratrum*, see Zeman, *Anabaptists and the Czech Brethren*, 22–26. The *Bohemica* bibliography (pp. 370–85) in Zeman's work is first-rate. The three definitive works on the history of the Brethren are Anton Gindely, *Geschichte der Böhmischen Brüder*, 2d ed., 2 vols. (Prague: Bellmann, 1861–1862); Joseph Th. Müller, *Geschichte der Böhmischen Brüder*, 3 vols. (Herrnhut: Missionsbuchhandlung,

1922–1931); and Rudolf Rícan, *The History of the Unity of Brethren*, trans. C. Daniel Crews (Bethlehem, Penn.: Moravian Church in America, 1992).

6. Unity of Brethren, *Unitas Fratrum*, Brethren, and Bohemian Brethren are used interchangeably throughout this book to refer to the same group.

7. Jan Hus (ca. 1372–1415) was a Czech reformer and central figure in the early Bohemian Reformation. The definitive biography is Matthew Spinka, *John Hus* (Princeton: Princeton University Press, 1968). For a concise discussion of the renewal movements that proceeded from Hus, see Rícan, *History of the Unity of Brethren*, 5–11.

8. This name came from their practice of administering Communion *sub utraque specie* ("under both kinds") to the laity.

9. See Murray L. Wagner, *Petr Chelcicky*, Studies in Anabaptist and Mennonite History 25 (Scottdale, Penn.: Herald Press, 1983), for a thorough treatment of Chelcicky.

10. Members of the Brethren believed that at the moment of reception of the eucharistic elements they "blindly through faith eat the true body of Lord Jesus," which "hung on the cross and is joined to his divinity" (*Acts of the Synods and Inner Council of the Jednota Bratrská*, I.66, as cited in Rícan, *History of the Unity of Brethren*, 31).

11. Cf. Heiko A. Oberman, *The Harvest of Medieval Theology* (Cambridge: Harvard University Press, 1963), 221, where he refers to the *Unitas Fratrum* as "part of a larger pan-European Donatist upsurge."

12. Cf. Milos Strupl, "Confessional Theology of the Unitas Fratrum," *Church History* 33 (September 1964): 291–93. Strupl was following Ferdinand Hresjsa, "Nábozensky svéráz Jednoty bratrské," *Zásady Jednoty ceskych bratrí* (Prague: n.p., 1939), 7–109.

13. Amédeo Molnár, "The Brethren's Theology," in Rudolf Rícan, *The History of the Unity of Brethren*, trans. C. Daniel Crews (Bethlehem, Penn.: Moravian Church in America, 1992), 392.

14. Strupl, "Confessional Theology of the Unitas Fratrum," 283.

15. For a fuller discussion, see Molnár, "Brethren's Theology," 390–420. For a more concise description, see Strupl, "Confessional Theology of the Unitas Fratrum," 283–86. Lukas, like the Unity of Brethren in general, presented his theology according to the trinitarian structure of the Apostles' Creed.

16. Cf. Molnár, "Brethren's Theology," 403, 405.

17. Strupl, "Confessional Theology of the Unitas Fratrum," 284.

18. Interestingly, Lukas defended and used the traditional pericopal system of Gospel and Epistle texts, though some of the Brethren objected.

19. E. Peschke, *Theologie der Bömischen Brüder in ihrer Frühzeit* (Stuttgart: Kohlhammer, 1935), who has a good discussion of the place of the Lord's Supper in Czech thought during the fifteenth and sixteenth centuries.

20. Pelikan, *Obedient Rebels*, 128.

21. See especially S. Harrison Thomson, "Luther and Bohemia," *ARG* 44 (1953): 164–73. See also Pelikan, *Obedient Rebels*, 125–27.

22. See, for example, Thomson, "Luther and Bohemia," 164–65; Müller, *Geschichte der Böhmischen Brüder*, 1:369; and F. Bartos, "Das Auftreten Luthers und die Unität der bömischen Brüder," *ARG* 31 (1934): 103–20. Lukas's *Apologia* was published in Nürnberg and caused something of a sensation. Emperor Maximilian I heard of it and requested a copy. Two written replies offered negative responses. The first, by Jacob Ziegler, was published in Leipzig in 1512. It also contained the text of Lukas's 1503 *Excusatio fratrum Waldensium contra binas lit-*

teras doctoris Augustini. The second reply was Jerome Dungersheim's *Confutatio*, which was published in 1514. It reproduced almost the entire *Apologia* within the text.

23. Thomson, "Luther and Bohemia," 168–70, following Bartos, "Das Auftreten," 106ff.

24. Thomson, "Luther and Bohemia," 173–76, cites the pertinent facts from a comprehensive study in J. Cihula, "Pomêr Bratrí ceskych k Martinovi Lutherovi," *VKCSN* (1897): 4–36. See also Rícan, *History of the Unity of Brethren*, 111–16; and Pelikan, *Obedient Rebels*, 125–32.

25. Pelikan, "Luther's Negotiations," 509–10, demonstrates from Weisse's hymnody that he had a spiritualistic and moralistic understanding of the Lord's Supper. Later, Weisse and Roh became official delegates from the Brethren to Luther.

26. "Luther to Speratus (May 16, 1522)," WABr 2:531.

27. "Luther to Speratus (June 13, 1522)," WABr 2:560–61: "[N]o one denies, not even the Brethren . . . that the body and blood of Christ are present there."

28. Luther mentions this booklet in the introduction of "Adoration of the Sacrament," LW 36:275–76 (= WA 11:431). Rícan, *History of the Unity of Brethren*, 113, suggests that the work in question was the 1520 booklet "O poklonê" ("On Bowing").

29. "Adoration of the Sacrament," LW 36:275–76 (= WA 11:431).

30. "Adoration of the Sacrament," LW 36:276 (= WA 11:431–32) (*author's emphasis*).

31. "Adoration of the Sacrament," LW 36:304 (= WA 11:455).

32. "But I suppose you will find some things lacking in the *Apologia* of our Philip, just as we find some things lacking in your *Apologia*" ("Adoration of the Sacrament," LW 36:276–77 [= WA 11:432]). The *Apologia* to which Luther referred was *Adversus Furiosum Pariensium Theologastrorum Decretrum, Phillipi Melanchthonis Pro Luthero Apologia* (1521). It can be found in C. G. Bretschneider and H. E. Bindseil, eds., *Corpus Reformatorum* (Halle: C. A. Schwetschke, 1834–1860), 1:398–416. An English translation can be found in Philipp Melanchthon, *Selected Writings*, ed. Elmer Ellsworth Flack and Lowell J. Satre, trans. Charles Leander Hill (Minneapolis: Augsburg, 1962), 69–87.

33. Thomson, "Luther and Bohemia," 167.

34. The page numbers are according to "Adoration of the Sacrament," LW 36.

35. "There has come from your midst a little book in German and Bohemian, 'Christian Instruction for Young Children,' in which among other things it is stated that in the sacrament Christ is not present substantially and naturally . . . . For you doubtless know that through your messengers to me I requested that you would prepare a special treatise to clarify this article of faith" ("Adoration of the Sacrament," LW 36:275 [= WA 11:431]). "So, in order to bring the matter to a conclusion and to silence the offense occasioned by the little book which you published in German, I shall set forth this article, for you and for everybody, just as clearly as I possibly can" ("Adoration of the Sacrament," LW 36:276 [= WA 11:431]).

36. "Adoration of the Sacrament," LW 36:287–88 (= WA 11:441).

37. "Adoration of the Sacrament," LW 36:279 (= WA 11:434).

38. "Adoration of the Sacrament," LW 36:289 (= WA 11:442).

39. "Adoration of the Sacrament," LW 36:277 (= WA 11:432).

40. "Adoration of the Sacrament," LW 36:289 (= WA 11:443).

41. "Adoration of the Sacrament," LW 36:295 (= WA 11:448). Luther allowed the adoration of the Sacrament because he believed in the bodily presence of Christ. Because Christ was present in the Eucharist, he could be worshiped there: "For

I must always confess that Christ is present when his body and blood are present" ("Adoration of the Sacrament," LW 36:294 [= WA 11:447]).

42. Luther later expressed his personal preference about the adoration of the Sacrament: "I really think that it would be better to follow the example of the apostles and not worship, than to follow our custom and worship. Not that adoration is wrong, but simply because there is less danger in not adoring than in adoring; because human nature tends so easily to emphasize its own works and to neglect God's work, and the sacrament will not admit of that" ("Adoration of the Sacrament," LW 36:297 [= WA 11:449]).

43. "Adoration of the Sacrament," LW 36:298 (= WA 11:450).

44. The phrases "for our trespasses" and "for our justification" are taken from Rom. 4:25. It is noteworthy that Luther also used Rom. 4:25 to interpret the Second Article of the Apostles' Creed in the Schmalkald Articles. See SA II, 2, 1. See *The Ecumenical Luther*, chapter 5, for more on the Schmalkald Articles and Luther's doctrinal hermeneutic.

45. "Adoration of the Sacrament," LW 36:298 (= WA 11:450–51).

46. "Adoration of the Sacrament," LW 36:298 (= WA 11:450–51).

47. "Adoration of the Sacrament," LW 36:298–99 (= WA 11:451).

48. "Adoration of the Sacrament," LW 36:299 (= WA 11:451).

49. "Adoration of the Sacrament," LW 36:299 (= WA 11:451).

50. "Adoration of the Sacrament," LW 36:299–300 (= WA 11:452).

51. "Adoration of the Sacrament," LW 36:300 (= WA 11:452).

52. "Adoration of the Sacrament," LW 36:300 (= WA 11:452).

53. "Adoration of the Sacrament," LW 36:300 (= WA 11:452).

54. "Adoration of the Sacrament," LW 36:300–301 (= WA 11:452–53).

55. "Adoration of the Sacrament," LW 36:301 (= WA 11:452–53). Luther's argument was based on Matt. 19:14, where Jesus said of the children he was blessing that the kingdom of heaven belonged to "such as these." Because the New Testament consistently taught that one enters the kingdom of heaven only through faith, Luther concluded that little children must enter it in the same way. Such faith in little children occurred simultaneously with Baptism and was a gift of God, the same gift that God had given to Jewish children through circumcision.

56. "Adoration of the Sacrament," LW 36:301 (= WA 11:453).

57. "Adoration of the Sacrament," LW 36:303 (= WA 11:455).

58. "Adoration of the Sacrament," LW 36:301–2 (= WA 11:453).

59. "Adoration of the Sacrament," LW 36:302 (= WA 11:454).

60. "Adoration of the Sacrament," LW 36:303 (= WA 11:454).

61. These were confirmation, penance, marriage, ordination, and extreme unction.

62. "Adoration of the Sacrament," LW 36:303 (= WA 11:454).

63. "Adoration of the Sacrament," LW 36:303 (= WA 11:454–55)

64. "Adoration of the Sacrament," LW 36:303 (= WA 11:454–55).

65. Rícan, *History of the Unity of Brethren*, 114–16, summarizes Lukas's "Answer of the Brethren to the Writing of M. Luther."

CHAPTER 4

1. On Philipp of Hesse, see Hans Hillerbrand, *Landgrave Philipp of Hesse, 1504–1567*, Reformation Essays and Studies, vol. 1 (St. Louis: Foundation for Reformation Research, 1967).

2. Luther's party included the Wittenberg theologians Justus Jonas (1493–1555), Caspar Cruciger (1504–1548), and Georg Rörer (1492–1557); also Gotha pastor Friedrich Myconius (1490–1546), the theologian Justus Menius (1499–1558), and a layman, Captain E. von der Thann of Eisenach attended the colloquy in Marburg. These men arrived with Luther on September 30. Andreas Osiander (1498–1552) of Nuremberg, Stephan Agricola (1491–1547) of Augsburg, and Johannes Brenz (1499–1570) of Schwäbisch-Hall arrived in the afternoon on October 2. It is also generally supposed that Veit Dietrich (1506–1549) of Wittenberg was in attendance, serving as Luther's *famulus*.

3. On Zwingli's theology and life, see W. P. Stephens, *The Theology of Huldrych Zwingli* (Oxford: Clarendon, 1986); W. P. Stephens, *Zwingli* (Oxford: Clarendon, 1992); Ulrich Gäbler, *Huldrych Zwingli*, trans. Ruth C. L. Gritsch (Philadelphia: Fortress, 1986); G. R. Potter, *Zwingli* (Cambridge: Cambridge University Press, 1976); Gottfried W. Locher, *Die Zwinglische Reformation im Rahmen der europäischen Kirchengeschichte* (Göttingen: Vandenhoeck & Ruprecht, 1979); and Gottfried W. Locher, *Zwingli's Thought*, Studies in the History of Christian Thought 25 (Leiden: Brill, 1981).

4. For Oecolampadius's life and theology, see Ernst Staehlin, *Briefe und Akte zum Leben Oekolampads*, 2 vols. (Leipzig: M. Heinsius Nachfolger Eger & Sievers, 1927–34); E. Gordon Rupp, *Patterns of Reformation* (Philadelphia: Fortress, 1969); and Thomas A. Fudge, "Icarus of Basel?" *Journal of Religious History* 21:3 (October 1997): 268–84.

5. On Martin Bucer's life, theology, and the reformation of Strasbourg, see Christian Krieger and Marc Lienhard, eds., *Martin Bucer and Sixteenth Century Europe*, Studies in Medieval and Reformation Thought, vols. 52–53 (Leiden: Brill, 1993); Martin Greschat, *Martin Bucer* (München: Beck, 1990); D. F. Wright, ed., *Martin Bucer* (Cambridge: Cambridge University Press, 1994); D. F. Wright, trans. and ed., *Common Places of Martin Bucer*, The Courtenay Library of Reformation Classics, vol. 4 (Berkshire, England: Sutton Courtenay Press, 1972); James Atkinson, "Martin Bucer (1491–1551)," *The Churchman* 79 (1965): 19–28; and Hastings Eells, *Martin Bucer* (New Haven: Yale University Press, 1931).

6. On Capito's life and contributions to the reformation at Strasbourg, see James M. Kittelson, *Wolfgang Capito*, Studies in Medieval and Reformation Thought 17 (Leiden: Brill, 1975).

7. The following is an extremely brief summary of a complex political situation. In spring 1529, at the second Diet of Speyer, the 1521 Edict of Worms had been reimplemented, which again forbade the evangelical doctrine. This, of course, was totally unacceptable to the evangelical minority at the diet, which included the elector of Saxony and Landgrave Philipp of Hesse. These princes, along with some of the imperial cities, issued a formal protest, which was read at the diet on April 19. Three days later, the leaders of the minority forged a secret defensive alliance to defend their faith in case it was attacked by those faithful to Rome. Immediately, Philipp of Hesse tried to include Zurich in the alliance and wrote Zwingli to ask for his assistance in bringing this about. The elector of Saxony and Margrave George of Brandenburg-Ansbach rejected the plan to include Zurich in the alliance, arguing that a political federation was possible only where unity in doctrine existed. Such unity did not exist, they argued, as long as the Swiss insisted on their view of the Eucharist. Therefore, in July, George of Brandenburg-Ansbach suggested drawing up a united confession that would form the basis of doctrinal unity with the Swiss and the South Germans loyal to them, as well as detailing the differences between the North Germans loyal to Luther's doctrine and the Swiss. The Wittenbergers complied with this proposal and completed the statement, now known as the Schwabach Articles, in mid-September. It was in this political and theological context that the elector

encouraged Luther to attend the Marburg Colloquy. For a more complete account, see Johann M. Reu, *The Augsburg Confession* (Chicago: Wartburg, 1930), 1:1–32; 2:32–44. See also Walther Köhler, *Die religiöse und politische Entwicklung bis zum Marburger Religionsgespräch*, vol. 1 of *Zwingli und Luther*, Quellen und Forschungen zur Reformationsgeschicte 6 (Leipzig: Verein für Reformationsgeschichte, 1924); and Walther Köhler, *Vom Beginn der Marburger Verhandlungen 1529 bis zum Abschluss der Wittenberger Konkordie von 1536*, vol. 2 of *Zwingli und Luther*, Quellen und Forschungen zur Reformationsgeschicte 7 (Gütersloh: Bertelsmann, 1953), 1–163.

8. "Letter to Landgrave Philip of Hesse, June 23, 1529," LW 49:231 (= WABr 5:101–2).

9. WABr 105:125. Cf. Preserved Smith and Charles M. Jacobs, trans. and eds., *Luther's Correspondence and Other Contemporary Letters* (Philadelphia: Lutheran Publication Society, 1913), 2:477. In another letter, Luther urged Johannes Brenz, who had been invited to the colloquy, not to attend, which would give the Wittenberg party an excuse not to attend. See WABr 105:141. Cf. Smith and Jacobs, *Luther's Correspondence*, 2:493–94.

10. "The Marburg Colloquy *and* The Marburg Articles, 1529," LW 38:15 (= WA 30/3:110–11).

11. Roland Bainton, "Luther and the *Via Media* at the Marburg Colloquy," *LQ* 1 (November 1949): 395–96. It is interesting to note that Luther's comment about the "different spirit" was specifically spoken not to the Swiss, but to South German Martin Bucer, a member of the Strasbourg delegation. Bucer had said of Luther two years earlier: "Let Luther acknowledge that he is being led by a spirit far different from that of Christ" (cited in Bucer's 1527 "Preface to the Fourth Volume of Luther's Postil," StL 17:1601).

12. See *The Ecumenical Luther*, chapter 4 n. 20.

13. This does not mean the Lord's Supper was viewed in isolation, unrelated to other doctrines. Nor do we ignore the fact that Luther was suspicious that the Swiss and South Germans were in error on other important teachings, such as the Trinity, the person of Christ, original sin, Baptism, justification, the ministry of the Word, and purgatory. Luther clearly announced his concerns at the beginning of the Marburg Colloquy. See "Marburg Colloquy," LW 38:36 (= WA 30/3:111). Moreover, the Wittenberg theologians came to Marburg with the Schwabach Articles in hand, a statement of seventeen articles that they had drafted to serve as a platform for unity to be presented at Marburg.

14. Reu, *Augsburg Confession*, 28–31. Reu thinks that Justus Jonas was a third collaborator. Reu's book includes an English translation of the Schwabach Articles in part 2, pp. 40–44.

15. Wilhelm Maurer, *Historical Commentary on the Augsburg Confession*, trans. H. George Anderson (Philadelphia: Fortress, 1986), 7–10, 20–27. Maurer traces the line of dependence that runs from Luther's Confession to the Schwabach Articles to the first section of the Augsburg Confession of 1530, noting the differences between Luther's Confession and the Schwabach Articles. Concerning the authorship of the Schwabach Articles, though Maurer sees Luther's imprint on the document, he still can say about Melanchthon, "We may certainly consider him the chief author of the Schwabach Articles" (24).

16. Gäbler, *Huldrych Zwingli*, 136.

17. Unlike the other two case studies considered in this book, which were literary dialogues, Marburg was a face-to-face colloquy. Thus what was actually spoken by Luther at the colloquy must be examined. Unfortunately, there is no official transcript of the proceedings because at Luther's request no official minutes were taken. Multiple unofficial notes of the colloquy's sessions were recorded, and

these form an adequate account of what was said by Luther and the other dialogue participants. There are seven texts related to Marburg: (1) The report by Caspar Hedio of Strasbourg, written in Latin, is widely considered the most important source of the colloquy as a whole. (2) The Latin report of Anonymous was apparently written by someone within Luther's circle. (3) Rudolph Collin, Zwingli's colleague from Zurich, provided a report in Latin. (4) Osiander's German report in the form of a letter to the city council of Nürnberg is especially valuable for insights about the end of the colloquy. (5) Brenz wrote a letter in Latin (with a small portion in German) to Schradin and the people of Reutlingen. (6) *Rhapsodies on the Marburg Colloquy* was also by an unknown author. (7) The *Summary Report Concerning the Marburg Colloquy* by Heinrich Utinger was written in German. For brief discussions of these texts, see Hermann Sasse, *This Is My Body* (Minneapolis: Augsburg, 1959), 178–80; and LW 38:10–12. The texts themselves are in LW 38:15–89 (= WA 30/3:110–71). Various attempts have been made to reconstruct the colloquy by harmonizing these texts. The most thorough of these is in Köhler, *Zwingli und Luther*, 2:66–163. The best attempt in English is Sasse, *This Is My Body*, 180–220.

18. For both the Eucharistic Controversy and the Marburg Colloquy, the most thorough examination is Köhler, *Zwingli und Luther*. Sasse, *This Is My Body*, is also an excellent source that highlights Luther's theology. Martin Brecht, *Martin Luther: Shaping and Defining the Reformation, 1521–1532*, trans. James L. Schaaf (Minneapolis: Fortress, 1990), 293–334, is a thorough summary of both events, as well as a good reference for secondary literature. See also Heinrich Bornkamm, *Luther in Mid-Career, 1521–1530*, ed. Karin Bornkamm, trans. E. Theodore Bachmann (Philadelphia: Fortress, 1983), 501–51, 631–53. Finally, Bernhard Lohse, *Martin Luther's Theology*, trans. and ed. Roy A. Harrisville (Minneapolis: Fortress, 1999), is highly recommended. It includes concise but accurate treatments of Luther's theology as related to both the controversy and the colloquy (169–77, 306–13), as well as excellent bibliographies (364, 375–76).

19. October 1–3, counting the preliminary discussions held on October 1 between Luther and Oecolampadius, on the one hand, and between Melanchthon and Zwingli on the other. See Sasse, *This Is My Body*, 180–84.

20. The formula, recorded by Oecolampadius, is: "We confess, that, by virtue of the words 'This is my body, this is my blood,' the body and blood are truly—*hoc est: substantive et essentialiter, non autem quantitative vel qualitative vel localiter* [that is: substantively and essentially, however not quantitatively nor qualitatively nor locally]—present and distributed in the Lord's Supper." The formula is in Sasse, *This Is My Body*, 214–15. See also Köhler, *Zwingli und Luther*, 2:131ff. The negative phrase was meant to appease Zwingli and Oecolampadius's concern that Luther and his party were holding to a "capernaitic," that is, a carnal, local presence in the bread.

21. "Marburg Colloquy," LW 38:88–89 (= WA 30/3:170).

22. Even this consensus is questionable. Zwingli's signing of the Marburg Articles appears duplicitous when nine months later—in his *Fidei Ratio*, which was delivered to the emperor at the Diet of Augsburg—he contradicted what he supposedly agreed to at Marburg. For example, whereas at Marburg (Article 8) Zwingli had agreed that the Holy Spirit works and creates faith through the oral Word and preaching, in *Fidei Ratio* (Article 7), he said that "[m]oreover, a channel or vehicle is not necessary to the Spirit, for He Himself is the virtue and energy by whom all things are borne, and has no need of being borne." Whereas at Marburg (Articles 9, 15) Zwingli had agreed that God creates and increases faith through Baptism and the Lord's Supper, in *Fidei Ratio* (Article 7), he stated that "I believe, indeed I know, that all the sacraments are so far from conferring grace, that they do not even convey or dispense it. . . . From this it follows . . . that the sacraments are given as a public testimony of that grace which is previ-

ously present to every individual." Either Zwingli changed his mind, interpreted the Marburg Articles in his own way, or was duplicitous. Whatever the explanation, this contradiction injects an element of doubt into the validity of the consensus. The quotations are from Ulrich Zwingli, *On Providence and Other Essays*, eds. S. M. Jackson and W. J. Hinke (Durham, N.C.: Labyrinth Press, 1983), 46–47. See also Sasse, *This Is My Body*, 223–27.

23. WABr 5:155. Cf. Smith and Jacobs, *Luther's Correspondence*, 2:495–96. This same attitude is expressed in Luther's October 4 letter to his wife (LW 49:236) and in the first sermon that he preached after his return to Wittenberg. "Things look rather hopeful. I do not say that we have attained brotherly unity, but a kindly and friendly concord . . . . If you pray diligently, the concord may become a brotherly one" (WA 28:668ff., quoted in Sasse, *This Is My Body*, 221).

24. I am indebted in what follows to Sasse's discussion in *This Is My Body*, 17–48. See also Carter Lindberg, *The European Reformations* (Cambridge, Mass.: Blackwell, 1996), 181–91.

25. Sasse, *This Is My Body*, 24.

26. Lindberg, *European Reformations*, 184–85. Sasse, *This Is My Body*, 26.

27. Also pointed out in James M. Kittelson, *Luther the Reformer* (Minneapolis: Augsburg, 1986), 196. It must be said that Berengar and Wycliffe went beyond Augustine by denying that grace is given through the Supper.

28. Quoted in Sasse, *This Is My Body*, 28.

29. For a list of publications that attacked Luther's position in the controversy, see LW 37:8– 11. For more comprehensive lists of the literary combatants, see Sasse, *This Is My Body*, 109–15; Brecht, *Shaping and Defining the Reformation*, 293–324; Bornkamm, *Luther in Mid-Career*, 501–51; Lindberg, *European Reformations*, 191–94; and Mark U. Edwards Jr., *Luther and the False Brethren* (Stanford: Stanford University Press, 1975), 82–104.

30. Lohse, *Martin Luther's Theology*, 171.

31. Lohse, *Martin Luther's Theology*, 169.

32. For example, W. P. Stephens has convincingly shown that it is quite difficult to pin down Zwingli's early sacramental views. In his earliest published work on the Lord's Supper, *An Exposition of the Articles* (1523), Zwingli made statements that seemed to grant the bodily presence ("there is no dispute here about whether the body and blood of Christ are eaten and drunk, for no Christian doubts that") and statements that seemed to take it away ("it is not a matter of bodily eating but of faith"). Zwingli definitely claimed that forgiveness is given to the believer through the Sacrament and that it was given for the strengthening of faith. He also seemed to make the presence of Christ in the Sacrament dependent on personal faith. See Stephens, *Theology of Huldrych Zwingli*, 218–27. Köhler thinks that by June 1523, Zwingli's early sacramental theology had moved from transubstantiation to one representative of Erasmus's mystical understanding. See Köhler, *Zwingli und Luther*, 1:83–87.

33. Hoen's treatise, *A Most Christian Letter* (published by Zwingli in 1525), is translated in Heiko A. Oberman, *Forerunners of the Reformation* (New York: Holt, Rinehart, & Winston, 1966), 268–76.

34. According to Lohse, *Martin Luther's Theology*, 170, Hoen's letter seems to have been stimulated by *De sacramento Eucharistiae*—a tract written by Wessel Gansfort (d. 1489)—and by Erasmus.

35. "The Adoration of the Sacrament, 1523" LW 36:279 (= WA 11:434).

36. "Adoration of the Sacrament," LW 36:275 (= WA 11:431).

37. "Adoration of the Sacrament," LW 36:277 (= WA 11:432). This is a position that Luther had held consistently since 1520 and his treatise "The Babylonian

Captivity of the Church." See LW 36:44 (= WA 6:518): "And as there is greater power in the word than the sign, so there is greater power in the testament than in the sacrament." Especially clear is this passage from "Receiving Both Kinds in the Sacrament, 1522": "For these words are a thousand times more important than the elements of the sacrament; without them the sacrament is not a sacrament but a mockery before God" (LW 36:254 [= WA 10/2:29]). See also "Receiving Both Kinds," LW 36:244–45 (= WA 10/2:19–20).

38. This will be explored in *The Ecumenical Luther*, chapter 4, "Evidence for Luther's Doctrinal Hermeneutic," which begins on p. 96.

39. "Adoration of the Sacrament," LW 36:278 (= WA 11:433).

40. "Adoration of the Sacrament," LW 36:279 (= WA 11:434). The dangers of human reason in matters of faith had been Luther's constant refrain since "Babylonian Captivity of the Church": "For my part, if I cannot fathom how the bread is the body of Christ, yet I will take my reason captive to the obedience of Christ, and clinging simply to his words, firmly believe not only that the body of Christ is in the bread, but that the bread is the body of Christ" (LW 36:34 [= WA 6:511]). Luther expressed the same thought in a more pointed fashion: "Even though philosophy cannot grasp this, faith grasps it nonetheless. And the authority of God's Word is greater than the capacity of our intellect to grasp it" ("Babylonian Captivity of the Church," LW 36:35 [= WA 6:511]). Luther continued to use this argument often, accusing his opponents of rejecting the bodily presence because reason could not understand how such a thing could be. He denounced Andreas Bodenstein von Karlstadt for this: "Furthermore he teaches us what Frau Hulda, natural reason, has to say in the matter, just as if we did not know that reason is the devil's prostitute and can do nothing else but slander and dishonor what God does and says" ("Against the Heavenly Prophets in the Matter of Images and Sacraments, 1525," LW 40:174–75 [= WA 18:164]). See especially the section in "Against the Heavenly Prophets" entitled "Concerning Frau Hulda, Dr. Karlstadt's Shrewd Reason, in This Sacrament," LW 40:192ff. (= WA 18:182ff.).

41. This is more fully developed in *The Ecumenical Luther*, chapter 4, "Andreas Bodenstein von Karlstadt," which begins on p. 83.

42. "Adoration of the Sacrament," LW 36:279 (= WA 11:434).

43. "Adoration of the Sacrament," LW 36:289 (= WA 11:443). Luther had long held this position. For example, he had stated in the 1520 treatise "Babylonian Captivity of the Church": "With unheard-of perversity we mock the mercy of the giver by giving as a work the thing we receive as a gift, so that the testator, instead of being a dispenser of his own goods, becomes the recipient of ours. Woe to such sacrilege!" (LW 36:48 [= WA 6:520]). Also in the same treatise: "For, since the word of divine promise in this sacrament sets forth the forgiveness of sins, let every one draw near fearlessly, whoever he may be, who is troubled by his sins, whether by remorse or by temptation. For this testament of Christ is the one remedy against sins, past, present and future, if you but cling to it with unwavering faith and believe that what the words of the testament declare is freely granted to you" (LW 36:57 [= WA 6:526]).

44. "Adoration of the Sacrament," LW 36:295 (= WA 11:448).

45. "Adoration of the Sacrament," LW 36:298 (= WA 11:450). Already in "Babylonian Captivity of the Church," Luther could say: "Even so each one can derive personal benefit from the mass only by his own personal faith. It is absolutely impossible to commune on behalf of anyone else" (LW 36:49 [= WA 6:521]). See also "The Misuse of the Mass, 1521," LW 36:177 (= WA 8:519).

46. "Adoration of the Sacrament," LW 36:282 (= WA 11:437). Luther had used the red-hot iron analogy once before to demonstrate from nature that it was not contrary to reason for Christ's body to be one with the bread, in opposition to

the claims of transubstantiation ("Babylonian Captivity of the Church," LW 36:32 [= WA 6:510]). See also "Against the Heavenly Prophets," LW 40:196–97 (= WA 18:186). For an explicit mention of the "sacramental union," see the discussion in *The Ecumenical Luther*, pp. 103–4.

47. Luther learned about Karlstadt's visit to Strasbourg from a November 22 letter from Gerbel (WABr 3:378–81) and from a November 23 letter from the Strasbourg clergy (WABr 3:381–90).

48. Lindberg, *European Reformations*, 139–40. See also Ulrich Bubenheimer, "Karlstadt," *Theologische Realenzykopädie* 17 (1988): 649–57.

49. "Letter to the Christians at Strassburg in Opposition to the Fanatic Spirit, 1524," LW 40:68 (= WA 15:394).

50. Two years later, Luther was still referring to "Against the Heavenly Prophets" as a definitive statement of his view of the Supper, a statement that he believed had not yet been answered by anyone who opposed the bodily presence. See "That These Words of Christ, 'This Is My Body,' etc., Still Stand Firm against the Fanatics, 1527," LW 37:18–19 (= WA 23:71, 73). In 1528, Luther was still referring to the treatise in "Confession Concerning Christ's Supper," LW 37:193 (= WA 26:296–97).

51. For example, Karlstadt offered the opinion that "This is my body" was grammatically discontinuous with the rest of the sentence because the *Hoc* began with a capital letter and was preceded by a period. Therefore, he argued that "This is my body" had nothing to do with "Take, eat" and was superfluous. In another argument, Karlstadt stated that the Greek pronoun τουτο could not refer to the bread because bread in Greek (αρτος) was masculine, but τουτο was neuter, like the Greek word for body, σομα. Therefore, τουτο must refer to σομα. See the discussion in "Against the Heavenly Prophets," LW 40:154–77 (= WA 18:144–66).

52. "Against the Heavenly Prophets," LW 40:177 (= WA 18:166–67).

53. "Against the Heavenly Prophets," LW 40:179 (= WA 18:170). On Karlstadt's denial of this, see WABr 18:170.

54. See Carter Lindberg, *The Third Reformation* (Macon, Ga.: Mercer University Press, 1983), 62.

55. Carter Lindberg, "The Conception of the Eucharist According to Erasmus and Karlstadt," in *Les dissidents du XVIᵉ siècle entre l'humanisme et le catholicisme*, ed. Marc Lienhard (Baden-Baden: Koerner, 1983), 79–94.

56. "Against the Heavenly Prophets," LW 40:202 (= WA 18:192).The consequences of Luther's argument for his doctrinal hermeneutic will be expanded in *The Ecumenical Luther*, chapter 4, "Huldrych Zwingli," which begins on p. 87.

57. "Against the Heavenly Prophets," LW 40:203 (= WA 18:193).

58. In "That These Words of Christ," Luther dealt with John 6:63 in a lengthy section; see LW 37:78–102 (= WA 23:167–207). See also LW 37:46, 129–34 (= WA 23:115, 251–59). The reformer took up the question of John 6:63 again in "Confession Concerning Christ's Supper," LW 37:237–52 (= WA 26:353–78).

59. See *The Ecumenical Luther*, pp. 85–86.

60. "Against the Heavenly Prophets," LW 40:146, 147 (= WA 18:136, 137).

61. "Against the Heavenly Prophets," LW 40:213–14 (= WA 18:203–4).

62. On the theology of Zwingli, see Stephens, *Theology of Huldrych Zwingli*, 5–50; Brecht, *Shaping and Defining the Reformation*, 294; Sasse, *This Is My Body*, 92–95; and Lindberg, *European Reformations*, 170–73.

63. "Marburg Colloquy," LW 38: 55 (= WA 30/3:118). Cf. LW 38:21. Luther responded to this by saying: "Furthermore, when you say that God does not

propose to us anything incomprehensible, I could not admit this. [Consider] the virginity of Mary, the forgiveness of sins, and many similar matters" (LW 38:22 [= WA 30/3:119]).

64. See *The Ecumenial Luther*, p. 91–92.

65. "Marburg Colloquy," LW 38:55 (= WA 30/3:118).

66. Zwingli clearly gave the Greek New Testament priority. On Zwingli's use of the church fathers, see Stephens, *Theology of Huldrych Zwingli*, 17–21. What we know of Zwingli's opinion and use of the church fathers comes from marginal notes that he made in his editions of their writings. On the basis of these marginal notes, it is clear that before 1522 Zwingli often consulted Origen, Augustine, and Jerome. Augustine's tractates on John are especially heavily annotated by Zwingli.

67. Köhler has argued, however, that Zwingli's distinction between the body and spirit was a result of the influence of Augustine's Neoplatonism. Cited in Stephens, *Theology of Huldrych Zwingli*, 19–20.

68. Fritz Büsser, "Zwingli the Exegete," in *Probing the Reformed Tradition*, ed. Elsie Anne McKee and Brian G. Armstrong (Louisville: Westminster/John Knox, 1989), 192.

69. Referred to in Stephens, *Theology of Huldrych Zwingli*, 26–27, 45–46.

70. Brecht, *Shaping and Defining the Reformation*, 294.

71. Stephens, *Theology of Huldrych Zwingli*, 45.

72. Franz Kolb, the preacher in Wertheim, had written to Luther in August 1524 to tell him that Zwingli was teaching a symbolic view of the Lord's Supper (WABr 3:78ff., no. 769). From that time on, Luther suspected the worst. In a November 17, 1524, letter to Nikolaus Hausmann (before the Wittenberg reformer could have seen Zwingli's *Letter to Matthew Alber*), Luther associated Zwingli with Karlstadt: "Among the Swiss, Zwingli at Zürich and Leo Jud share the same opinion as Karlstadt, so widespread is this evil. But Christ reigns—to say nothing of the fact that he fights back" (LW 49:88–90 [= WABr 3:373]).

73. Z 3:335–54. The English translation appears in Ulrich Zwingli, *Writings*, ed. H. Wayne Pipkin and Edward J. Furcha, Pittsburgh Theological Monographs, new ser., vol. 13 (Allison Park, Penn.: Pickwick, 1984), 2:131–45. *Commentary on True and False Religion* is in Z 3:628ff. The English translation is Ulrich Zwingli, *Commentary on True and False Religion*, ed. Samuel Macauley Jackson and Clarence Nevin Heller (Durham, N.C.: Labyrinth Press, 1981).

74. Köhler held that Hoen's letter decisively moved Zwingli from an Erasmian view of a mystical presence of Christ to a symbolic view in which the bodily presence was completely rejected. See Köhler, *Zwingli und Luther*, 1:61–63, 84–87. Stephens disagreed with this, stating that it is "impossible to say how important the letter of Cornelius Hoen in 1524 was in the development of Zwingli's eucharistic theology. Zwingli argued that he already held a symbolic view when he read it . . . Whether or not this is the case, there are certainly different notes in Zwingli's eucharistic writings from the end of 1524" (Stephens, *Theology of Huldrych Zwingli*, 227, 256–57).

75. For both Zwingli and Oecolampadius, the sixth chapter of John and especially John 6:63 convinced them that the bodily presence of Christ in the Sacrament was impossible. At Marburg, this was the first argument that Oecolampadius used against the bodily presence: "Chapter 6 explains the other passages of Scripture. Christ is not present there locally" ("Marburg Colloquy," LW 38:16 [= WA 30/3:113]). It is also noteworthy that the first time Zwingli spoke in the colloquy, he also spoke at length about John 6:63: "Even if we do not have [a passage that says], 'This is the figure of my body,' we do have [a passage] which leads us away from the bodily eating. . . . [W]e ought to consider the passage [in

John 6] because it leads away from bodily eating. Hence it follows that in the Supper Christ did not give himself in bodily fashion" ("Marburg Colloquy," LW 38:20 [= WA 30/3:117–18]). In fact, the first morning session was basically a standoff. Luther took his stand on the Words of Institution, and Zwingli and Oecolampadius took theirs on John 6:63.

76. Erasmus's position can be seen in "The Enchiridion," ed. and trans. Ford Lewis Battles, Library of Christian Classics 14 (Philadelphia: Westminster, 1953), 335–39. See also Stephens, *Theology of Huldrych Zwingli*, 15–17.

77. Zwingli, *Writings*, 132.

78. Zwingli, *Writings*, 132

79. Zwingli, *Writings*, 136.

80. In his March 1525 *Commentary on True and False Religion*, Zwingli referred to John 6:63 as his "buckler" and "wall of bronze" that would turn aside all "engines of war, catapults, battering-rams, sheds, and every kind of weapon." He claimed that it alone, without any further argument, would be enough to show that *is* must mean "signifies" (Zwingli, *Providence and Other Essays*, 212; Z 3:784–86, 791, 801, 816). Zwingli also argued against interpreting John 6:63 by the words "This is my body" because John 6:63 was "perfectly clear" and less offensive to reason than the notion that Christ's body was essentially present. See Zwingli, *Providence and Other Essays*, 220–21; Z 3:792.

81. Zwingli, *Writings*, 138.

82. Zwingli, *Writings*, 139.

83. Zwingli, *Writings*, 139.

84. Zwingli, *Writings*, 139.

85. Zwingli, *Writings*, 143.

86. Zwingli, *Writings*, 143.

87. Zwingli, *Writings*, 137–38. This quote is representative: "[S]alvation can come in no other way than through Christ, and therefore not through the sacramental eating of bread and wine" (137).

88. Zwingli, *Writings*, 136: "You believe that Christ is eaten here in bodily shape, and since you have no such Scripture, you undoubtedly see that this whole notion is at the same time dead and the most damnable invention of idolatry. For who has not worshipped this sacrament?"

89. *Subsidium sive coronis de eucharistia*, also known as "Rearguard" or "The Eucharist" in Z 4:458–504. A German translation appeared in fall 1525 and again in 1526.

90. More specifically, Zwingli defined the trope in the Words of Institution as metaphor. He did this in response to his opponents' argument that the Words of Institution involved a metonymy and, therefore, *is* could not mean "signifies." Zwingli, *Writings*, 203–4.

91. "This was just what I wanted, that you should display your ignorance, namely that you do not know the difference between a parable and a trope. A parable is an analogy or a comparison. A trope is the transferring and changing of a word from its natural meaning, and the adaptation of it to another having some affinity with it, as a plant is transferred from its native soil to another . . . So also in our passage, 'This is my body,' the word 'is' is put tropically for 'signifies,' so that the sense is 'This signifies or typifies that my body has been given for you,' or 'This is a symbol of my body that has been given for you' " (Zwingli, *Writings*, 208–9).

92. Zwingli described the dream and interpreted Exod. 12:11 in detail in Zwingli, *Writings*, 209–14.

93. Bornkamm, *Luther in Mid-Career*, 511: "This gave him an excuse to part company with Karlstadt and his 'amply forced' exegesis, something over which Zwingli felt relieved, especially in view of Karlstadt's mounting popularity in Anabaptist groups."

94. Zwingli, *Writings*, 218.

95. In *Subsidiary Essay on the Eucharist*, Zwingli had written, "They know that flesh sits at the right hand of the Father and moves not thence until it comes back for the final reckoning with the whole world" (Zwingli, *Writings*, 197).

96. Zwingli, *Writings*, 205–6. According to Zwingli, the threefold distinction of Christ's body originally had been proposed by Heinrich Engelhardt, doctor of Pontifical Law, during the April 11 meeting of the Council of the Two Hundred. Zwingli enthusiastically adopted and recommended the argument, however.

97. Johannes Bugenhagen (1485–1558), a trusted friend of Luther throughout the reformer's life, was one of the principal figures in the Lutheran Reformation and one of its greatest theologians. He is known as the great organizer of the Lutheran Church because he successfully introduced the Reformation into many towns and principalities, including Hamburg, Brunswick, Pomerania, and Denmark. He also was pastor of the Wittenberg congregation from 1523 to 1528; was Luther's cherished confessor; officiated at Luther's wedding in 1525; was the sponsor of Luther's firstborn son, John; and preached Luther's funeral sermon.

98. StL 20:500–05.

99. For example, see Luther's November 5 letter to Gregory Casel. In October, the Strasbourg clergy, including Martin Bucer, had sent Casel, the Hebrew language instructor in Strasbourg, to Wittenberg to work for unity in the question of the Lord's Supper. Luther's letter to Casel, which was intended to be read to the Strasbourg clergy, made it clear that, though he also desired peace, he denounced the eucharistic teaching of Zwingli and Oecolampadius. Smith and Jacobs, *Luther's Correspondence*, 2:346–50; WABr 3:599–612.

100. WA 19:113–25. In this short letter, Luther's only new contribution to the Eucharistic Controversy, he stressed that the disunity among the Sacramentarians proved that their doctrine was not of the Holy Spirit.

101. The English translation appears in G. W. Bromiley, ed. and trans., *Zwingli and Bullinger*, Library of Christian Classics 24 (Philadelphia: Westminster, 1953), 176–238.

102. Bromiley, *Zwingli and Bullinger*, 191.

103. Bromiley, *Zwingli and Bullinger*, 196. The following quote is also illustrative: "For if the 'is' is to be taken literally, then we must eat the body of Christ with its flesh, bones, veins, nerves, marrow and other members which I will forbear to mention: for God cannot lie. If Christ spoke literally and not figuratively, then of necessity it follows that his body is eaten literally and perceptibly, as Berengarius was forced to confess: but all believers know very well that they do not eat the body of Christ in that way. Hence the very nature and truth of the matter will not allow us to take the words literally" (199).

104. Bromiley, *Zwingli and Bullinger*, 199.

105. Bromiley, *Zwingli and Bullinger*, 213.

106. The doctrine of the *communicatio idiomatum*, or the communication of properties, was an interpretation of the doctrine of the two natures of Christ adopted at the Council of Chalcedon in A.D. 451. Chalcedon had condemned the views of Nestorius and Eutyches. Nestorius (d. ca. 451), patriarch of Constantinople, had condemned the teaching that Mary was *theotokos* (mother of God), saying instead that she was *Christotokos* (mother of Christ). He held that there was no

communion of the two natures in Christ, that the two natures were sharply separated. Eutyches (ca. 378–454), a monk in Constantinople, taught that after the incarnation there was only one nature in Christ, that the human nature was swallowed up by the divine. This became known as Monophysitism. Chalcedon condemned both of these positions, instead confessing that the one Christ was "in two natures, unconfusedly, immutably, indivisibly, indistinctly." Because of the unity of the person of Christ, the two natures must not be separated from each other or mixed or changed into one or the other. Only this understanding would preserve the miracle of the incarnation. Because of the unity of the person of Christ, what pertains to one nature is communicated to or exchanged with the other. The human nature is born, is hungry, dies, etc. The divine nature has omnipotence and omnipresence, among other qualities. The *communicatio idiomatum* teaches, for example, that God died on the cross or that God was swaddled and placed in the manger. On the other hand, it teaches that the human Jesus is all-powerful, created the world, and is present everywhere.

107. Zwingli, *Writings*, 320.

108. Zwingli, *Writings*, 321. A little later, Zwingli wrote, "But in reality expressions of this kind involve a leap and are not literal" (Zwingli, *Writings*, 328).

109. Zwingli, *Writings*, 324.

110. *A Friendly Exegesis*, February 1527; *A Friendly Answer*, March 1527; *Zwingli's Christian Reply*, June 1527; and *Two Replies to Luther's Book*, August 1528.

111. Stephens, *Theology of Huldrych Zwingli*, 242.

112. Zwingli, *Writings*, 247.

113. " '[Quoting Bucer] Without detriment to faith,' he says, 'one may hold different views in this matter.' I do not agree in this, but I do not find fault with him for writing it. For the excellent man wished to relieve the disease by making it appear less serious" (Zwingli, *Writings*, 281).

114. Zwingli, *Writings*, 282.

115. As did Erasmus and Karlstadt before him.

116. The first of these was a June 1526 preface that Luther wrote for the *Syngramma Seuvicum* written by Johannes Brenz the previous October. This document, signed by fourteen Swabian preachers from southwestern Germany, sharply rejected the Swiss doctrine of the Eucharist as articulated by Oecolampadius. The preface is in WA 19:447–61. Luther's second publication was a September 13, 1526, letter to Johann Herwagen, the publisher of Luther's postil translation. In the letter, Luther bitterly complained that Martin Bucer, who was translating Luther's postil into Latin, had taken certain liberties: Bucer had attached a preface in which he highly praised Zwingli and Oecolampadius, and he had added comments to the sermon for Septuagesima Sunday (on 1 Cor. 9:24–10:6) that warned the reader not to follow Luther's authority in the Eucharistic Controversy. The letter to Herwagen is in WA 19:462–74.

117. Oecolampadius had written that if the Spirit of God had not left Luther, then the Wittenberg reformer would make a new contribution to the problem of the Lord's Supper. See Oecolampadius's July 1526 *Reasonable Answer to Dr. Martin Luther's Instruction Concerning the Sacrament* (StL 20:582ff.).

118. LW 36:335–61 (= WA 19:482–523).

119. LW 37:13–150 (= WA 23:38–320).

120. Brecht, *Shaping and Defining the Reformation*, 310–11.

121. LW 37:161–372 (= WA 26:240–509).

122. The year 1527 had been difficult for Luther. On July 6, he had experienced intense spiritual *Anfechtungen*, followed by a severe sickness (Luther described

this in WABr 4:248), which among other things included fainting spells. (He mentioned this in a July 13, 1527, letter to Nikolaus Hausmann [LW 49:168–69 (= WABr 4:222)]). The plague had hit Wittenberg, killing many. As of November, he was greatly concerned for his wife, who was due to give birth, and his infant son, Hans, who was seriously ill. For Luther's frame of mind in November 1527, see his letter to Justus Jonas (LW 49:171–77 [= WABr 4:279–80]).

123. WA 26:249.

124. "To the Christian Nobility of the German Nation Concerning the Reform of the Christian Estate, 1520," LW 44:199 (= WA 6:456).

125. "Against the Heavenly Prophets," LW 40:222 (= WA 18:213).

126. "That These Words of Christ," LW 37:42 (= WA 23:109).

127. Cf., Capito, *Proper Attitude*, 1525, StL 20:349f.; and Bucer, *Defense and Explanation*, 1524, StL 20:408f.

128. "Now that we have preserved the treasure, and not allowed the kernel to be taken out of the shell so that we have only chaff left instead of grain, we must now preach on the second part, namely, how one should make use of the sacrament and derive benefit from it. For it is not sufficient that we know what the sacrament is, namely, that Christ's body and blood are truly present, but it is also necessary to know why they are present and for what reason they are given to us" ("Sacrament of the Body and Blood of Christ," LW 36:346–47 [= WA 19:501]). "But here is where our opponents cause anguish. The devil cannot leave it alone; he must besmirch God's works and words. If he cannot tear it away completely, he makes an empty nut of it. The pope took away from us one element of the sacrament. These people, however, leave us both elements; but they make a hole in the nut, in order that we may lose the body and blood of Christ" ("Sacrament of the Body and Blood of Christ," LW 36:347 [= WA 19:501–2]).

129. Irving L. Sandberg, trans., *The 1529 Holy Week and Easter Sermons of Dr. Martin Luther* (St. Louis: Concordia Academic Press, 1999), 38, from the March 21, Palm Sunday afternoon sermon.

130. "That These Words of Christ," LW 37:16 (= WA 23:69).

131. "That These Words of Christ," LW 37:130 (= WA 23:253).

132. "That These Words of Christ," LW 37:28 (= WA 23:87).

133. "To believe that Christ is in the bread is an opinion, not faith" ("Marburg Colloquy," LW 38:54 [= WA 30/3:114]).

134. Sandberg, *1529 Holy Week and Easter Sermons*, 64–65. From the March 24, Wednesday Morning of Holy Week sermon.

135. Sasse, *This Is My Body*, 152–53.

136. "That These Words of Christ," LW 37:29 (= WA 23:87).

137. "Babylonian Captivity of the Church," LW 36:33 (= WA 6:510).

138. "That These Words of Christ," LW 37:65 (= WA 23:145).

139. "For I heard your messengers testify verbally that you unanimously hold that Christ is truly present in the sacrament with his flesh and blood as it was born of Mary and hung on the holy cross, just as we Germans believe" ("Adoration of the Sacrament," LW 36:275 [= WA 11:431]). "We know what Christ's body is, namely, that which was born of Mary, suffered, died, and rose again" ("Sacrament of the Body and Blood of Christ," LW 36:338 [= WA 19:485]). Luther's wording follows closely that of *Ego Berengarius* (1079), which was the official doctrine of the Roman Church.

140. "Confession Concerning Christ's Supper," LW 37:195, 196, 197 (= WA 26:298, 299, 300).

141. The formula is in Sasse, *This Is My Body*, 214–15. See also Köhler, *Zwingli und Luther*, 2:131ff.

142. Matt. 26:26–28; Mark 14:22–24; Luke 22:19–20; and 1 Cor. 11:23–25. Luther used a conflated text in public worship and instruction.

143. "Marburg Colloquy," LW 38:17 (= WA 30/3:114). At the colloquy, Luther spoke this in German for emphasis.

144. "Confession Concerning Christ's Supper," LW 37:272 (= WA 26:406).

145. Sandberg, *1529 Holy Week and Easter Sermons*, 48. From the March 22, Monday Morning of Holy Week sermon.

146. "That These Words of Christ," LW 37:19 (= WA 23:73).

147. "Marburg Colloquy," LW 38:57 (= WA 30/3:123).

148. "Confession Concerning Christ's Supper," LW 37:163 (= WA 26:262).

149. "Babylonian Captivity of the Church," LW 36:30 (= WA 6:509).

150. "Confession Concerning Christ's Supper," LW 37:270 (= WA 26:403).

151. "Marburg Colloquy," LW 38:43 (= WA 30/3:128). Sasse's reconstruction of this statement is: "I insist that there must be a trope in the Lord's Supper. This can be shown, as also the Article of the Creed demands it: 'He ascended into heaven and sitteth on the right hand of God the Father.' Otherwise, a great difficulty would arise, namely, that, while Christ says he is in heaven, we should seek him in the Supper. For one and the same body cannot be in several places at the same time" (Sasse, *This Is My Body*, 200).

152. "That These Words of Christ," LW 37:112–13 (= WA 23:225).

153. "Now, however, since he does not say here, 'My flesh is of no avail,' but simply, 'Flesh is of no avail,' you really find yourself in trouble and distress because you must prove it means Christ's flesh here. There is a very great difference between Christ's flesh and ordinary flesh" ("That These Words of Christ," LW 37:79 [= WA 23:169]). "Our position is that where the two words, "flesh" and "spirit," are placed in opposition to one another in the Scriptures, flesh cannot mean Christ's body but always means the old flesh which is born of the flesh, John 3: 'That which is born of the flesh is flesh' " ("That These Words of Christ," LW 37:95 [= WA 23:193, 195]).

154. Luther was especially referring to the philosophy of Occam, which he had learned while a student at Erfurt. See the discussion in Sasse, *This Is My Body*, 125–27.

155. This discussion is found in "Confession Concerning Christ's Supper," LW 37:214–16 (= WA 26:327–29).

156. "Confession Concerning Christ's Supper," LW 37:216 (= WA 26:329).

157. Sandberg, *1529 Holy Week and Easter Sermons*, 47, from the March 22, Monday Morning of Holy Week sermon. As Luther also stated in "That These Words of Christ": "But I shall put my finger still more accurately upon their real argument which leads them to such an error . . . . This one factor moves them above all others: that according to reason it is altogether absurd to believe that we should eat and drink Christ's body and blood physically in the Supper" (LW 37:51 [= WA 23:123]).

158. "This is the rancor and hatred of natural reason, which wants nothing to do with this article and therefore spits and vomits against it, and then tries to wrap itself in Scripture so that it may avoid being recognized. Not a single article of faith would remain if I followed the rancor of reason" ("That These Words of Christ," LW 37:53 [= WA 23:127]).

159. Consider this exchange at Marburg: "Luther: . . . 'Furthermore, when you say that God does not propose to us anything incomprehensible, I could not admit

this. [Consider] the virginity of Mary, the forgiveness of sins, and many similar matters. So also, "This is my body" [is incomprehensible.'] . . . Zwingli: . . . 'It is not true that God places many incomprehensible matters before us. That Christ is true God and man is not unknown to the faithful' " ("Marburg Colloquy," LW 38:22, 23).

160. Zwingli, "Friendly Exegesis," in *Writings*, 277.

161. "Confession Concerning Christ's Supper," LW 37:299–300 (= WA 26:442–43).

162. Cf. Sasse, *This Is My Body*, 129–30.

163. "Against the Heavenly Prophets," LW 40:197–98 (= WA 18:187–88).

164. "Confession Concerning Christ's Supper," LW 37:301–3 (= WA 26:444–45).

165. Zwingli asked, "What is the principle of difference by which we admit a synecdoche, but reject a metonymy which is just as good a trope as the other?" (Zwingli, "Friendly Exegesis," in *Writings*, 338). It should be noted, however, that Zwingli had been insisting on the Words of Institution as metaphor not metonymy.

166. "Oecolampadius: . . . You do not admit a trope in the words of institution, and yet you make it a synecdoche. Thus you introduce a new meaning contrary to the understanding of the teachers of the church universal" ("Marburg Colloquy," LW 38:30 [= WA 30/3:133]).

167. This reconstructed text is found in Sasse, *This Is My Body*, 204.

168. Because Zwingli was Luther's chief opponent in the Eucharist Controversy, this exploration only addresses Zwingli's figurative argument. However, Luther regarded Oecolampadius's argument—that the metaphor was to be found in the word *body* (that is, "Take eat, this is the sign of my body")—to be the same argument as Zwingli's: "In the first place, it is certain that Zwingli and Oecolampadius agree in their understanding of the text, even though their words differ. For Zwingli's expression, 'This represents my body,' is exactly the same as Oecolampadius' 'This is a sign of my body' " ("That These Words of Christ," LW 37:34 [= WA 23:95]).

169. Luther had responded briefly to the signification argument of Hoen and had examined several of the passages in his 1523 "Adoration of the Sacrament." See LW 36:280–82 (= WA 11:434–36).

170. "That These Words of Christ," LW 37:34 (= WA 23:95).

171. "That These Words of Christ," LW 37:34–35 (= WA 23:95).

172. For example, "the rock was Christ" (1 Cor. 10:4); "it is the Lord's passover" (Exod. 12:11); "I am the true vine" (John 15:1); and "I am the door" (John 10:7, 9).

173. "That These Words of Christ," LW 37:38–39 (= WA 23:99).

174. "Confession Concerning Christ's Supper," LW 37:171 (= WA 26:271).

175. "Confession Concerning Christ's Supper," LW 37:172 (= WA 26:271–72).

176. This is a reference to 1 John 4:1–3: "Dear friends, do not believe every spirit, but test the spirits to see whether they are from God, because many false prophets have gone out into the world. This is how you can recognize the Spirit of God: Every spirit that acknowledges that Jesus Christ has come in the flesh is from God, but every spirit that does not acknowledge Jesus is not from God. This is the spirit of the antichrist, which you have heard is coming and even now is already in the world."

177. "That These Words of Christ," LW 37:150 (= WA 23:283).

178. "Adoration of the Sacrament," LW 36:298 (= WA 11:450).

179. "That These Words of Christ," LW 37:82 (= WA 23:173).

180. "That These Words of Christ," LW 37:83 (= WA 23:175).

181. Luther had argued similarly against Karlstadt in "Against the Heavenly Prophets": "Tell me, where is the flesh of Christ of avail? On the cross? In heaven? In the mother's womb? Where then? I suppose I'll soon hear that he cannot be anywhere, since his flesh is of no avail. For if it follows that Christ is not in the sacrament since the flesh of Christ is of no avail, it follows equally well that he is nowhere" (LW 40:202 [= WA 18:192]). Luther also believed that his opponents' John 6:63 argument could lead to Docetism: "For if their fanaticism continues, that Christ's flesh is of no avail, soon Marcion, Mani, and Valentinus will come teaching that Christ had no real body but an apparition of a body, because it is not compatible for Christ's body to be of no avail and yet for him to have a real body" ("That These Words of Christ," LW 37:99 [= WA 23:201, 203]).

182. As Zwingli put it at Marburg: "Christ therefore is finite, as we are finite" ("Marburg Colloquy," LW 38:60 [= WA 30/3:136]).

183. "Marburg Colloquy," LW 38:60 (= WA 30/3:136).

184. "Confession Concerning Christ's Supper," LW 37:229 (= WA 26:340–41).

185. Often referred to as the ubiquity of Christ's human nature.

186. "Confession Concerning Christ's Supper," LW 37:210, 211 (= WA 26:321, 322).

187. This is what later theologians would call the *genus auchematicum* or *majestaticum*.

188. Johann Anselm Steiger argues that Luther's use of the *communicatio idiomatum* did not merely apply to the reformer's Christology and eucharistic theology, but it drove all of Luther's theology, including anthropology, Scripture, justification, rhetoric, ethics, and pastoral care. See Steiger, "The *communicatio idiomatum* as the Axle and Motor of Luther's Theology," *LQ* 14 (Summer 2000): 125–58.

189. "Confession Concerning Christ's Supper," LW 37:218–19 (= WA 26:332–33). "Secondly, the spirit should answer thus: Christ is God and man, and his humanity has become one person with God, and is thus wholly and completely drawn into God above all creatures, so that he remains perfectly united with him. How is it possible, then, for God to be somewhere where Christ as man is not? How can it happen, without dividing the person, that God may be here without the humanity and there with the humanity?—especially since we have not two Gods but only one God, and yet this God is wholly and perfectly man according to one person, viz. his Son" ("Confession Concerning Christ's Supper," LW 37:218–19 [= WA 26:332–33]).

190. For more information on Nestorianism and Monophysitism, see *The Ecumenical Luther*, chapter 4 n. 106. See also Justo González, *A History of Christian Thought* (Nashville: Abingdon, 1970), 1:363–92.

191. "They raise a hue and cry against us, saying that we mingle the two natures into one essence. This is not true. We do not say that divinity is humanity, or that the divine nature is the human nature, which would be confusing the natures into one essence. Rather, we merge the two distinct natures into one single person, and say: God is man and man is God. We in turn raise a hue and cry against them for separating the person of Christ as though there were two persons. If Zwingli's alloeosis stands, then Christ will have to be two persons, one a divine and the other a human person, since Zwingli applies all the texts concerning the passion only to the human nature and completely excludes them from the divine nature. But if the works are divided and separated, the person will also have to be separated, since all the doing and suffering are not ascribed to natures but to persons. It is the person who does and suffers everything, the one thing according to this nature and the other thing according to the other nature, all of which scholars know perfectly well. Therefore we regard our Lord Christ as God and man in one person, 'neither confusing the natures nor dividing the person' "

("Confession Concerning Christ's Supper," LW 37:212–13 [= WA 26:324]).

192. "That These Words of Christ," LW 37:56 (= WA 23:131). Later in the same treatise, Luther repeated this belief: "It is our belief, of course, as the Scriptures teach us, that our Lord Jesus Christ is in essence and by nature true God, and 'in him the fulness of the Godhead dwells bodily,' as St. Paul says in Colossians 2[:9]. Thus, apart from Christ there is simply no God or Godhead at all" ("That These Words of Christ," LW 37:61 [= WA 23:139]).

193. "Marburg Colloquy," LW 38:46 (= WA 30/3:132–33).

194. Sasse, *This Is My Body*, 123.

195. See *The Ecumenical Luther*, pp. 68, 82–83.

196. "Babylonian Captivity of the Church," LW 36:56 (= WA 6:525).

197. "Order of Mass and Communion," LW 53:25 (= WA 12:211).

198. "Confession Concerning Christ's Supper," LW 37:192 (= WA 26:294) (*Luther's emphasis*). A year later, Luther continued to set forth this distinction: "Our enemies get stuck in this work: Christ died on the cross, not in the Lord's Supper. Therefore the forgiveness of sins is on the cross, not in the Lord's Supper. But how do I acquire it? When I believe, they answer. They attach themselves to this last work on the cross. But then must faith be only in the place where Christ was crucified? One cannot come to faith if it is not preached, as Paul says: 'And how are they to believe in one of whom they have never heard? And how are they to hear without someone to proclaim him?' (Romans 10:14). So if Christ were crucified a hundred times in a day and no one preached it, then the forgiveness of sins would be lost. For this reason the work completed on the cross must be contained in the Word and be offered to the people through the Word" (Sandberg, *1529 Holy Week and Easter Sermons*, 67, from the March 24, Wednesday Morning of Holy Week sermon).

199. See the discussion in *The Ecumenical Luther*, chapter 4 n. 22.

200. For example: "They are words of life and salvation, so that whoever believes in them has all his sins forgiven through that faith; he is a child of life and has overcome death and hell. Language cannot express how great and mighty these words are, for they are the sum and substance of the whole gospel. This is why these words are far more important than the sacrament itself, and a Christian should make it a practice to give far more attention to these words than to the sacrament" ("Adoration of the Sacrament," LW 36:277 [= WA 11:432]). This understanding would find its way into the Small Catechism: "Answer: The words "given for you" and "shed for you for the forgiveness of sins" show us that forgiveness of sin, life, and salvation are given to us in the sacrament through these words, because where there is forgiveness of sin, there is also life and salvation" (K-W, 362).

201. "That These Words of Christ," LW 37:86 (= WA 23:179).

202. "See, then, what a beautiful, great, marvelous thing this is, how everything meshes together in one sacramental reality. The words are the first thing, for without the words the cup and the bread would be nothing. Further, without bread and cup, the body and blood of Christ would not be there. Without the body and blood of Christ, the new testament would not be there. Without the new testament, forgiveness of sins would not be there. Without forgiveness of sins, life and salvation would not be there" ("Confession Concerning Christ's Supper," LW 37:338 [= WA 26:478–79]).

203. "That These Words of Christ," LW 37:133 (= WA 23:257).

204. "That These Words of Christ," LW 37:124–25 (= WA 23:245).

205. "That These Words of Christ," LW 37:129–30 (= WA 23:251).

206. Lindberg, *European Reformations*, 190.

207. It has often been stated that Zwingli could not agree to Luther's last-minute compromise because of the sociopolitical situation in Zurich. Because of the strong Catholic opposition in the city, the bodily presence was viewed as crass papalism among Zwingli's followers. Moreover, Luther's bodily presence doctrine was viewed in Zurich as a relapse into Catholicism. Had he adopted the bodily presence at Marburg, Zwingli would have been accused of relapsing. See, for example, Sasse, *This Is My Body*, 101–2, 231; and Lindberg, *European Reformations*, 174, 196.

208. "Oecolampadius said: They think it is faith because Christ is in the bread. This is an opinion, not faith" ("Marburg Colloquy," LW 38:18 [= WA 30/3:114]).

209. "Zwingli: . . . In fact, you yourself recognize that spiritual eating gives comfort. And since there is agreement on this point, which is the main one, he begs, for the sake of the love of Christ, [that no one be accused of heresy on account of his dissension]. The early fathers, even if they disagreed, nevertheless did not condemn one another in such a way" ("Marburg Colloquy," LW 38:20 [= WA 30/3:117]).

210. "That These Words of Christ," LW 37:23, 25 (= WA 23:79, 81, 83).

211. "That These Words of Christ," LW 37:27 (= WA 23:85, 87).

212. One way this can be observed is in part three of "Confession Concerning Christ's Supper." Part three contains a point-by-point confession of Luther's faith, structured around the three articles of the Apostles' Creed. In this confession, Luther placed the Lord's Supper within the Third Article of the creed and stressed that it was a means of grace through which the Spirit worked. Although Luther didn't specifically mention the Lord's Supper in the Second Article, it is noteworthy that Luther expanded the section on the incarnation, especially stressing that the man Jesus Christ was "one eternal, indivisible person, of God and man, so that Mary the holy Virgin is a real, true mother not only of the man Christ, as the Nestorians teach, but also of the Son of God, as Luke says" (LW 37:362, [= WA 26:501]). Given Luther's earlier accusation that Zwingli had (like Nestorius) separated Christ into two persons, it is likely that the Wittenberg reformer had the Lord's Supper in mind in the Second Article also. It was Sasse's opinion that in part three of Luther's "Confession Concerning the Supper": "[T]he article on the Lord's Supper is brought into connection with the entire Christian doctrine" (Sasse, *This Is My Body*, 153).

CHAPTER 5

1. John F. Johnson, "Polemicism or Ecumenism," in *Promoting Unity: Themes in Lutheran-Catholic Dialogue*, ed. H. George Anderson and James R. Crumley Jr. (Minneapolis: Augsburg, 1989), 40.

2. "The perceptive Roman Catholic will see behind the form of Luther's remarks, behind the sharp, bitter, angry, and sometimes insulting language, what Luther is really concerned about . . ." (H. P. Hamann, "The Smalcald Articles as a Systematic Theology," *Concordia Theological Quarterly* 52 [January 1988]: 38).

3. For the road the Schmalkald Articles followed to confessional status and inclusion in the 1580 Book of Concord, see Robert Kolb, *Confessing the Faith* (St. Louis: Concordia, 1991), 119ff.

4. For a brief description of Luther's health problems during this period, see William R. Russell, *Luther's Theological Testament* (Minneapolis: Fortress, 1995), 24–33. See also Mark U. Edwards Jr., *Luther's Last Battles* (Ithaca: Cornell University Press, 1983), 9. For a general description of Luther's health history, see Friedrich Küchenmeister, *Dr. Martin Luthers Krankengeschichte* (Leipzig: n.p., 1881).

5. Russell, *Luther's Theological Testament*, 24.

6. "Appellatio F. Martini Luther ad Concilium," WA 2:36–40. This was written shortly after Luther's meeting with Cardinal Cajetan at Augsburg. It also was made public without Luther's permission.

7. Of course, such a free, general council meant different things for the evangelicals and the Catholics. "For the Protestants [evangelicals], including Luther, it meant a council free of papal control, in which the laity might participate and vote and the clergy were freed of their oaths of obedience to the pope and, most important of all, in which all decisions were made on the basis of Scripture. For the Catholics, on the other hand, it meant a council that followed the traditional procedures and in which the authority of the pope was not challenged and only the clergy had votes. For Protestants a 'true council' would reform the abuses of the papacy and sustain the Protestant teachings; for Catholics a 'true council' would reform the abuses of the church and, once and for all, pass judgment on the Protestant heresy" (Edwards, *Luther's Last Battles*, 74).

8. For a thorough treatment of these diets and developments, see Hubert Jedin, *A History of the Council of Trent*, trans. Ernest Graf (London: Nelson, 1957), 1:197–281. See also Johann M. Reu, *The Augsburg Confession* (Chicago: Wartburg Publishing House, 1930), 2:32–33.

9. AC, Preface (German text), 21 (K-W, 34).

10. AC, Preface (German text), 21 (K-W, 34).

11. "The Recess of Augsburg, September 22, 1530" is translated in Reu, *Augsburg Confession*, 1:390–92. See also WABr 6:480.

12. Actually, some progress was made toward the end of Clement's pontificate. He and Charles met in Bologna from December 13, 1532, to February 28, 1533, to discuss the council. The pope agreed to send nuncios to sound out the attitudes of the various European rulers toward a council. Count Ugo Rangoni, bishop of Reggio-Emilia, was sent to Germany. In Weimar, on June 3, 1533, Rangoni delivered orally and in writing to the Elector of Saxony, Prince John Frederick, eight articles from the pope that detailed the conditions under which a council would meet. The conditions included the demand that the council would meet in an Italian city, that it would meet "according to the established custom of the Church," and that the participants would agree in advance to submit to the council's decisions. The conditions made it clear that the pope was demanding full control over the council. In a series of opinions that sought to advise the elector, Luther and his colleagues cautioned John Frederick against rejecting the council because the evangelicals had been asking for such a gathering for so long. Nor could the evangelicals support a counter-council because this would either lead to or give the appearance of schism. They made it clear, however, that many of the pope's conditions were unacceptable. Luther was overruled, and on June 30, John Frederick and the Schmalkald League, though not completely closing the door on the council, rejected the pope's proposal and had the eight papal articles and the league's reply published. In fall 1533, thanks to the insistence of the French king, Francis I, Pope Clement gave up the idea of a council for the remainder of his life. See LW 50:82 n. 4, and WABr 6:480ff. See also Martin Brecht, *Martin Luther: The Preservation of the Church, 1532–1546*, trans. James L. Schaaf (Minneapolis: Fortress, 1993), 173–74; and Edwards, *Luther's Last Battles*, 75–76.

13. See WABr 7:317–18, 322; Julius Köstlin, *Life of Luther* (New York: Scribner's, 1911), 463–66; and Brecht, *Preservation of the Church*, 174–76. For an excellent picture of Luther's understanding of a council at this time, see his 1536 disputation "On the Power of the Council," WA 39/1:184–87, which is translated in Edwards, *Luther's Last Battles*, 226–27.

14. Brecht, *Preservation of the Church*, 176.

15. *UuA*, 15–17.

16. See James L. Schaaf, "The Smalcald Articles and Their Significance," in *Interpreting Luther's Legacy*, ed. Fred W. Meuser and Stanley D. Schneider (Minneapolis: Augsburg, 1969), 70.

17. F. Bente, *Historical Introductions to the Book of Concord* (St. Louis: Concordia, 1965), 47. See also Schaaf, "Smalcald Articles," 70. This bull did not refer to the council. See Willard Dow Allbeck, *Studies in the Lutheran Confessions* (Philadelphia: Muhlenberg, 1952), 187.

18. A copy of the official text of the bull was forwarded to John Frederick by Margrave George of Brandenburg on July 6. See LW 50:145 n. 13.

19. The papal legate, Peter van der Vorst, didn't officially present the bull to John Frederick until February 1537. See LW 50:145 n. 13.

20. (1) On July 24, John Frederick requested an opinion from his Wittenberg scholars concerning how or whether he should receive the papal legate. Would such reception constitute submission to the pope? What if the elector was cited as a party to the council rather than merely being invited? For this letter, see CR 3:119. (2) Before the Wittenberg professors had a chance to respond, John Frederick issued his own statement in which he gave several reasons for not attending the council. See CR 3:99ff. (3) An opinion, probably authored by Melanchthon and signed by Luther and the other theologians, was returned to John Frederick on August 6. This opinion cautioned against declining the council, even if the Lutherans were cited. Regardless, the elector should await the wording of the bull. If the evangelicals were cited to present their teaching, they should attend. If they were cited to be condemned, they should decline. Furthermore, the opinion stated that the pope had the right to proclaim a council, but the judgment and decision belonged to the council. Neither should the elector decline because of the site of the council (CR 3:119). For a partial translation of this opinion, see Bente, *Historical Introductions*, 50. (4) John Frederick was not convinced by the arguments of his theologians. Therefore, he dispatched his chancellor, Dr. Gregor Brück, to a gathering of theologians at Luther's house on August 30. Brück delivered a scolding on behalf of John Frederick because the theologians had allowed themselves to be unduly influenced by the jurists and had not approached the subject with the proper diligence nor had they weighed the dangers. Such an invitation, John Frederick said, could only be accepted under protest. Thus he requested a second opinion (CR 3:147; Bente, *Historical Introductions*, 51). Because of Melanchthon's absence from Wittenberg in the autumn of 1536, this second opinion was not finished until December 6.

21. *UuA*, 22–24, which is translated in Bente, *Historical Introductions*, 52.

22. For example, John Frederick wrote a December 11 letter to Luther and the Wittenberg theologians. It officially commissioned Luther to write what would become the Schmalkald Articles. Luther began the document soon after receiving this letter and finished it in two weeks. See *UuA*, 26–29.

23. Per the prince's order, Luther submitted his original draft to the opinion of Justus Jonas, Johannes Bugenhagen, Caspar Cruciger, Melanchthon, Georg Spalatin, Nikolaus von Amsdorf, and Johann Agricola in Wittenberg after Christmas 1536. Each article was read, then discussed. One major addition at this point was a section on the adoration of the saints. Some unnecessary doctrines mentioned for discussion were ordination, adiaphora, and whether the evangelicals should stop preaching against one kind in the Sacrament if the pope conceded to them the use of both kinds. These nonessential matters were not included. On this, see Bente, *Historical Introductions*, 58. The Schmalkald Articles were subscribed by all. Spalatin then prepared a written copy, which he personally delivered to the elector in early January 1537.

24. There is an indication of this, for example, in the elector's January 7, 1537, letter to Luther: "[A]ccordingly we shall also confess them and have them confessed

freely and publicly before the council, before the whole world, and whatever may come, and we shall ask God that He would vouchsafe grace to our brother and to us, and also to our posterity, that steadfastly and without wavering we may abide and remain in them." The entire letter is in *UuA*, 83–87.

25. "Articles of Christian doctrine which were to have been presented by our side at the council in Mantua—or wherever else it was to have met—and which were to indicate what we could or could not accept or give up" (K-W, 297).

26. SA Preface, 1: "Pope Paul III called a council to meet at Mantua last year around Pentecost. . . . We on our side had to prepare for the eventuality that, whether summoned to the council or not, we would be condemned. I was therefore instructed to compose and assemble articles of our teaching in case it came to negotiations about what and how far we would or could compromise with the papists, and in which things we definitely intended to persist and remain firm" (K-W, 297).

27. SA I, 4 (K-W, 300).

28. SA, II, 2, 10: "This article on the Mass will be the decisive issue in the council because, were it possible for them to give in to us on every other article, they could not give in on this one" (K-W, 303). SA II, 4, 15: "These four articles will furnish them with enough to condemn at the council. They neither can nor will concede to us the tiniest fraction of these articles" (K-W, 310). SA II, 4, 16: "At the council, we will not stand (as at Augsburg) before the emperor or the secular authority . . . . We will stand before the pope and the devil himself, who does not intend to listen but only to damn us on the spot, to murder us, and to force us into idolatry" (K-W, 310).

29. Luther regularly employs the words *weichen* and *nachgeben* in this connection.

30. SA II, 1, 5; SA II, 2, 1, 10, 17, 20, 21, 24, 29; and SA II, 4, 15.

31. Both the council and testamentary purposes are evident. This question was debated in the 1950s by Hans Volz and Ernst Bizer in *Zeitschrift für Kirchengeschichte*. This debate showed that the Schmalkald Articles was both Luther's personal theological testament of faith and a public confessional document written to prepare for deliberations at the Mantua council. Volz built his argument largely on Chancellor Brück's September 3, 1536, letter to Elector John Frederick, which mentioned a note that the elector had asked Brück to give to Luther. The note apparently asked Luther to work on a document that would be Luther's testament. This letter can be found in *UuA*, 18–22. For the debate between Volz and Bizer, see Ernst Bizer, "Zum geschichtlichen Verständnis von Luthers Smalcaldischen Artikeln," *ZKG* 67 (1955–56): 61–92; Hans Volz, "Luthers Smalcaldischen Artikel," *ZKG* 68 (1957): 259–86; and Ernst Bizer, "Noch einmal: Die Smalcaldischen Artikel," *ZKG* 68 (1957): 287–94. For a summary of this debate, see Russell, *Luther's Theological Testament*, 38–41.

32. The council did not meet until June 1545 in Trent.

33. In fact, Luther's articles were never used for the purpose of the council. They were not even considered in plenary session by the Schmalkalden *Bundestag* in February 1537. The Schmalkald League decided that no new statement of faith was needed because they already had the Augsburg Confession and the Wittenberg Concord. The league also decided to decline Pope Paul III's invitation to attend the council. On this and the question of the theologians' subscriptions, see *UuA*, 145–75; Volz, "Luthers Smalcaldischen Artikel," 279ff.; and Schaaf, "Smalcald Articles," 78–80.

34. Hence the statements in SA Preface, 3; SA III, 15, 3. It should be noted that in SA Preface, 3, Luther gives the reason he decided to publish the articles not the reason he originally wrote the document. This testamentary purpose for the Schmalkald Articles would also explain why Luther added SA III, 3, 42–45 and

SA III, 8, 3–13 to the published version, additions that seem to address the fanatics, antinomians, and enthusiasts, as well as the papists. If Luther now perceived the articles to be a statement of his core theology, it would make sense to address these opponents as well.

35. Schaaf, "Smalcald Articles," 81–82.

36. For example, "Why should we poor Christians be forced to believe whatever the pope and his papists think, even when it is not necessary to salvation? Has papal authority the power to make unnecessary matters necessary articles of faith, and can it make heretics of people in matters which are not necessary for salvation?" ("Defense and Explanation of All the Articles, 1521," LW 32:79–80 [= WA 7:429]).

37. "Against Latomus, 1521," LW 32:154 (= WA 8:54).

38. For various theological analyses, see Russell, *Luther's Theological Testament*, 59–114; Allbeck, *Studies in the Lutheran Confessions*, 194–212; Thomas M. McDonough, *The Law and the Gospel in Luther*, Oxford Theological Monographs (Oxford: Oxford University Press, 1963), 130–45; Karl Thieme, *Luthers Testament wider Rom in seinem Schmalkaldischen Artikeln* (Leipzig: Deichert, 1900); and Robert Kolb, "Luther's Smalcald Articles," *Concordia Journal* 14 (April 1988): 115–37.

39. SA I (K-W, 300) (*Luther's emphasis*).

40. For an exposition of the ecumenical creeds, see "The Three Symbols or Creeds of the Christian Faith, 1538," LW 34:201–29.

41. K-W, 300.

42. Luther does show this connection in "Confession Concerning Christ's Supper, 1528," LW 37:360–72; and in "On the Councils and the Church, 1539," LW 41:103ff.

43. Allbeck is on target: "But if there is no dispute in these matters, why are they named? . . . Luther is conscious of being part of the church universal both in doctrine and practice. He was presenting his Articles, not as a heretic, schismatic, or sectarian, but as an ecumenical Christian" (Allbeck, *Studies in the Lutheran Confessions*, 195).

44. Article 1 is on justification by faith in Christ; article 2 is on the Mass; article 3 is on the chapters and monasteries; article 4 is on the papacy. Article 2 also has seven subarticles: purgatory, spirit manifestations, pilgrimages, fraternities, relics, indulgences, and the invocation of saints.

45. SA II (K-W 300).

46. SA II, 1, 1–4 (K-W, 301).

47. SA II, 1, 5 (K-W, 301).

48. SA II, 1, 5 (K-W, 301). It is on the basis of this passage that Lutherans have long referred to the doctrine of justification as the *articulus stantis et candentis ecclesiae*. This phrase is attributed to Valentin Löscher, the champion of Lutheran orthodoxy. See Gerhard Sauter, "Rechtfertigung," *TRE* 28 (1992): 315 (the English translation appears in *LQ* 11 [1997]: 17–102, here 44).

49. *Hauptartikel* is a technical term that Luther uses throughout the Schmalkald Articles.

50. As Robert Preus has pointed out, the doctrine of justification had a much larger role to play for Luther and the Lutheran confessors than the hermeneutical one. "The centrality of the article of justification and its key function in exegesis, hermeneutics, confession, preaching, and holy living is not merely a quirk of Luther's which chanced to find its way into the theology of Melanchthon and the Lutheran Confessions at various points. It is rather a veritable and overarch-

ing principle which explains the theology and structure of Lutheranism" (Preus, *Justification and Rome* [St. Louis: Concordia Academic Press, 1997], 18).

51. "Luther spoke indiscriminately of the article of Christ, the article of justification, and the article of faith in Christ as we have seen. This practice was neither deliberate nor haphazard, but natural. Luther and the Lutheran Confessions never considered justification narrowly as a mere formulation or definition. The justification of a sinner, whether considered as an article of faith or an event, cannot be separated from the grace of God, the redeeming work of Christ, the work of the Spirit through the means of grace and faith in Christ. The article of justification entails all these biblical motifs and cannot be presented or confessed in isolation from them" (Preus, *Justification and Rome*, 117 n. 6).

52. They are Rom. 4:25; John 1:29; Isa. 53:6; Rom. 3:23–25; Rom. 3:28; Rom. 3:26; Acts 4:12; and Isa. 53:5.

53. SA II, 2, 2 (K-W, 301–2).

54. SA II, 2, 8–9 (K-W, 302–3).

55. SA II, 2, 11–29 (K-W, 303–6).

56. SA II, 2, 13–15 (K-W, 304). The Latin translation is significant here: "We have a different rule, namely, that . . ."

57. SA II, 2, 13–15 (K-W, 304).

58. SA II, 2, 18 (K-W, 304).

59. SA II, 2, 21 (author's translation from *BSLK*).

60. SA II, 2, 22–23 (author's translation from *BSLK*).

61. SA II, 2, 24 (author's translation from *BSLK*).

62. SA II, 2, 25 (author's translation from *BSLK*).

63. SA II, 3, 2 (author's translation from *BSLK*).

64. SA II, 4, 1 (K-W, 307).

65. SA II, 4, 5 (K-W, 308).

66. SA II, 2, 1 (K-W, 301).

67. SA II, 2, 7 (K-W, 302).

68. SA II, 2, 12 (K-W, 303).

69. SA II, 2, 19 (K-W, 304).

70. SA II, 2, 21 (K-W, 305).

71. SA II, 2, 23 (K-W, 305).

72. SA II, 2, 24 (K-W, 305).

73. SA II, 2, 25 (K-W, 305).

74. SA II, 3, 2 (K-W, 306).

75. SA II, 4, 3 (K-W, 307).

76. The most extreme example of this was Boniface VIII's bull *Unam Sanctam* (1302): "It is altogether necessary to salvation for every human creature to be subject to the Roman pontiff" (Colman J. Barry, ed., *Readings in Church History* [Westminster, Md.: Newman, 1960], 1:467).

77. SA II, 4, 4 (K-W, 307).

78. SA II, 4, 10, 12 (K-W, 309).

79. See, for example, SA II, 4, 2. "Behind each article is that pastoral concern . . . This is a confession of a pastor, not a schoolman . . . The Smalcald Articles focus our confession on Jesus only, for the sake of His people, that they might receive good pastoral care. That is what Luther's Reformation was all about" (Kolb,

"Luther's Smalcald Articles," 122, 136).

80. Many discussions of Schmalkald Articles part III do not attempt any cohesive explanation. They merely quote the first part of Luther's heading: "We could discuss the following matters or articles with learned, reasonable people or among ourselves" (K-W, 310). A sampling would include Eric W. Gritsch and Robert W. Jenson, *Lutheranism* (Philadelphia: Fortress, 1976), 25; H. William Jordan, "The Smalcald Articles and the Treatise on the Power and Primacy of the Pope," *Currents in Theology and Mission* 4 (Fall 1977): 23; and Hamann, "Smalcald Articles," 30–31, who later qualified this as an "ostensible division." McDonough considered part III, articles 1–8 as restating Luther's basic evangelical principles and part III, articles 9–15 (except for 13) as stating negatively his Law-Gospel scheme by condemning Roman practices. "In any event, the gist of the articles, in their essential content and purpose, is a reavowal and defense of the pure Word of God and the right use of the Sacraments" (McDonough, *The Law and the Gospel*, 134–36). Thieme sees SA III, 4 as holding the key to understanding part III (Thieme, *Luthers Testament*, 49).

81. "These are the articles on which I must stand and on which I intend to stand, God willing, until my death. I can neither change nor concede anything in them. If anybody desires to do so, it is on that person's conscience" (K-W, 326).

82. The articles discussed in SA III are: I. Sin; II. The Law; III. Repentance; IV. The Gospel; V. Baptism; VI. The Sacrament of the Altar; VII. The Keys; VIII. Confession; IX. Excommunication; X. Ordination and Vocation; XI. The Marriage of Priests; XII. The Church; XIII. How Man Is Justified and Good Works; XIV. Monastic Vows; and XV. Human Traditions.

83. Allbeck, *Studies in the Lutheran Confessions*, 198.

84. Russell, *Luther's Theological Testament*, 114.

85. SA III (K-W, 310).

86. SA III, 15, 3 (K-W, 326).

87. "Against the Heavenly Prophets in the Matter of Images and Sacraments, 1525," LW 40:130 (= WA 18:114).

88. "Against the Heavenly Prophets, 1525," LW 40:122 (= WA 18:105).

89. See *The Ecumenical Luther*, pp. 48ff.

90. SA III, 4 (K-W, 319).

91. SA III, 12, 2 (K-W, 324–25).

92. SA III, 13, 2–3 (K-W, 325).

93. SA III, 14, 1 (K-W, 325).

94. SA III, 14, 1 (K-W, 325).

95. SA III, 15, 1 (K-W, 326).

96. SA III, 1, 3 (K-W, 311).

97. SA III, 1, 11 (K-W, 311).

98. SA III, 3, 12 (K-W, 314).

99. SA III, 3, 14 (K-W, 314).

CHAPTER 6

1. "In ecclesiology everything hinges on a few crucial distinctions, and the most crucial distinction of all is that between the church as the interior fellowship of faith and the church as the exterior fellowship in the means of grace" (Kurt E. Marquart, *The Church and Her Fellowship, Ministry, and Governance*, Confessional Lutheran Dogmatics 9 [Waverly: The International Foundation for Confes-

sional Lutheran Research, 1990], 8). This twofold aspect of the one church is also referred to as visible/invisible. The Apology of the Augsburg Confession clearly states the inner and outer aspects of the church: "For we grant in this life hypocrites and evil people are mingled with the church and are members of the church according to the external association of the church's signs—that is, Word, confession of faith, and sacraments—especially if they have not been excommunicated. . . . However, the church is not only an association of external ties and rites like other civic organizations, but it is principally an association of faith and the Holy Spirit in the hearts of persons. It nevertheless has its external marks so that it can be recognized, namely the pure teaching of the gospel and the administration of the sacraments in harmony with the gospel of Christ" (Ap. VII–VIII 3, 5 [K-W, 174]).

2. The words *ecumenism* and *ecumenical* come from the Greek word *oikoumene*, which in the Greco-Roman world and in the Greek New Testament meant "the inhabited world" or "worldwide." In the sixteenth century, the Apostles', Nicene, and Athanasian Creeds were called "ecumenical" creeds because Christians throughout the world confessed them. It was in the twentieth century that the word *ecumenical* began to be used for the unity of the church worldwide. For a lexical study of the word *ecumenical*, see Ruth Rouse and Stephen Charles Neill, eds., *A History of the Ecumenical Movement*, vol. 1, *1517–1948*, 2d ed. (Philadelphia: Westminster, 1968), 735–40.

3. Rouse and Neill, *History of the Ecumenical Movement*, 1:353–63.

4. Rouse and Neill, *History of the Ecumenical Movement*, 1:360–61, 406–41.

5. Rouse and Neill, *History of the Ecumenical Movement*, 1:545ff.

6. On the history and formation of the WCC, see Robert S. Bilheimer, *Breakthrough: The Emergence of the Ecumenical Tradition* (Grand Rapids: Eerdmans, 1989). The WCC is the largest ecumenical organization in the world today, numbering 342 churches in more than 120 countries.

7. On the formation of the LWF, see E. Clifford Nelson, *The Rise of World Lutheranism: An American Perspective* (Philadelphia: Fortress, 1982). As of 2003, the LWF included 136 member church bodies, representing 61.7 of 65.4 million Lutherans worldwide. The 2.5 million-member Lutheran Church—Missouri Synod (LCMS) is not a member of the LWF.

8. As seen, for example, in the 1928 papal encyclical *Mortalium Animos*, in which Pope Pius XI forbid all Catholics from participating in the Ecumenical Movement. He wrote that such participation denied that the Roman Catholic Church alone is the true church and that unity can occur only when Christian denominations return to Rome and to papal obedience. This was repeated in two subsequent encyclicals of Pope Pius XII: *Mysticus Corporis Christi* (1943) and *Humani Generis* (1950). In Rouse and Neill, *History of the Ecumenical Movement*, 1:677–93.

9. "The restoration of unity among all Christians is one of the principal concerns of the Second Vatican Council . . . Certainly, such division openly contradicts the will of Christ, scandalizes the world, and damages the most holy cause, the preaching of the Gospel to every creature. . . . The sacred Council exhorts, therefore, all the Catholic faithful to recognize the signs of the times and to take an active and intelligent part in the work of ecumenism" (Second Vatican Ecumenical Council, "Decree on Ecumenism *Unitatis Redintegratio*," 1, 4, in *The Ecumenical Movement*, ed. Michael Kinnamon and Brian E. Cope [Geneva: WCC Publications, and Grand Rapids: Eerdmans, 1997], 27, 30).

10. The ultimate goal is full communion, in which ministries are recognized and the Eucharist is shared.

11. Described in Gerard Kelly, *Recognition*, American University Studies, ser. VII,

vol. 186 (New York: Peter Lang, 1996), 104–5.

12. This was clarified at the 1975 Assembly at Nairobi in "Breaking Barriers," II.4, in *The Ecumenical Movement*, ed. Michael Kinnamon and Brian E. Cope (Geneva: WCC Publications, and Grand Rapids: Eerdmans, 1997), 110.

13. This was the critique of the LWF. See Kelly, *Recognition*, 113.

14. "Breaking Barriers," II.6, in *Ecumenical Movement*, 111.

15. Statement on "The Unity We Seek," in *The Ecumenical Movement*, ed. Michael Kinnamon and Brian E. Cope (Geneva: WCC Publications, and Grand Rapids: Eerdmans, 1997), 122.

16. "2.2. Diversities which are rooted in theological traditions, various cultural, ethnic or historical contacts are integral to the nature of communion. . . . In communion diversities are brought together in harmony as gifts of the Holy Spirit, contributing to the richness and fullness of the church of God" (Kinnamon and Cope, *Ecumenical Movement*, 125).

17. "2.1 The unity of the church to which we are called is a koinonia given and expressed in the common confession of the apostolic faith; a common sacramental life entered by one baptism and celebrated together in one eucharistic fellowship; a common life in which members and ministries are mutually recognized and reconciled; and a common mission witnessing the gospel of God's grace to all people and serving the whole of creation" (Kinnamon and Cope, *Ecumenical Movement*, 124).

18. From "A Declaration of Ecumenical Commitment: A Policy Statement of the Evangelical Lutheran Church in America," adopted at the ELCA Churchwide Assembly on 31 August 1991 by a vote of 919 for, 67 against, and 4 abstaining. See *Ecumenism: The Vision of the ELCA* (Chicago: ELCA, Office of the Secretary, 1991), 37.

19. Jon Nilson, *Nothing beyond the Necessary* (New York: Paulist, 1995), v.

20. Harding Meyer, "Fundamental Difference—Fundamental Consensus," *MidStream* 25 (July 1986): 247.

21. Two representative examples are Joseph A. Burgess, ed., *In Search of Christian Unity* (Minneapolis: Fortress, 1991); and Robert W. Jenson, *Unbaptized God: The Basic Flaw in Ecumenical Theology* (Minneapolis: Fortress, 1992).

22. Gerhard O. Forde, "The Catholic Impasse: Reflections on Lutheran-Catholic Dialogue Today," in *Promoting Unity: Themes in Lutheran-Catholic Dialogue*, ed. H. George Anderson and James R. Crumley Jr. (Minneapolis: Augsburg, 1989), 67, 68. Robert Jenson echoes this observation: "It has come to seem that the traditional conflicts between any two of the great confessions must be only symptoms and manifestations of difference hidden at some conceptual level deeper than that occupied by the traditional matters of controversy" (Jenson, *Unbaptized God*, 6).

23. George A. Lindbeck, *The Nature of Doctrine* (Philadelphia: Westminster, 1984), 7.

24. This is discussed, for example, by Hermann Sasse in *Here We Stand: Nature and Character of the Lutheran Faith*, trans. Theodore G. Tappert (Adelaide: Lutheran Publishing House, 1979), 83–92.

25. Eusebius, *Church History* 5.24.13. Philip Schaff and Henry Wace, eds., *Nicene and Post-Nicene Fathers of the Christian Church*, 2d ser., vol. 1 (Grand Rapids: Eerdmans, 1982), 243. These words were contained in a letter that Bishop Ireneaus wrote to Victor, the bishop of Rome, in about A.D. 190. Victor had excommunicated all the churches in Asia because they celebrated the Paschal Fast (the celebration of Christ's death and resurrection) on the 14th of Nissan, rather than on the Friday and Sunday following the first full moon after the vernal equinox, as did the rest of the churches. Ireneaus admonished Victor not to

destroy the unity of the church over such a thing.

26. John Paul II, *Ut Unum Sint* (Washington, D.C.: United States Catholic Conference, 1996), 89.78.

27. Kelly, *Recognition*, 226.

28. After decades of ambiguity concerning this phrase, in 1991 the WCC Faith and Order Commission released a study entitled "Confessing One Faith." It explained and recommended the Nicene-Constantinopolitan Creed of A.D. 325 as a summary of the apostolic faith. However, "Confessing the Faith" was not meant to be a definitive statement; instead, it was a working document that solicited response from the churches.

29. The introduction of the 1982 WCC Faith and Order Commission document "Baptism, Eucharist, and Ministry" asked churches to prepare an official response that would inform the commission of "the extent to which your church can recognize in this text the faith of the Church through the ages." See Kinnamon and Cope, *Ecumenical Movement*, 178.

30. John Paul II, *Ut Unum Sint*, 23.18, 65.57, 92.81, 105.94.

31. John Paul II, *Ut Unum Sint*, 24.18.

32. John Paul II, *Ut Unum Sint*, 42.36.

33. John Paul II, *Ut Unum Sint*, 43.36.

34. "Decree on Ecumenism," in *The Documents of Vatican II*, ed. Walter M. Abbott, trans. ed. Joseph Gallagher (Piscataway: New Century, 1966), 354.11: "When comparing doctrines, they [Catholic theologians] should remember that in Catholic teaching there exists an order or 'hierarchy' of truths, since they vary in their relationship to the foundation of the Christian faith." This quote implies that truths are not of the same importance because not all relate to the foundation of the faith in the same way. Yet "the foundation of the Christian faith" is not defined; therefore, the hierarchy of truths becomes meaningless for ecumenism. This is discussed in Nilson, *Nothing beyond the Necessary*, 66–74.

35. John Paul II, *Ut Unum Sint*, 24.18.

36. John Paul II, *Ut Unum Sint*, 43.36.

37. Heinrich Fries and Karl Rahner, *Unity of the Churches: An Actual Possibility*, trans. Ruth C. L. Gritsch and Eric W. Gritsch (Philadelphia: Fortress, and New York: Paulist, 1985), 13.

38. Cited in Nilson, *Nothing beyond the Necessary*, 29–39. Also dissenting was Joseph Cardinal Ratzinger, prefect of the Vatican's Congregation for the Doctrine of the Faith, who is arguably the most influential Roman Catholic theologian today. He argued that thesis one of the Fries-Rahner proposal was "ecumenism in reverse" that returns to A.D. 400 and ignores everything that has happened since then. Also cited in Nilson, *Nothing beyond the Necessary*, 41.

39. Nilson, *Nothing beyond the Necessary*, 68.

40. "What is decisively new in Luther over against the medieval tradition is that . . . in the course of his dispute with Rome he was forced more and more to give Scripture critical value against specific traditions and doctrinal positions in tension with or actually opposed to Scripture" (Bernhard Lohse, *Martin Luther's Theology*, trans. and ed. Roy A. Harrisville [Minneapolis: Fortress, 1999], 187).

41. "Proceedings at Augsburg, 1518," LW 31:282 (= WA 2:21).

42. "Against Latomus, 1521," LW 32:230 (= WA 8:108).

43. "Defense and Explanation of All the Articles, 1521," LW 32:11–12 (= WA 7:317).

44. "Defense and Explanation," LW 32:81 (= WA 7:429–30).

45. "The Gospel for the Sunday after Christmas, Luke 2," LW 52:146 (= WA 10/1:446).

46. "Defense and Explanation," LW 32:96 (= WA 7:453).

47. "Answer to the HyperChristian, Hyperspiritual, and Hyperlearned Book by Goat Emser in Leipzig—including Some Thoughts Regarding His Companion, the Fool Murner, 1521," LW 39:164 (= WA 7:638–39).

48. "Defense and Explanation," LW 32:11 (= WA 7:315).

49. "The Babylonian Captivity of the Church, 1520," LW 36:107 (= WA 6:560–61).

50. "The Bondage of the Will, 1525," LW 33:90–91 (= WA 18:652).

51. Norvald Yri, *Quest for Authority: An Investigation of the Quest for Authority within the Ecumenical Movement from 1910 to 1974 and the Evangelical Response* (Kisumu: Evangel Publishing House, 1978), 243.

52. An excellent primer on the more recent critical interpretive methods is Janice Capel Anderson and Stephen D. Moore, eds., *Mark and Method: New Approaches in Biblical Studies* (Minneapolis: Fortress, 1992).

53. Carl E. Braaten and Robert W. Jenson, eds., introduction to *Reclaiming the Bible for the Church* (Grand Rapids: Eerdmans, 1995), ix–xi.

54. Braaten and Jenson, *Reclaiming the Bible*, 69–78. Alister McGrath refers to this hijacking of the study of Scripture by the contemporary culture as "the Babylonian captivity of Scripture."

55. "The most holy Synod of Trent, perceiving that this truth and instruction is contained in the written books and in the unwritten traditions, which, after they had been received by the apostles from the mouth of Christ Himself or from the apostles themselves, the Holy Spirit dictating, have come down to us, transmitted as it were from hand to hand; and following the example of the orthodox fathers, it receives and venerates with equal devotion and reverence all the books of the Old and the New Testament (since God is the author of both) and also said traditions, both those pertaining to faith, and those pertaining to morals, as dictated either orally by Christ or by the Holy Spirit and preserved by a continuous succession in the Catholic Church" (The First Decree of the Fourth Session of the Council of Trent). About this decree, Martin Chemnitz remarked: "It is truly a Pandora's box, under whose cover every kind of corruption, abuse, and superstition has been brought into the church. For what fiction will not be allowed, if once this postulate is granted, that proof and confirmation of the Scripture are not necessary?" (Martin Chemnitz, *Examination of the Council of Trent*, trans. Fred Kramer [St. Louis: Concordia, 1971], 1:219).

56. "Dogmatic Constitution on Divine Revelation (*Dei Verbum*)," in *Documents of Vatican II*, 117.9, 10; 125.21.

57. The *magisterium* is the pope and the bishops collectively.

58. "Dogmatic Constitution on Divine Revelation," in *Documents of Vatican II*, 118.10.

59. When a question of truth was at stake, the apostles always pointed their congregations backward to the apostolic doctrine already given—not to a new unfolding of tradition. The reference point was always the past. Cf. Rom. 16:17; 1 Cor. 11:1, 23–25; Gal. 1:8-9; Col. 2:6–7; Heb. 13:8–9; Jude 1:3.

60. John Paul II, *Ut Unum Sint*, par. 78, p. 90.

61. Declared church dogma by Pope Pius IX in the bull *Ineffabilis* on 8 December 1854.

62. Declared church dogma by Pope Pius XIII in the apostolic constitution *Munificentisimus* on 1 November 1950.

63. John Paul II, *Ut Unum Sint*, 107–8.97.

64. "If anyone says that the Roman Pontiff has only the office of inspection and direction, but not the full and supreme power of jurisdiction over the whole Church, not only in matters that pertain to faith and morals, but also in matters that pertain to the discipline and government of the Church throughout the whole world; or if anyone say that he has only a more important part and not the complete fullness of the supreme power; or if anyone says that this power is not ordinary and immediate either over each and every Church or over each and every shepherd and faithful, anathema sit." Quoted in Carl E. Braaten and Robert W. Jenson, eds., *Church Unity and the Papal Office* (Grand Rapids: Eerdmans, 2001), 65.

65. See John Paul II, *Ut Unum Sint*, 98.88–108.97.

66. John Paul II, *Ut Unum Sint*, 105.94.

67. "But the college of bishops has no authority unless it is simultaneously conceived of in terms of its head, the Roman Pontiff, Peter's successor, and without any lessening of his power or primacy over all, pastors as well as general faithful. For in virtue of his office, that is, as Vicar of Christ and pastor of the whole Church, the Roman Pontiff has full, supreme, and universal power over the Church. And he can always exercise this power freely" ("Dogmatic Constitution on the Church," in *Documents of Vatican II*, 43.22).

68. See the essay in Braaten and Jenson, *Church Unity and Papal Office*, as an example of the "hands off" approach that often passes for scholarship in the Ecumenical Movement. Stressing the positive is one thing—but not at the expense of accuracy and honesty.

69. "And I tell you that you are Peter, and on this rock I will build my church, and the gates of Hades will not overcome it. I will give you the keys of the kingdom of heaven; whatever you bind on earth will be bound in heaven, and whatever you loose on earth will be loosed in heaven."

70. For a historical survey on how the Petrine Ministry of the Bishop of Rome was understood in the first centuries of the church, see Brian E. Daley, "The Ministry of Primacy and the Communion of Churches," in *Church Unity and the Papal Office*, ed. Carl E. Braaten and Robert W. Jenson (Grand Rapids: Eerdmans, 2001), 27–58.

71. "Defense and Explanation," LW 32:67–68 (= WA 7:409). Luther was commenting on Article 25.

72. "The Judgment of Martin Luther on Monastic Vows, 1521," LW 44:317 (= WA 8:617).

73. 1 Cor. 9:5.

74. 1 Tim. 3:2; cf. also Titus 1:5–6.

75. 1 Tim. 4:1–5.

76. Matt. 19:10–12; 1 Cor. 7:7.

77. See "Decree on the Ministry and Life of Priests," in *Documents of Vatican II*, 566.16.

78. Namely, Matt. 19:10; Luke 20:36; 1 Cor. 7:32–34. See "Decree on Priestly Formation," in *Documents of Vatican II*, 446–47.10.

79. William A. Norgren and William G. Rusch, *"Toward Full Communion" and "Concordat of Agreement"* (Minneapolis: Augsburg, and Cincinnati: Forward Movement Publications, 1991).

80. Anglicans have defined this variously from the sixteenth through the nineteenth centuries. John Henry Newman, speaking for the Tractarian movement, understood the historic episcopate to be an unbroken chain of the laying on of hands from Peter to the current bishops. This view seems to have influenced the

Chicago Lambeth Quadrilateral. See Robert J. Goeser, "Augustana 28 and Lambeth 4: Episcopacy as Adiaphoron or Necessity" in *Concordat of Agreement: Supporting Essays*, ed. Daniel F. Martensen (Minneapolis: Augsburg, and Cincinnati: Forward Movement Publications, 1995), 31–54.

81. It is so described in chapter 1 of Norgren and Rusch, *"Toward Full Communion,"* 19ff.

82. The other three being the Holy Scriptures, the Apostles' and Nicene Creeds, and the sacraments of Baptism and Eucharist. As cited in Norgren and Rusch, *"Toward Full Communion,"* 19.

83. In the Lutheran-Episcopal dialogue, the Ordinal of 1662 has often been cited. It declares that only bishops who stand in the historic episcopate can ordain persons into the priesthood.

84. See, for example, Eric W. Gritsch, "Episcopacy: the Legacy of the Lutheran Confessions," in *Concordat of Agreement: Supporting Essays*, ed. Daniel F. Martensen (Minneapolis: Augsburg, and Cincinnati: Forward Movement Publications, 1995), 101–12; and Goeser, "Augustana 28 and Lambeth 4," 31–54.

85. Norgren and Rusch, *"Toward Full Communion,"* 100.

86. Norgren and Rusch, *"Toward Full Communion,"* 100.

87. "While the two churches will fully acknowledge the authenticity of each other's ordained ministries from the beginning of the process, the creation of a common, and therefore fully interchangeable, ministry will occur with the full incorporation of all active bishops in the historic episcopate by common joint ordinations" ("Concordat of Agreement," E.14, in Norgren and Rusch, *"Toward Full Communion,"* 104).

88. Edward D. Schneider, "A Response," *Dialog* 32 (Summer 1993): 223.

89. "Call to Common Mission," 13.

90. "For The Episcopal Church, full communion, although begun at the same time, will not be fully realized until both churches determine that in the context of a common life and mission there is a shared ministry of bishops in the historic episcopate" ("Call to Common Mission," 14).

91. Representative of this debate are two articles that appeared in the fall 2000 issue of *Dialog*. The articles are Carl E. Braaten, "Episcopacy and the E.L.C.A.," *Dialog* 39 (Fall 2000): 214–21; and Vitor Westhelle, "Augsburg Confession VII and the Historic Episcopate," *Dialog* 39 (Fall 2000): 222–28. Braaten argues for the agreement with ECUSA. Westhelle argues against it.

92. "And it is enough for the true unity of the church to agree concerning the teaching of the gospel and the administration of the sacraments. It is not necessary that human traditions, rites, or ceremonies instituted by human beings be alike everywhere" (AC VII, 2–4, Latin text [K-W, 43]).

93. Braaten, "Episcopacy and the E.L.C.A.," 216.

94. "With no mention of the canonical Scriptures as the Word of God, no mention of the ordained ministry to the Word and Sacraments, and no mention of the Ecumenical Creeds of the Ancient Church, let us not for a moment suppose that Article VII can bear the entire weight of eucharistic fellowship" (Braaten, "Episcopacy and the E.L.C.A.," 216). This is a perplexing statement. It is self-evident that all the articles of faith, including the ones that Braaten mentions here, are included in the phrase *doctrina evangelii* (doctrine of the Gospel), which are then made explicit in the articles of the Augsburg Confession and in the remainder of the Lutheran Confessions.

95. Westhelle, "Augsburg Confession VII and the Historic Episcopate," 224.

96. The old misunderstanding that Augsburg Confession VII has nothing to do with

doctrinal formulations or confessions is, unfortunately, still with us and is still repeated in certain Lutheran circles. It is also a total misunderstanding of the reformers' emphasis on doctrine, as this study has shown. For example, Leif Grane writes: "There can be no doubt that the phrase *consentire de doctrina evangelii* (to agree concerning the teaching of the Gospel), refers to proclamation, not to 'correct doctrine' or something similar" (Grane, *The Augsburg Confession: A Commentary*, trans. John H. Rasmussen [Minneapolis: Augsburg, 1987], 96–97). Kurt Marquart has well said, "[A]ttempts to turn AC VII into an attractive ecumenical slogan by jettisoning unwelcome dogmatic ballast, continue unabated" (Marquart, *Church and Her Fellowship*, 56).

97. K-W, 640.

98. *The Joint Declaration on the Doctrine of Justification in Confessional Lutheran Perspective* (St. Louis: LCMS Commission on Theology and Church Relations, 1999), 20, 21.

99. The "Joint Declaration on the Doctrine of Justification" was written by theologians of the LWF and the Roman Catholic Church in 1997. It claimed to represent a "consensus in the basics truths of the doctrine of justification," with the result that the doctrine of justification was no longer considered to be church-dividing. Because of this agreement, the mutual condemnations between Lutherans and Catholics concerning justification no longer applied. The ELCA adopted the text at its August 1997 Worldwide Assembly. Amid great pomp and publicity, leaders of the LWF and the Catholic Church signed the document on 31 October 1998 in Augsburg, Germany. It continues to be heralded as a major ecumenical breakthrough and a major step toward unity between Lutherans and Catholics.

100. *Joint Declaration on the Doctrine of Justification in Confessional Lutheran Perspective*, 53; "Joint Declaration on the Doctrine of Justification," 18.

101. "Response of the Roman Catholic Church to the Joint Declaration," *One in Christ* 36 (January 2000): 81.

102. The other major difference is that the language of the "Joint Declaration" shows that Catholics continue to think of justification, at least in part, as an ongoing internal transformation. Lutherans teach that justification is a forensic act: God declares the sinner righteous for Christ's sake through faith. For Lutherans, justification is an immediate verdict that happens outside the sinner. For an excellent analysis of the "Joint Declaration," see *Joint Declaration on the Doctrine of Justification in Confessional Lutheran Perspective*.

103. Edward Yarnold, *In Search of Unity* (Collegeville: Liturgical Press, 1988), 85–86.

104. 1 Cor. 14:34 (ESV): "[W]omen should keep silent in the churches. For they are not permitted to speak, but should be in submission, as the Law also says." 1 Tim. 2:12 (ESV): "I do not permit a woman to teach or to exercise authority over a man; rather, she is to remain quiet." Obviously, a more complex argument can be made. For example, that of the order of creation vs. the order of redemption, that the Son of God became man, that Christ chose only men to be his apostles, that the apostles did not choose women to succeed them, etc. For a summary of the issues involved in the ordination of women, see Marquart, *Church and Her Fellowship*, 166–71.

105. This is stated in AC V, 1–3: "To obtain such faith God instituted the office of preaching, giving the gospel and the sacraments. Through these, as through means, he gives the Holy Spirit who produces faith, where and when he wills, in those who hear the gospel" (K-W, 40).

106. LCMS Commission on Theology and Church Relations, *A Lutheran Stance Toward Ecumenism* (St. Louis: Concordia, 1974), 12 (*original emphasis*).

107. *Formula of Agreement in Confessional Lutheran Perspective* (St. Louis: LCMS,

1999), 35–36.

108. Keith F. Nickle and Timothy F. Lull, eds., *A Common Calling: The Witness of Our Reformation Churches in North American Today* (Minneapolis: Augsburg Fortress, 1993), 66.

109. "Joint Declaration on the Doctrine of Justification," 50.

110. Robert Preus, *Justification and Rome* (St. Louis: Concordia Academic Press, 1997), 111–12.

BIBLIOGRAPHY

PRIMARY SOURCES

Bromiley, G. W., ed. and trans. *Zwingli and Bullinger.* Library of Christian Classics 24. Philadelphia: Westminster, 1953.

Luther, Martin. *D. Martin Luthers Werke. Kritische Gesamtausgabe. Briefwechsel.* 18 vols. Weimar: Hermann Böhlaus Nachfolger, 1930–1985.

——. *D. Martin Luthers Werke. Kritische Gesamtausgabe. Deutsche Bibel.* Weimar. 12 vols. in 15. Weimar: Hermann Böhlaus Nachfolger, 1906–1961.

—— . *D. Martin Luthers Werke. Kritische Gesamtausgabe. Schriften.* 68 vols. Weimar: Hermann Böhlaus Nachfolger, 1883–1999.

——. *D. Martin Luthers Werke. Kritische Gesamtausgabe. Tischreden.* Weimar: Hermann Böhlaus Nachfolger, 1912–1921. Reprinted in 2000.

——. *Dr. Martin Luthers Sämmtliche Schriften.* 2d ed. 23 vols. in 24. Edited by Johann Georg Walch. St. Louis: Concordia, 1881–1910.

——. *Luther's Works.* American Edition. General editors Jaroslav Pelikan and Helmut T. Lehmann. 56 vols. St. Louis: Concordia, and Philadelphia: Muhlenburg and Fortress, 1957–1986.

——. *Sermons of Martin Luther.* Edited by John Nicholas Lenker. Translated by John Nicholas Lenker et al. 8 vols. Reprint, Grand Rapids: Baker, 1983.

Rupp, E. Gordon, and Philip S. Watson, eds. and trans. *Luther and Erasmus: Free Will and Salvation.* Library of Christian Classics 17. Philadelphia: Westminister, 1969.

Smith, Preserved, and Charles M. Jacobs, eds. and trans. *Luther's Correspondence and Other Contemporary Letters.* 2 vols. Philadelphia: Lutheran Publication Society, 1913–18.

Zwingli, Ulrich. *Commentary on True and False Religion.* Edited by Samuel Macauley Jackson and Clarence Nevin Heller. Durham, N. C.: Labyrinth Press, 1981.

——. *Huldreich Zwinglis sämtliche Werke.* Edited by Emil Egli and Georg Finsler. Corpus Reformatorum, vols. 88ff. Reprint, Zurich: Theologischer Verlag Zurich, 1983.

——. *On Providence and Other Essays.* Edited by S. M. Jackson and W. J. Hinke. Durham, N. C.: Labyrinth Press, 1983.

——. *Writings.* Vol. 2, *In Search of True Religion, Reformation, Pastoral and Eucharistic Writings.* Edited by H. Wayne Pipkin and Edward J. Furcha. Pittsburgh Theological Monographs, new ser., vol. 13. Allison Park, Penn.: Pickwick, 1984.

SECONDARY SOURCES

Allbeck, Willard Dow. *Studies in the Lutheran Confessions*. Philadelphia: Muhlenberg, 1952.

Althaus, Paul. *The Ethics of Martin Luther*. Translated by Robert C. Schultz. Philadelphia: Fortress, 1972.

―――. *Die Theologie Martin Luthers*. Gütersloh: Gütersloher, 1962.

―――. *The Theology of Martin Luther*. Translated by Robert C. Schultz. Philadelphia: Fortress, 1966.

Anderson, H. George, T. Austin Murphy, and Joseph A. Burgess, eds. *Justification by Faith*. Lutherans and Catholics in Dialogue 6. Minneapolis: Augsburg, 1985.

Atkinson, James. "Martin Bucer (1491–1551): Ecumenical Pioneer." *The Churchman* 79 (1965): 19–28.

Bagchi, David V. N. *Luther's Earliest Opponents: Catholic Controversialists, 1518–1525*. Minneapolis: Fortress, 1991.

Bainton, Roland, H. *Erasmus of Christendom*. New York: Scribner's, 1969.

―――. *Here I Stand: A Life of Martin Luther*. New York: Mentor, 1957.

―――. "Luther and the *Via Media* at the Marburg Colloquy." *The Lutheran Quarterly* 1 (November 1949): 395–96.

Barge, Hermann. *Andreas Bodenstein von Karlstadt*. 2 vols. 1905. Reprint, Nieuwkoop: De Graaf, 1968.

Barry, Colman J., ed.. *Readings in Church History*. Vol. 1, *From Pentecost to the Protestant Revolt*. Westminster, Md.: Newman, 1960.

Bayer, Oswald. "Luther's Ethics as Pastoral Care." *Lutheran Quarterly* 4 (1990): 125–42.

Baylor, Michael G., ed. and trans. *The Radical Reformation*. Cambridge: Cambridge University Press, 1991.

Beisser, Friedrich. *Claritas scripturae bei Martin Luther*. Göttingen: Vandenhoeck & Ruprecht, 1966.

Die Bekenntnisschriften der evangelisch-lutherischen Kirche. 11th edition. Göttingen: Vandenhoeck & Ruprecht, 1992.

Bente, F. *Historical Introductions to the Book of Concord*. St. Louis: Concordia, 1965.

Bizer, Ernst. "Zum geschichtlichen Verständnis von Luthers Smalcaldischen Artikeln." *Zeitschrift für Kirchengeschichte* 67 (1955–56): 61–92.

―――. "Noch einmal: Die Smalcaldischen Artikel." *Zeitschrift für Kirchengeschichte* 68 (1957): 287–94.

Blickle, Peter. *Communal Reformation: The Quest for Salvation in Sixteenth-Century Germany*. Atlantic Highlands: Humanities Press, 1992.

Bornkamm, Heinrich. *Luther in Mid-Career, 1521–1530*. Edited by Karin Bornkamm. Translated by E. Theodore Bachmann. Philadelphia: Fortress, 1983.

Bouwsma, William J. *John Calvin: A Sixteenth Century Portrait*. New York: Oxford University Press, 1988.

Braaten, Carl E., and Robert W. Jenson, eds. *Church Unity and the Papal Office.* Grand Rapids: Eerdmans, 2001.

Brecht, Martin. *Martin Luther: His Road to Reformation, 1483–1521.* Translated by James L. Schaaf. Minneapolis: Fortress, 1985.

———. *Martin Luther: The Preservation of the Church, 1532–1546.* Translated by James L. Schaaf. Minneapolis: Fortress, 1993.

———. *Martin Luther: Shaping and Defining the Reformation, 1521–1532.* Translated by James L. Schaaf. Minneapolis: Fortress, 1990.

Bubenheimer, Ulrich. *Consonantia Theologiae et Jurisprudentiae: Andreas Bodenstein von Karlstadt als Theologe and Jurist zwischen Scholastik und Reformation.* Tübingen: J. C. B. Mohr, 1977.

———. "Karlstadt," *Theologische Realenzyklopädie* 17 (1988): 649–57.

Burgess, Joseph A., ed. *In Search of Christian Unity: Basic Consensus, Basic Differences.* Minneapolis: Fortress, 1991.

Büsser, Fritz. "Zwingli the Exegete: A Contribution to the 450th Anniversary of the Death of Erasmus." Pages 175–96 in *Probing the Reformed Tradition: Historical Studies in Honor of Edward A. Dowey, Jr.* Edited by Elsie Anne McKee and Brian G. Armstrong. Louisville: Westminster/John Knox, 1989.

Cantor, Norman. *Inventing the Middle Ages: The Lives, Works, and Ideas of the Great Medievalists of the Twentieth Century.* New York: William Morrow, 1991.

Chemnitz, Martin. *Examination of the Council of Trent.* Vol. 1. Translated by Fred Kramer. St. Louis: Concordia, 1971.

———. *Examination of the Council of Trent.* Vol. 2. Translated by Fred Kramer. St. Louis: Concordia, 1978.

Commission on Theology and Church Relations, LCMS. *The Joint Declaration on the Doctrine of Justification in Confessional Lutheran Perspective.* St. Louis: LCMS Commission on Theology and Church Relations, 1999.

Denzinger, H., and A. Schönmetzer, eds. *Enchiridion Symbolorum definitionum et declarationuim de rebus fidei et morum.* Freiberg: Herder, 1965.

Dickens, A. G. *The English Reformation.* 2d ed. University Park, Penn.: Pennsylvania State University Press, 1991.

———. *The German Nation and Martin Luther.* New York: Harper & Row, 1974.

Duke, Alastair. *Reformation and Revolt in the Netherlands.* London: Hambledon, 1990.

Ebeling, Gerhard. *Luther: An Introduction to His Thought.* Translated by R. A. Wilson. Philadelphia: Fortress, 1964.

———. *Word and Faith.* Translated by James W. Leitch. Philadelphia: Fortress, 1963.

Edwards, Mark U. Jr. *Luther and the False Brethren.* Stanford: Stanford University Press, 1975.

———. *Luther's Last Battles: Politics and Polemics, 1531–1546.* Ithaca: Cornell University Press, 1983.

———. *Printing, Propaganda, and Martin Luther.* Berkeley: University of California Press, 1994.

————. "Catholic Controversialist Literature, 1518–1555: Some Statistics." *Archiv für Reformationsgeschichte* 79 (1988): 189–204.

————, and George Tavard. *Luther, Reformer for the Churches: An Ecumenical Study Guide.* Philadelphia: Fortress, 1983.

Eells, Hastings. *Martin Bucer.* New Haven: Yale University Press, 1931.

Enders, Ernst Ludwig, ed. *Luther und Emser: Ihre streitschriften as dem jahre 1521.* 2 vols. Halle: Niemeyer, 1890–1892.

Evennett, H. Outram. *The Spirit of the Counter-Reformation.* Edited with a postscript by John Bossy. South Bend, Ind.: University of Notre Dame Press, 1970.

Forde, Gerhard O. *Where God Meets Man: Luther's Down-to-Earth Approach to the Gospel.* Minneapolis: Augsburg, 1973.

Fraenkel, P. "An der Grenze vor Luthers Einfluss: Aversion gegen Umwertung." *Zeitschrift für Kirchengeschichte* 89 (1978): 21–30.

————. "John Eck's Enchiridion of 1525 and Luther's Earliest Arguments against Papal Primacy." *Studia theologica* 21 (1967): 110–63.

Fudge, Thomas A. "Icarus of Basel? Oecolampadius and the Early Swiss Reformation." *Journal of Religious History* 21:3 (October 1997): 268–84.

Gäbler, Ulrich. *Huldrych Zwingli: His Life and Work.* Translated by Ruth C. L. Gritsch. Philadelphia: Fortress, 1986.

Gensichen, Hans-Werner. *Damnamus: Die Verwerfung von Irrlehre bei Luther und im Luthertum des 16. Jahrhunderts.* AGTL 1. Berlin: Lutherisches, 1955.

Gerrish, Brian A. *Grace and Gratitude: The Eucharist in John Calvin's Theology.* Minneapolis: Fortress, 1993.

————. "The Lord's Supper in the Reformed Confessions." In *Major Themes in the Reformed Tradition.* Edited by Donald K. McKim. Grand Rapids: Eerdmans, 1992.

Gindely, Anton. *Geschichte der Böhmischen Brüder.* 2 vols. 2d ed. Prague: Bellmann, 1861–1862.

Goertz, Hans-Jürgen. *Thomas Müntzer: Apocalyptic, Mystic and Revolutionary.* Edinburgh: T & T Clark, 1993.

González, Justo L. *A History of Christian Thought.* Vol. 1. Nashville: Abingdon, 1970.

Greschat, Martin. *Martin Bucer: ein Reformator und seine Zeit.* München: Beck, 1990.

Gritsch, Eric W. *Thomas Müntzer: A Tragedy of Errors.* Minneapolis: Fortress, 1989.

————. "Lutheran Teaching Authority Past and Present." In *Teaching Authority and Infallibility in the Church.* Edited by Paul C. Empie, T. Austin Murphy, and Joseph A. Burgess. Lutherans and Catholics in Dialogue 6. Minneapolis: Augsburg, 1978.

————, and Robert W. Jenson. *Lutheranism: The Theological Movement and Its Confessional Writings.* Philadelphia: Fortress, 1976.

Hamann, H. P. "The Smalcald Articles as a Systematic Theology." *Concordia Theological Quarterly* 52 (January 1988): 38.

Headley, J. M. "The Reformation as Crisis in the Understanding of Tradition." *Archiv für Reformationsgeschichte* 78 (1987): 5–22.

Hendrix, Scott. *Luther and the Papacy: Stages in a Reformation Conflict.* Philadelphia: Fortress, 1981.

Hermann, Ruldoph. *Von der Klarheit der Heiligen Schrift: Untersuchungen und Erörterungen über Luthers Lehre von der Schrift in De servo arbitrio.* Berlin: Evangelische Verlagsanstalt, 1958.

Hillerbrand, Hans J. *Landgrave Philipp of Hesse, 1504–1567.* Reformation Essays and Studies, vol. 1. St. Louis: Foundation for Reformation Research, 1967).

———, ed. *The Oxford Encyclopedia of the Reformation.* 4 vols. New York: Oxford University Press, 1996.

———. "Andreas Bodenstein of Carlstadt, Prodigal Reformer." *Church History* 35 (1966).

Janz, D. R. *Luther on Thomas Aquinas: The Angelic Doctor in the Thought of the Reformer.* Veröffentlichungen des Instituts für europäische Geschichte Mainz 140. Stuttgart: Franz Steiner, 1989.

Jedin, Hubert. *A History of the Council of Trent.* Vol. 1. Translated by Ernest Graf. London: Nelson, 1957.

John Paul II, *Ut Unum Sint.* Washington, D.C.: United States Catholic Conference, 1996.

Johnson, John F. "Polemicism or Ecumenism: Another Look at the Smalcald Articles." In *Promoting Unity: Themes in Lutheran-Catholic Dialogue.* Edited by H. George Anderson and James R. Crumley Jr. Minneapolis: Augsburg, 1989.

Jordan, H. William. "The Smalcald Articles and the Treatise on the Power and Primacy of the Pope." *Currents in Theology and Mission* 4 (Fall 1977): 23.

Jüngel, Eberhard. "Um Gottes willen—Klarheit! Kritische Bemerkungen zur Verharmlosung der kriteriologischen Funktion des Rechtfertigungsartikels-aus Anlass einer–kumenischen 'Gemeinsamen Erklärung zur Rechtfertigungslehre.' " *Zeitschrift für Theologie und Kirche* 94 (1997): 394–406.

Kelly, Gerard. *Recognition: Advancing Ecumenical Thinking.* American University Studies, ser. VII, vol. 186. New York: Peter Lang, 1996.

Kingdon, Robert M. "The Geneva Consistory in the Time of Calvin." In *Calvinism in Europe 1540–1620,* ed. by Andrew Pettegree, Alastair Duke, and Gillian Lewis. Cambridge: Cambridge University Press, 1994.

Kinnamon, Michael, and Brian E. Cope, eds. *The Ecumenical Movement: An Anthology of Key Texts and Voices.* Geneva: WCC Publications, and Grand Rapids: Eerdmans, 1997.

Kittelson, James M. *Luther the Reformer: The Story of the Man and His Career.* Minneapolis: Augsburg, 1986.

———. *Wolfgang Capito: From Humanist to Reformer.* Studies in Medieval and Reformation Thought 17. Leiden: Brill, 1975.

Klug, Eugene F. A. *Church and Ministry: The Role of Church, Pastor, and People from Luther to Walther.* St. Louis: Concordia, 1993.

Köhler, Walther. *Zwingli und Luther: Ihr Streit uber das Abendmahl nach seinen politischen und religiösen Beziehungen.* Vol. 1, *Die religiöse und politische Entwicklung bis zum Marburger Religionsgespräch.* Quellen und Forschungen zur Reformationsgeschicte 6. Leipzig: Verein für Reformationsgeschichte, 1924.

————. *Zwingli und Luther: Ihr Streit über das Abendmahl nach seinen politischen und religiösen Beziehungen.* Vol. 2, *Vom Beginn der Marburger Verhandlungen 1529 bis zum Abschluss der Wittenberger Konkordie von 1536.* Quellen und Forschungen zur Reformationsgeschichte 7. Gütersloh: Bertelsmann, 1953.

Kohls, Ernst Wilhelm. *Die Theologie des Erasmus.* 2 vols. Basel: Friedrich Reinhardt, 1966.

Kolb, Robert. *Confessing the Faith: Reformers Define the Church, 1530–1580.* St. Louis: Concordia, 1991.

————. "Luther's Smalcald Articles: Agenda for Testimony and Confession." *Concordia Journal* 14 (April 1988): 115–37.

Köstlin, Julius. *Life of Luther.* New York: Scribner's, 1911.

————. *The Theology of Luther in Its Historical Development and Inner Harmony.* Vol. 2. Translated by Charles E. Hay. Philadelphia: Lutheran Publication Society, 1897.

Krause, G., and G. Müller, gen. eds. "Lehre." *Theologische Realenzyklopädie.* Berlin: de Gruyter, 1977–.

Krieger, Christian, and Marc Lienhard, eds. *Martin Bucer and Sixteenth Century Europe: actes du colloque de Strasbourg (28–31 août 1991).* Studies in Medieval and Reformation Thought, vols. 52–53. Leiden: Brill, 1993.

Küchenmeister, Friedrich. *Dr. Martin Luthers Krankengeschichte.* Leipzig: n.p. 1881.

Lange, Albert. "Der Bedeutungswandel der Begriffe 'fides' und 'hairesis' und die dogmatische Wertunge der Konzilentscheidungen von Vienne und Trient." *Münchener Theologische Zeitschrift* 4 (1953): 133–46.

Le Goff, Jacques. *Intellectuals in the Middle Ages.* Oxford: Blackwell, 1993.

Lindbeck, George A. *The Nature of Doctrine: Religion and Theology in a Postliberal Age.* Philadelphia: Westminster, 1984.

Lindberg, Carter. *Beyond Charity: Reformation Initiatives for the Poor.* Minneapolis: Fortress, 1993.

————. *The European Reformations.* Cambridge, Mass.: Blackwell, 1996.

————. *The Third Reformation: Charismatic Movements and the Lutheran Tradition.* Macon, Ga.: Mercer University Press, 1983.

————. "The Conception of the Eucharist According to Erasmus and Karlstadt." In *Les Dissidents du XVIᵉ siècle entre l'humanisme et le catholicisme.* Edited by Marc Lienhard. Baden-Baden: Koerner, 1983.

————. "Luther's Critique of the Ecumenical Assumption That Doctrine Divides but Service Unites." *Journal of Ecumenical Studies* 27 (Fall 1990): 679–96.

Locher, Gottfried W. *Die Zwinglische Reformation im Rahmen der europäischen Kirchengeschichte.* Göttingen: Vandenhoeck & Ruprecht, 1979.

Lohse, Bernhard. *Luthers Theologie in ihrer historischen Entwicklung und in ihrem systematischen zusammenhang.* Göttingen: Vandenhoeck & Ruprecht, 1995.

————. *Martin Luther: An Introduction to His Life and Work.* Translated by Robert C. Schultz. Philadephia: Fortress, 1986.

————. *Martin Luther's Theology: Its Historical and Systematic Development.* Translated and edited by Roy A. Harrisville. Minneapolis: Fortress, 1999.

————. "Cajetan und Luther." In *Evangelium in der Geschichte.* Göttingen: Vandenhoeck & Ruprecht, 1988.

Lortz, Joseph. *The Reformation in Germany.* Translated by Ronald Walls. New York: Herder & Herder, 1968.

Luther, Martin. *Studienausgabe.* 6 vols. Edited by Hans-Ulrich Delius. Berlin: Evangelische Verlagsanstalt, 1979–1999.

Lynch, Joseph H. *The Medieval Church: A Brief History.* London: Longman, 1992.

Maltby, William S., ed. *Reformation Europe: A Guide to Research II.* St. Louis: Center for Reformation Research, 1992.

Manns, Peter, Harding Meyer, Carter Lindberg, and Harry McSorley, eds. *Luther's Ecumenical Significance: An Interconfessional Consultation.* Philadelphia: Fortress, and New York: Paulist, 1984.

Marquart, Kurt E. *The Church and Her Fellowship, Ministry, and Governance.* Confessional Lutheran Dogmatics 9. Waverly: The International Foundation for Lutheran Confessional Research, 1990.

Martikainen, Eeva. *Doctrina: Studien zu Luthers Begriff der Lehre.* Helsinki: Luther-Agricola-Gesellschaft, 1992.

————. "Future Emphases in Ecumenical Research: New Trends in the Study of Luther." *Lutheran World Federation Documentation* 32 (March 1993): 102–3.

Maurer, Wilhelm. *Historical Commentary on the Augsburg Confession.* Translated by H. George Anderson. Philadelphia: Fortress, 1986.

McDonough, Thomas M. *The Law and the Gospel in Luther: A Study of Martin Luther's Confessional Writings.* Oxford Theological Monographs. Oxford: Oxford University Press, 1963.

McGrath, Alister E. *The Genesis of Doctrine: A Study in the Foundations of Doctrinal Criticism.* Oxford: Basil Blackwell, 1990.

McSorley, Harry. *Luther: Right or Wrong? An Ecumenical-Theological Study of Luther's Major Work, The Bondage of the Will.* New York: Newman, and Minneapolis: Augsburg, 1969.

Meyer, Carl S., ed. *Luther for an Ecumenical Age: Essays in Commemoration of the 450th Anniversary of the Reformation.* St. Louis: Concordia, 1967.

Meyer, Harding, "Fundamental Difference—Fundamental Consensus." *Mid-Stream* 25 (1986): 247–57.

Mirbt, Carl. *Quellen zur Geschichte des Papsttums und des römischen Katholizismus.* 4th ed. Tübingen: J. C. B. Mohr, 1924.

Molnár, Amedeo. "The First Reformation." *Moravian Theological Seminary Bulletin* (1972–1977): 103–7.

Müller, Joseph Th. *Geschichte der Böhmischen Brüder.* 3 vols. Herrnhut: Missionsbuchhandlung, 1922–1931.

Nilson, Jon. *Nothing Beyond the Necessary: Roman Catholicism and the Ecumenical Future.* New York: Paulist, 1995.

Norgren, William A., and William G. Rusch. *"Toward Full Communion" and "Concordat of Agreement."* Minneapolis: Augsburg, and Cincinnati: Forward Movement Publications, 1991.

Oberman, Heiko A. *Forerunners of the Reformation: The Shape of Late Medieval Thought Illustrated by Key Documents.* New York: Holt, Rinehart, & Winston, 1966.

———. *The Harvest of Medieval Theology: Gabriel Biel and Late Medieval Nominalism.* Cambridge: Harvard University Press, 1963.

———. *Luther: Man between God and the Devil.* Translated by Eileen Walliser-Schwarzbart. New Haven: Yale University Press, 1989.

———. *Werden und Wertung der Reformation: Vom Wegestreit zum Glaubenskampf.* Spätscholastik und Reformation 2. Tübingen: J. C. B. Mohr, 1979

O'Collins, Gerald. *The Case against Dogma.* New York: Paulist, 1975.

Ommen, Thomas B. *The Hermeneutic of Dogma.* American Academy of Religion Dissertation 11. Missoula: Scholars Press, 1975.

Ozment, Steven. *The Age of Reform (1250–1550).* New Haven: Yale University Press, 1980.

———. *When Fathers Ruled: Family Life in Reformation Europe.* Cambridge: Harvard University Press, 1983.

———, ed. *Reformation Europe: A Guide to Research.* St. Louis: Center for Reformation Research, 1982.

Pater, Calvin. *Karlstadt as the Father of the Baptist Movements: The Emergence of Lay Protestantism.* Toronto: University of Toronto Press, 1984.

Pelikan, Jaroslav. *Historical Theology: Continuity and Change in Christian Doctrine.* London: Hutchinson, 1971.

———. *Obedient Rebels: Catholic Substance and Protestant Principle in Luther's Reformation.* New York: Harper & Row, 1964.

———. *Reformation of Church and Dogma 1300–1700.* The Christian Tradition, vol. 4. Chicago: University of Chicago Press, 1984.

———. "Luther's Endorsement of the Confessio Bohemica." *Concordia Theological Monthly* 20 (November 1949): 829–43.

———. "Luther's Negotiations with the Hussites." *Concordia Theological Monthly* 20 (July 1949): 496–517.

Peschke, E. *Theologie der Bömischen Brüder in ihrer Frühzeit.* Stuttgart: Kohlhammer, 1935.

Pieper, Francis. *Christian Dogmatics.* Vol. 2. St. Louis: Concordia, 1951.

Potter, G. R. *Zwingli.* Cambridge: Cambridge University Press, 1976.

Preus, James S. *Carlstadt's "Ordinaciones" and Luther's Liberty: A Study of the Wittenberg Movement, 1521–22.* Harvard Theological Studies 26. Cambridge: Harvard University Press, 1974.

Preus, Robert D. *Justification and Rome.* St. Louis: Concordia Academic Press, 1997.

———. *The Theology of Post-Reformation Lutheranism.* Vol. 1, *A Study of Theological Prolegomena.* St. Louis: Concordia, 1970.

Rahner, Karl, and Karl Lehmann. *Kerygma and Dogma.* Mysterium salutis. New York: Herder & Herder, 1969.

Reu, Johann M. *The Augsburg Confession: A Collection of Sources with an Historical Introduction.* 2 vols. Chicago: Wartburg Publishing House, 1930.

Ríčan, Rudolf. *The History of the Unity of Brethren.* Translated by C. Daniel Crews. Bethlehem, Penn.: Moravian Church in America, 1992.

Rothen, Bernhard. *Die Klarheit der Schrift.* 2 vols. Göttingen: Vandenhoeck & Ruprecht, 1990–92.

Rouse, Ruth, and Stephen Charles Neill, eds. *A History of the Ecumenical Movement.* Vol. 1, *1517–1948.* 2d ed. Philadelphia: Westminster, 1968.

Rupp, E. Gordon. *Patterns of Reformation.* Philadelphia: Fortress, 1969.

Russell, William R. *Luther's Theological Testament: The Schmalkald Articles.* Minneapolis: Fortress, 1995. 2d ed. St. Louis: Concordia, forthcoming.

Sandberg, Irving L., trans. *The 1529 Holy Week and Easter Sermons of Dr. Martin Luther.* St. Louis: Concordia Academic Press, 1999.

Sasse, Hermann. *This Is My Body.* Minneapolis: Augsburg, 1959.

Schaaf, James L. "The Smalcald Articles and Their Significance." In *Interpreting Luther's Legacy: Essays in Honor of Edward C. Fendt.* Edited by Fred W. Meuser and Stanley D. Schneider. Minneapolis: Augsburg, 1969.

Scott, Tom and Bob Scribner, eds. *The German Peasants' War: A History in Documents.* Atlantic Highlands: Humanities Press, 1990.

Scribner, R. W. "Politics and the Institutionalization of Reform in Germany." In *The Reformation, 1520–1559.* Edited by G. R. Elton. 2d ed. New Cambridge Modern History 2. Cambridge: Cambridge University Press, 1990.

Sider, Ronald J. *Andreas Bodenstein von Karlstadt: The Development of His Thought, 1517–1525.* Leiden: Brill, 1974.

———. *Karlstadt's Battle with Luther: Documents in a Liberal-Radical Debate.* Philadelphia: Fortress, 1978.

Southern, R. W. *Western Society and the Church in the Middle Ages.* The Pelican History of the Church 2. Baltimore: Penguin, 1970.

Spinka, Matthew. *John Hus: A Biography.* Princeton: Princeton University Press, 1968.

Spitz, Lewis W. *The Protestant Reformation, 1517–1559.* New York: Harper & Row, 1985. Reprint, St. Louis: Concordia, 2001.

———. *The Renaissance and Reformation Movements.* Vol. 1, *The Renaissance.* Chicago: Rand McNally, 1971. Reprint, St. Louis: Concordia, 1980.

Staehlin, Ernst. *Briefe und Akte zum Leben Oekolampads.* 2 vols. Leipzig: M. Heinsius Nachfolger Eger & Sievers, 1934.

Stayer, James M. *The German Peasants' War and Anabaptist Community of Goods.* McGill-Queens Studies in the History of Religion 6. Montreal: McGill-Queens University Press, 1991.

Steck, Karl Gerhard. *Lehre und Kirche bei Luther.* München: Kaiser, 1963.

Steiger, Johann Anselm. "The *communicatio idiomatum* as the Axle and Motor of Luther's Theology." *Lutheran Quarterly* 14 (Summer 2000): 125–58.

Stephens, W. P. *The Theology of Huldrych Zwingli.* Oxford: Clarendon, 1986.

————. *Zwingli: An Introduction to His Thought*. Oxford: Clarendon, 1992.

Strupl, Milos. "Confessional Theology of the Unitas Fratrum." *Church History* 33 (September 1964): 291–93.

Stupperich, Robert. *Erasmus von Rotterdam und seine Welt*. De Gruyter Studienbuch. Berlin: de Gruyter, 1977.

Tappert, Theodore G., ed. *The Book of Concord*. Philadelphia: Fortress, 1959.

Thieme, Karl. *Luthers Testament wider Rom in seinem Schmalkadlischen Artikeln*. Leipzig: Deichert, 1900.

Thomson, S. Harrison. "Luther and Bohemia." *Archiv für Reformationsgeschichte* 44 (1953): 164–73.

Volz, Hans. "Luthers Smalcaldischen Artikel," *Zeitschrift für Kirchengeschichte* 68 (1957): 259–86.

————, and Heinrich Ulbrich, eds. *Urkunden und Aktenstücke zur Geschichte von Martin Luthers Schmalkaldischen Artikeln (1536–1574)*. Berlin: De Gruyter, 1957.

Wagner, Murray L. *Petr Chelcicky: A Radical Separatist in Hussite Bohemia*. Studies in Anabaptist and Mennonite History 25. Scottdale, Penn.: Herald Press, 1983.

Watson, Philip S. *Let God Be God! An Interpretation of the Theology of Martin Luther*. London: Epworth, 1947.

Weier, Reinhold. *Das Theologieverständnis Martin Luthers*. Konfessionskundliche und Kontroverstheologische Studien 36. Paderborn: Bonifacius-Druckerei, 1976.

Wicks, Jared. "Thomism between Renaissance and Reformation: The Case of Cajetan." *Archiv für Reformationsgeschichte* 68 (1977): 9–32.

Williams, George H. *The Radical Reformation*. 3d ed. Sixteenth Century Essays and Studies 15. Kirksville: Sixteenth Century Journal Publishers, 1992.

Wright, D. F., trans. and ed. *Common Places of Martin Bucer*. The Courtenay Library of Reformation Classics, vol. 4. Berkshire, England: Sutton Courtenay Press, 1972.

————, ed. *Martin Bucer: Reforming Church and Community*. Cambridge: Cambridge University Press, 1994.

Zeman, Jarold Knox. *The Anabaptists and the Czech Brethren in Moravia 1526–1628*. Studies in European History 20. The Hague: Mouton, 1969.

DATE DUE
